THE
MONT BLANC
MASSIF

THE 100 FINEST ROUTES

Emile Bayle, David Belden, Henri Bertholet, Georges Bertone, Albert Blanchard, René Bonnardel, André Braconnay, Joseph et Marcel Burnet, Claude Cassin, Jean-Paul Charlet, Alain de Chatellus, Joël Coquegniot, Michel Darbellay, Bernard Denjoy, Lino Donvito, Jean-Claude Droyer, Léonce Fourrès, Jean Franco, Maurice Gicquel, Yasuyu Komori, François Lespinasse, Ugo Manera, Hideo Miyazaki, Jean-Pierre Motti, Pierre Nava, Gabriel Ollive, Yves Pollet-Villars, A. Re, Vincent Renard, Paul Rouaix, Shigo Shirahata, Haroun Tazieff, Michel Vaucher, Bradford Washburn, Cosimo Zappelli, all these assisted in the production of this book, either by helping me with the technical descriptions or by allowing me to use their collections of photographs. I am most grateful to them all. Here was yet another way of being on the same rope, just as most of them had often been with me in the mountains.

My closest collaborator was Alex Lucchesi who did the line-drawings. He loves the mountains and loves drawing, and for a task so demanding, both were necessary qualifications. To him, of course, go my heartfelt thanks, but I know that he and I both enjoyed our partnership.

All alpinists will know the maps published by the Institut Géographique National (France), the Istituto Geografico Militare (Italy) and the Service Géographique Fédéral (Switzerland), the Vallot Guides so carefully edited by L. Devies and P. Henri, and the guides published by the Italian and Swiss Alpine Clubs. Sometimes alpinists may be slightly disconcerted to find heights differing by two or three metres for the same peak, but this seems to me of secondary importance; maps serve primarily to inspire dreams.

Kaye & Ward—Mont Blanc—8/9pt Univers—8264/2—24 ems—MJS——

First published by Editions Denoël 1973
First published in Great Britain by
Kaye & Ward Ltd
21 New Street, London EC2M 4NT
1975
First published in the USA by
Oxford University Press, Inc.
200 Madison Avenue,
New York, N.Y.10016
1975

English translation Copyright © Kaye & Ward, 1974

ISBN 0 7182 1098 0 (Great Britain)
ISBN 0 19 519789 5 (USA)
Library of Congress Catalogue Card No 73-93091 (USA)
Printed in France

TABLE OF CONTENTS

CHOOSING A ROUTE   7

MONT BLANC: THE PLAYGROUND   9

The Mont Blanc Range
40 Million Years Ago
Two Centuries of Mountain-Lovers

BECOMING AN ALPINIST   16

Preparations
Equipment
The Rules of the Game
Enthusiasm and Clear Thinking
Free and Artificial Climbing
The Choice of Routes
Keeping to Time
Gradings

ROUTES ARRANGED BY SUMMIT   24

THE 100 FINEST ROUTES   26

THE WOULD-BE MOUNTAINEER   238

The Frendo Spur on the
Aiguille du Midi.

CHOOSING A ROUTE

Which peak to climb? By what route? Why? When and how? This is the sort of question, serious, absorbing, that the climber asks himself, first of all in winter when he is dreaming of the climbs he will do and drawing up a programme for his next season, and then later on, when he has arrived in the mountains and has to adjust his plans and his ambitions to the weather and the conditions.

The ascent of any route begins, in dreams at least, the autumn before. Our minds ring, involuntarily, with the alluring names of mountains, aiguilles, faces and ridges. Is it the name itself which is so tempting, or the picture we have of the mountain itself, or does the appeal come from our feeling for the actual process of climbing? All of us have our reasons, innumerable, personal and complex. From many points of view, a climb is a challenge we must meet.

Whatever the reasons are, our anticipation is the first step in a confrontation not only with the climb but with ourselves. Which route are we to choose?

Which difficulties, of all kinds, are we to face? Indeed to hope for, since without such a hope a climber would confine himself to the easy routes, and it is surely characteristic of man to prefer challenge and difficulty.

What pleasures and delights are we to expect? Any climb is a red-letter day. True, the landscape is permanent, but the climber as it were controls and organises it for himself: the start in starlight, daybreak, the climb itself up to the rising sun: it is the climber who gives a new life and purpose to these realms of snow and rock . . . Then there is the physical process of climbing, a creative process, linking and co-ordinating the sense of balance with precise, elegant, delicate movements – if the climber fails to achieve this coordination, he is conscious of his failure as a lack in his enjoyment – the whole process arising from the climber's imagination or from the inspiration of the moment. And then there is the presence of his climbing companion – a friend, a brother – and their sense, at every belay, of shared confidence or shared uneasiness.

What advantages do we hope to gain? Naturally, there is the pleasure we get from the climbing process itself and from our victories, but as well as the delights of exercise in a mountain environment, there is also the process, coming every time as a surprise, of self-discovery, deepening a little further with every climb: who we are, how far we can go, what is our potential, where are the limits of our technique, our strength, our skill, our mountaineering sense: discoveries whose acceptance means that, if necessary, we may turn back (one step too far is already too far) and return another time, several times if need be – 'tomorrow is a new day'.

Self-discovery and discovery of the mountains, the two go together. Every route reveals some new secrets and deepens our relationship with the mountains; with each route, we may expect to make some new discovery. It is not just a question of climbing, it is a question of becoming an alpinist, a mountaineer: a continuous development.

Naturally, we want to climb well, to get to the top, but at the same time we feel a growing sense of unity with the high mountains. We need to be at one with the snow, the rock, the clouds, the winds. There will come a day, for instance, when all of a sudden, for no particular reason, partly of course because of conscious thought but mostly from that indefinable something called mountaineering sense, a sense of unity with the mountains, we choose the right face, the one where the snow-conditions are good whereas they are poor on the other face, or again, we choose the face where the snow is good and deep whereas just beside us, invisibly, there is only a light covering of snow over hard, glassy ice. And so we have had a climb which has been airy and exhilarating instead of laborious. True pleasure, lasting and elegant, comes from the sensation of climbing in a world in which we are at home.

Since the time of the first ascent of Mont Blanc in 1786, nearly two centuries ago, by Dr Paccard and the crystal-hunter Jacques Balmat, all the summits have been climbed – the mountains themselves, the *aiguilles, pointes, dents, pics, clochers, tours, gendarmes;* not only that, but each of them has been climbed by a number of different routes following different mountain features: walls, faces, ridges, pillars, spurs, *couloirs*, sometimes even by routes involving an ascent on one side and a descent on another.

Indeed, in the Mont Blanc range alone, there are more than two thousand possible routes, all described in admirably full detail in the Vallot guides (three volumes getting thicker with every new edition); but of course, as you might imagine, not all these routes are of equal interest.

Which peak to choose, and by which route? Why? These are questions I have asked myself time after time, even, perhaps particularly, when I was a young climber from the Calanques with no Alpine achievements to my name. And yet how can a young climber, however enthusiastic, pick out from the innumerable possibilities of this extraordinary playground the best climbs, those that will be the most enjoyable, those which will supply him with and encourage in him the technical experience which goes to make up the alpinist and mountaineer?

I, like all children, first came across Mont Blanc as a little greyish photograph in my geography textbook.

Only a few years later, seeing Mont Blanc more closely had become my great aim. Meanwhile, in the Calanques, out at sea, in Haute Provence, in Corsica, in the Oisans, I had been lucky enough to discover for myself the irresistible pull of the wild country, with its silence and its loneliness. I was ready for Mont Blanc.

I caught sight of the Mont Blanc range for the first time, at a distance, during a long walk which I and a group of friends, all about fifteen, did from Briançon to Chamonix, a walk during which every day brought new discoveries, fulfilling my every hope. From the Col du Bonhomme, from the Col de Voza, from the Brévent, which I had toiled up on foot, I stared at it and even started, unlikely as it may seem, to work out its possibilities. From the Montenvers (also a long walk), then from the Mer de Glace which I crossed in search of silence, I felt as though I was penetrating into some secret enclave; the Charmoz on the right, the Drus on the left, and in front of me the Mer de Glace itself, dividing at its head and soaring up towards those innumerable peaks; and then, in the distance, the Jorasses.

The Montenvers is a culmination; to go there is to pass into another world. I speak from experience. As well as passing through it frequently every summer, I was lucky enough in 1941 – no trains then, or tourists, nobody or practically nobody about – to live there for two consecutive months, as an instructor with *Jeunesse et Montagne*. I only went down three times to Chamonix, whereas every fine day I was off to the mountains. And yet even so I still had that same feeling of stepping into another world that I had had when I was fifteen on that fine August day in 1936, another world which, in spite of or because of its mystery, was made for happiness.

Back in Marseilles, I longed for that silence again and alternated between dreams and attempts to realise them. I pored over maps, visualising the mountains and their steepness. Not a day passed without my looking at some climbing book, or at the French Alpine Club's journal *La Montagne*, or at *Alpinisme*, whose front cover photographs were always so remarkably inspiring and which contained accounts of the great routes and first ascents done by the members of the Groupe de Haute Montagne. Carefully, I studied the illustrations; I would amuse myself by reading the text only afterwards to see whether I had guessed the right peak, the right face or ridge.

Everything tempted me: snow and ice routes, rock routes, mixed routes, ridges, faces or high-level traverses; I had every intention, sooner or later, of doing all of them. But the pressing problem was the coming summer: which route precisely was I to choose?

Compared with the enthusiastic or emotional slant of the stories, the technical descriptions had among other things the advantage of precision, of giving in an objective way the standard of the route, but there were still problems: in the first place, reading a description of a difficult route is often alarming, and in the second, there is also the fact that however useful and helpful such notes may be, they nevertheless have their limits; every description needs to be adapted to one's personal feelings and experience. As well as the precise, almost mathematical description of the pitches of the climb and their grading (III, IV, V, VI), there is the whole context of the climb: whether its name is intimidating or reassuring; whether the route is direct or whether it involves traverses which gain no height and may also be a serious handicap if bad weather makes the party turn back; the way the climb faces, its steepness and its features; whether it is open and exposed or whether it is sheltered and enclosed, giving the climber the feeling that he is imprisoned and shut in – as happens, for instance, on some of the routes on the South Face of Mont Blanc. Then again there is the question of the climb's situation with regard to the range itself and the valley, of its past history, of any legend attaching to it . . . all the things which come under the heading of its atmosphere or its 'aura'. In fact what we need, in between the individual account and the guidebook description, is something which would give some idea of the seriousness and 'substance' of the climb.

A further problem: as well as rock routes, where the standard of the climb can at least be given with some precision, we have snow routes and mixed routes where the difficulty varies according to the conditions: the snow, the temperature, the weather (a clear sky, or a cloudy sky which may keep out the heat of the sun and prevent melting, but which will also prevent verglas from melting), the winds which can, in a moment, totally change all these conditions.

And so the same question still remains: how are we to make a choice from so many peaks and so many routes?

My very first route in the Mont Blanc range was the Aiguille (or Pic) de Roc. Everything tempted me to it: its name, short and abrupt, its appearance, a granite spire, its situation on the Mer de Glace face of the Grépon, the account of the first ascent and the technical description given by Jacques de Lépiney (founder-member of the Groupe de Haute Montagne and the epitome of the ideal climber) and published with a superb photograph in June 1937 in *Alpinisme*. And then there was the possibility of carrying on from the Aiguille de Roc over the Grépon, following the route done in 1938 by Edouard Frendo (also much admired by the younger climbers, especially those from the Calanques). All these were irresistible temptations (even if not compelling reasons) for trying this particular route. And yet I realised, enjoyable though I found it, that this superb climb was not the best way for a beginner to make the acquaintance of the Mont Blanc range.

Two years later, I took a post as instructor with *Jeunesse et Montagne* at the climbing school at Les Frasserands, with its magnificent view. From then on I spent all year in the mountains, watching the ever-changing peaks, the wind, the clouds, the sky, living the true life of the high mountains, which is something quite apart from mere climbing and adds moreover another dimension to the latter. I was in daily contact too with the instructors at *Jeunesse et Montagne*, drawn from the best guides of Chamonix, the Vanoise, the Oisans, the Pyrenees, and who were all excellent mountaineers, highly individualistic. It was here that I realised the value of a course of Alpine training, and saw how a series of climbs could be designed to help the progress of the beginner.

Each course lasted a month and was divided into three stages:

1. Introduction to climbing techniques and to the mountains generally; this involved in the first place training in climbing itself, on rock, snow and ice, and included of course belaying techniques and carrying coils, and in the second place some easy routes (the Col du Géant, the Tour Ronde, the Trois Cols, the Petite Verte, the Tour Noir) to introduce the novice into that world of the mountains.
2. The application, on suitable routes, of the techniques learned in the first period, combined with training for the high mountains and leading gradually to the attainment of a high standard of physical and mental fitness.
3. More advanced climbing with some more difficult routes, planned and, more important, carried out by the pupils themselves, under the supervision, naturally, of the instructors.

In 1944, Edouard Frendo founded the Ecole Nationale d'Alpinisme and appointed me an instructor. It was both a joy and an honour to me to find myself working alongside not only Frendo himself (who was technical director) but also of Armand Charlet, chief instructor, and of the other instructors Lucien Amieux and René Rionda.

The instruction at the centre followed the same general lines as that at the *Jeunesse et Montagne* school, but its standard was considerably higher. We were now intending to train not climbers capable of leading a rope under the supervision of the instructors, but guides who would take full responsibility for a whole party.

It was exhilarating work. Part of my time could be spent planning the routes I would do on Sundays or between two courses, while the rest brought me the secret and well-founded satisfaction of watching those on the courses acquiring skills, balance, reflexes and mountaineering sense. And, an additional satisfaction, I could watch their pleasure in their own achievements.

And it was then that I had the idea of trying to communicate to others how to find that pleasure, that look of excitement in the eyes of those reaching a summit, of those becoming mountaineers – day by day, in spite of successes or initial failures, in fine or poor weather – that same pleasure I had felt myself when I was a novice and which I saw now in those I was teaching. There were after all eight long and well-filled years between the time when I myself had been a beginner, excited by accounts of climbs, intimidated by technical descriptions and puzzled when it came to choosing a route, and the time when, a fully qualified guide of four years' standing, I did an average of fifty routes a year. And it was then that I wrote *L'apprenti montagnard, les cinquante plus belles courses du massif du Mont Blanc**. This book drew on my experience both as a novice and as a guide and instructor and had as its aim to give a selection of routes which, if followed in order, would enable progress to be made. The routes worked up from the easiest to the most difficult, but each route represented the most interesting and most rewarding of its standard; I explained why I had chosen it, what skills the alpinist would need and what, from different points of view, he could expect to gain from it. Moreover, each route, more or less technically difficult, was linked with the routes before and after.

Two years later, in 1946, the book, original in intention and aims, was out of print. Today marks its reappearance, its emergence from a yet wider experience. It is designed to awake ambitions; to me, these have always seemed preferable to memories.

*Editions Grands Vents, 1946.

MONT BLANC: THE PLAYGROUND

THE MONT BLANC RANGE

What an extraordinary creation this is, wrought by earth and time! Magnificent seen from a distance, for climbers it is a real paradise. Nowhere else has the earth been so generous to them. There is an abundance of peaks, mountains and *aiguilles,* each one prodigal of ridges, pillars, buttresses, faces. And yet, in terms of area, the range is relatively small. If you look at it on a map of the Alps, it is only a small corner of that great range of mountains curving over several hundred kilometres, from the Mediterranean to Austria. The range is only 30 kilometres long and 12–15 kilometres broad; the Mont Blanc tunnel is only 11·6 kilometres long. Such an abundance in so small a compass could well have produced a feeling of clutter or chaos, but not here. On the contrary, here we have a sense of quite exceptional harmony: every peak in its place, linked to every other and yet separate, with its own separate identity and history, its own appeal, and all of them linked to the greatest, to that Mont Blanc which has lent its name to the range as a whole.

The French side of the range is awe-inspiring. It takes the form of massive yet shapely glaciers from which there emerge extraordinary *aiguilles,* soaring into the sky in a series of shoulders and soaring faces. At any time of the day or the year these glaciers are places of mystery, with a strange fascination. It is very understandable that once – and not so very long ago – they were a source only of fear or even terror, and that they were thought of only as errors of nature, a waste of the earth's energy. Even today, when routes cross them in all directions, they still inspire us with awe, wonder or amazement. The western end of the ridge, the Mont Blanc end, is composed principally of glaciers, whereas the eastern end has, silhouetted against the snow and the sky, those granite *aiguilles* whose soaring lines and glowing rock make them seem overflowing with new vitality. Ice and rock together are a unity, the one bringing out the beauty of the other; though each alone would have undeniable beauty, it would lose much of its character.

I have explored every part of the range, studied moreover and photographed it; I know every inch of it; and yet, even so . . .

How many times have I set off towards it? – certainly well over a thousand. Coming from Sallanches or from Pont Sainte-Marie higher up, or again from the Col des Montets, you know perfectly well that at a certain bend in the road the range will come into view. You are ready and waiting for it. You even know how, according to the time of day, it will look, what shadows there will be, what colourings it will have. Every detail of the landscape is imprinted on your mind. You expect nothing more thrilling than a rediscovery. And then there it is; but always, it is changed and made new, because it is so beautiful, so large in scale, that every time you see it is a new beginning; the range is recreated, unparalleled; and with a sense of shock, you discover it anew.

The Italian side is almost overwhelming. Above the Val Ferret to the North-East and the Val Veni to the South-West, both of them peaceful country valleys with their streams, their larch trees and their chalets, there towers in all its savage grandeur the great rock wall. This is a realm of granite, its great faces and its monstrous buttresses rearing up to the snows of the summit cornices. And yet there are also narrow, delicate ridges, whose elegance is all the more striking, as on the Aiguille Noire de Peuterey or the Aiguille de la Brenva, because it emerges from a world of brute force. What routes there are here for the experienced mountaineer! First-class routes like the ridges and pillars of the Brouillard, the Innominata, the Frêney, the Peuterey and the Brenva; names synonymous with climbing history, long routes where alpinists of the highest skill, like those on the Pillar of Frêney, have been defeated by the bad weather that is always hazardous and here particularly to be dreaded. And yet the valley with its cottages is a bare four kilometres away as the crow flies. If the mountains on the French side of Mont Blanc slope away, on the Italian side they obtrude, which explains why the latter seem to rise so close and so menacing above the Val Veni.

Further to the East the ridge becomes less abrupt. Around the Col du Géant there are several more popular (even crowded) summits, such as the Tour Ronde, the Dent du Géant and Rochefort Ridges; and then solitude returns again along the Jorasses ridge, to Mont Dolent and the Col Ferret.

The Swiss side is friendly, with less impressive, less over-powering peaks, with wooded valleys and pretty little chalets: the Trient Valley, Lac de Champex, and the Swiss Val Ferret follow to the East the ridge which goes from the Col de Balme to the Col Ferret, and includes the Aiguille du Tour, the Aiguille d'Argentière, the Tour Noir and Mont Dolent.

Mont Dolent is where three countries, Switzerland, Italy and France, meet and where their frontier ridges run together. Far from being a barrier, the ridges link the inhabitants of the valleys on all three sides. All of them breathe the pure, harsh, abundant air coming from the glaciers, from the *aiguilles* and from the high winds.

40 MILLION YEARS AGO

Under the pressure of the slow and irresistible forces of that time, which brought together the continents of Europe and Asia, the Mont Blanc range made its slow appearance in the middle of the tertiary era, forty million years ago.

Even before this, in the second half of the primary era, there had already been, where the present range stands, a chain of mountains. But even as it rose, the forces of erosion were already at work and in the course of time this chain disappeared again. Then the region sank below the surface of the oceans. The construction and destruction of this original chain occupied some hundred million years, but there are still visible traces of that long-ago Hercynian fold.

On top of the ocean-covered remains of these earlier mountains, sedimentary layers were deposited during the secondary and the first half of the tertiary eras – a total of some hundred and eighty million years. It was in this Oligocene era that the land masses, emerging from the sea, began to push back the seas. Little by little, as at the time of the Hercynian fold, the area where the Alps now stand was compressed between two tectonic plates, those huge slabs which, like a mosaic, cover the surface of the earth and

A sea of cloud below the 'dining room' at the
Dent du Géant; in the distance the Gran Paradiso
(below).
The Périades (left).

which here were forced together by the expansion of the ocean beds. The horizontal sedimentary strata laid down under the ocean which covered the base of the old vanished Hercynian fold were gradually folded, twisted, petrified and broken. And under these immense pressures, the old base was itself broken. A huge arched fold grew up, where the Mediterranean tectonic plate meeting the Hercynian plate of the Massif Central, Brittany, the Black Forest and Bohemia inserted itself under the latter and penetrated under it into the molten layer. This arched fold, a thousand kilometres long and two hundred wide, soon rose to sea-level and emerged at first in groups of archipelagos, then in a continuous chain; these were the new-born Alps.

The centre of the chain rose furthest, so that the effects of erosion were greatest on the oldest rocks. This explains why Mont Blanc and Mont Pelvoux, the Aar and the Belledonne, are made up of old metamorphosed rocks, gneiss and granite, whereas the more recent sedimentary layers are to be found on its edges, in the Préalpes, limestone massifs where there are fine, hard, serious climbs to be done when new snow or bad weather make conditions impossible in the high Alps. The birth of the Alps must have been an extraordinary spectacle, but it is one we can only imagine; the greatest pressures came from the east, Val Ferret – Val Veni, whereas westwards they were attenuated. Today, as the crow flies, it is 8 kilometres from the summit of Mont Blanc to the nearest point, Taconna, of the Arve Valley, whereas it is only 5 kilometres from Mont Blanc de Courmayeur to the nearest points of the Val Veni, Frêney or Miage. Such upheavals called for man to witness and record them, but the human race was not to make its appearance until forty million years later.

In the Miocene era, when there was considerable volcanic activity in Cantal and Velay and when, far to the east, almost on the opposite side of the planet, the Himalayas were emerging under intense orogenic pressures, the Alps were already fully formed and the forces of erosion, patient, persistent, unceasing, were sculpting them, shaping them, smoothing them.

In the quaternary era, the history of the Alps took a new turn with the formation of the glaciers; they covered the region with an immense ice-cap going down as far as Lyon. The highest summits were left clear, but the valley floors were scoured and smoothed, and one thousand metres of ice covered the Chamonix valley.

Finally, and very slowly, the glaciers retreated higher, the climate became less extreme and mankind's bolder spirits made their hazardous way into the high valleys. For centuries the high peaks were to be regarded simply as evil-bringers, as sources of rockfall, avalanche, mountain lakes breaking their banks, floods, and of course snowfalls which shut in the few inhabitants and cut them off, for those interminable winters, from the rest of the world.

In the sixteenth and seventeenth centuries, the so-called 'little ice-age', the growth of the Bossons, Argentière, and Tour Glaciers did much damage; the little soil there was on the steep fields was ruined, the barns were crushed and destroyed by the ice. In 1690 Jean d'Arenthon, Bishop of Geneva, came to Chamonix to exorcise the glaciers. The last few manifestations of this ice-age came in 1818, 1854 and in 1892 when the Bossons Glacier came as low as the road.

But long before this, a young Genevan naturalist and physicist had written emphatically: 'Since my childhood, I have had the most decided love for the mountains.' This was Horace-Benedict de Saussure, who was to 'invent' alpinism.

TWO CENTURIES OF MOUNTAIN-LOVERS

1760 – Horace Benedict de Saussure, aged twenty, feels a sense of vocation; he undertakes on foot the journey from his native town Geneva to the 'Glacières de Chamouny', as it was then spelt. On 24 July, he goes up to the Brévent: the beginning of a great adventure.

For the very first time, a man feels in his heart the quite irrational desire to climb – senselessly, illogically, for no purpose. Saussure has given birth to the idea of Mont Blanc as 'a summit to climb', and has created a whole new movement – Alpinism.

Back in Chamonix, he has an announcement made in all the parish churches of the valley, promising to give 'a very considerable reward to any who might be able to find a viable route to the summit of Mont Blanc.'

1761, 63, 67, 80 – Some guides are tempted by the reward, but there are no really serious attempts. The notion of going to the summit of Mont Blanc is too new and too revolutionary.

1775 – Four guides bivouac on the top of the Montagne de la Côte and reach the Grand Plateau, but, caught by bad weather and, even more alarming, by nightfall, scurry back to the valley. In his analysis of this attempt – he is keeping closely in touch with news relating to Mont Blanc – Saussure seizes on and emphasises the particular difficulty: how to get up and down in one day. 'I say in one day, since the peasants of the area do not believe that one can survive a night in the open in the snow' – a reference to the old superstition dating from the time, not then so very distant, when the range was known as the Montagnes Maudites (the accursed mountains) and it was generally believed that no-one who spent a night out on the glacier ever came back alive.

1786 – Attempts are made on the mountain in 1783, 84 and 85, but the attempt which is to point the way to success takes place on 8 June 1786. On that day, two parties of guides, one coming up by the Grands Mulets, the other by the Aiguille du Goûter, meet at the Dôme du Goûter. The weather begins to cloud over, leading to a general retreat. But 'not everyone retreated', writes Saussure. One of the group from the Grand Montets is a crystal-hunter who had joined the party at the last moment in spite of their reluctance. Saussure goes on: 'On the way back from the Dôme du Gouter, the crystal-hunter, whose relationship with his companions was none too friendly, walked separately and went off to one side to look for crystals in a rock off the track. When he wanted to rejoin the others or failing that to follow their tracks in the snow, he found that they had disappeared.' And it is thus that, at more than 4000 metres, a man finds himself alone, forgotten by his companions who had hurried off down to get to the valley before nightfall.

The man, alone, sets off on the descent, but at the Grand Plateau, caught by storm and nightfall, he has to stop. He is obliged to spend the night on the glacier, sitting on his sack and his snowshoes; but not only does he survive, he actually comes back, thus offering living disproof of the legend which had unnerved the peasants; from now on, it is clear that the way is open and that it is perfectly possible, if necessary, to take two days over the climb.

This man, robust, resolute, this crystal-hunter who, as it turns out, possesses an extraordinary mountaineering sense, an unerring instinct for the crevasses and seracs of the glaciers – had he fallen through a snow-bridge into a crevasse, this would have confirmed all existing superstitions and might well have put back the ascent of Mont Blanc by a number of years – this man is Jacques Balmat.

Another man, also a great character, has for some years taken an interest in Mont Blanc: the Chamonix doctor, Dr Paccard. Like Saussure a devotee of the natural sciences, he has a dream: to carry a barometer to the summit and take a reading there. An excellent mountaineer, he has already made several attempts.

As it happens, the doctor and the crystal-hunter are the best-qualified and the most determined and are, as a pair, ideally complementary. Paccard, while quite as tough as a guide, has no particular financial interest in the expedition so that Balmat is not obliged to share the prize offered by Saussure. On the other hand, if the doctor sets off with the crystal-hunter, whose knowledge of Mont Blanc is at that time unequalled, he stands the best chance of fulfilling his ambition by becoming the first man of science to reach the summit. The two men are thus an ideal team.

Two months later, on 8 August 1786, Paccard and Balmat succeed in that greatest of first ascents, the first ascent of Mont Blanc.

1787 – Fired with enthusiasm, in spite of his forty-seven years, Saussure in his turn sets off with the same goal. On 1 August, at 11 am, after having bivouacked at the Grand Plateau, Saussure with eighteen guides reached the summit.

Saussure's ascent arouses considerable interest and in educated circles is discussed all over Europe. Mont Blanc becomes fashionable and there is a series of ascents.

1808 – Marie Paradis, a peasant girl from Chamonix, reaches the summit thus completing, if not without difficulty, the first feminine ascent of Mont Blanc; the second will be accomplished by Henriette d'Angeville in 1838.

1820 – The first disaster. In poor weather the guides are reluctant to set out, but Dr Hamel, councillor at the Imperial Russian court, refuses to take no for an answer and the guides weakly agree. Not far above the Grand Plateau, the party is caught in an avalanche which sweeps five guides into a crevasse. Three of them cannot climb out; forty-one years later their bodies emerge far down the mountain from the Glacier des Bossons.

1823 – A code of practice for the Guides' Company at Chamonix is drawn up and circulated.

1857 – The first mountaineering club, the Alpine Club, is founded in London. Its members will participate like pilgrims in a new crusade. Except for Mont Blanc itself and the Aiguille du Midi, *all* the peaks are unclimbed; the modern climber can scarcely imagine such a situation. This is the golden age of alpinism. Led by guides from Chamonix, from the Valais and the Oberland, the members of the Alpine Club are to climb, one after another, all the highest and most attractive peaks of the range: the Aiguille de Trélatête, the Aiguille de Bionnassay, the Grandes Jorasses, the Aiguille d'Argentière, the Aiguille du Chardonnet, the Mont Dolent, the Aiguille Verte by the Whymper Couloir, by the Moine ridge and by the Grande Rocheuse spur, Mont Blanc by the Brenva . . . The period is dominated by two men: Edward Whymper, an English artist, and Michel Croz, an admirable guide. In 1866 in a single week, from 8–15 July, they did: 8 July, the first traverse of the Col du Triolet; 12 July, the first ascent of the Aiguille de Trélatête; 15 July, the first ascent of the Aiguille d'Argentière.

1880 – This marks the beginning of a more gymnastic sort of climbing, with Mummery and his guides Burgener and Venetz leading the field – the latter was a quite exceptional rock-climber. They climb the Drus, the Grands Charmoz, the Grépon and the Dent du Requin. Mummery, humorously and accurately, foresaw the following series of descriptions for the Grépon: 'An inaccessible peak – The most difficult climb in the Alps – An easy day for a lady'. Yet even today the Grépon is a serious climb and the Venetz crack (which can be avoided on the right) is still an obstacle. I have seen well-known climbers, perfectly at home on grade six, nevertheless fail on it.

1886 – In the century since the first ascent of Mont Blanc, some three thousand people have made the attempt and rather over half have succeeded, including sixty-seven women.

Nearly all the peaks have been climbed and a new trend is emerging on Mont Blanc and the Aiguille Verte: that of climbing each individual peak by several different routes. No longer is it simply a question for the alpinist of getting to the top; the mountain as a whole is now his playground and each summit must be reached by all its faces and all its ridges.

1935 to today – While it is often the North faces that hold out longest against assault, there are certain other faces of extreme difficulty, either rock faces like the East Face of the Grand Capucin, the West Face of the Drus or the South Face of the Aiguille du Fou which require intensive and delicate use of artificial techniques, or ice faces like the North Face of the Droites, or high mixed routes like the Frêney pillar. Rock routes whose ascent involves not only

route-finding but the banging in of one to two hundred pitons are 'downgraded' fairly soon after all the pitons are in place. Ice routes and mixed routes maintain their high standard of difficulty rather longer. But now that techniques have been so much improved and equipment so far developed, the new generation is making first solo ascents and first winter ascents of all these faces – a way for young climbers to get back to the pioneering past. There are also certain climbers who try to climb artificial routes free, or at least to climb free the artificial pitches on free routes – a very interesting development and one which represents a return to earlier standards. They are worthy successors, perhaps, to the Maquignaz brothers who, in 1882, climbed the Dent du Géant and left their equipment in place to lead the Sella brothers up it (later, unfortunately, the Dent du Géant was draped with fixed ropes, which will certainly have to be removed sooner or later); to Captain Ryan and his guide Franz Lochmatter who did the first ascent of the Ryan-Lochmatter Ridge on the Aiguille du Plan, starting from the Montenvers; and to G. W. Young and his guide Joseph Knubel who in ten days completed the following programme: 9 August 1911, first ascent of Mont Blanc by the Brouillard Ridge; 11 August, first descent (first traverse) of the Hirondelles Ridge on the Grandes Jorasses; 14 August, first ascent of the West Ridge of the Grandes Jorasses; 19 August, first ascent of the Mer de Glace face of the Grépon, including the Knubel Crack; all this at a time when there was neither a tunnel or a téléphérique to make the journey from Courmayeur to Chamonix quick and easy.

We can be justly proud of our grandparents; across the generations we can share with them the same passions. Starting that summer day in 1760 when a man looked out from the Brévent and for the first time in history took a fresh look at Mont Blanc and wanted to climb it, the history of Mont Blanc over two centuries is that of a love affair. Here men have given of their best, their most enthusiastic, most virile and most generous selves. They have given as they might have given in wartime, but here, in time of peace – freely.

Rows of seracs.

North Face of the Aiguille d'Argentière (left).

The Brenva Spur (below).

14

The rock triangle on Mont Blanc du Tacul (left).

The bergschrund on the Walker Spur, on the North Face of the Grandes Jorasses (below).

BECOMING AN ALPINIST

PREPARATIONS

There are two quite different sorts of danger inherent in climbing. There are in the first place the objective dangers due to poor rock and rockfalls; to snow with its crevasses and snow-bridges, cornices, seracs and avalanches; to bad weather, with mist, wind (the föhn especially), storms and thunderstorms. Then there are the subjective dangers arising from the climber's own competence and personality. Serious training is required for an Alpine season. Rock outcrops can give an excellent grounding in rock-climbing techniques – including such things as abseiling (it should be remembered that every year a certain number of serious accidents happen while abseiling).

As far as ice climbing is concerned, it is a very good idea to spend some time on one of the lower glaciers, the Bossons for instance, practising techniques. Walking in crampons, for example, is awkward and requires a different sort of balance and flexibility, as well as being rather tiring for the ankles. The climber will also need to learn how to use an ice axe, a technique which will vary according to the angle of the slope and the quality of the ice or snow. The ice axe is also used for cutting steps and this too the climber should learn at low altitudes so that he will be able to cut steps efficiently and with relative ease at 4000 metres or more. Finally, cramponning practice and step-cutting on snow or on a snow glacier are not enough; he should try out ice slopes and learn how to move on the ice of a glacier.

The old Couvercle Hut.

Training in rock and ice techniques (not forgetting belaying and dynamic belays) must be accompanied by training for general fitness. The climber will need considerable stamina as well as being well acclimatised. He will be helped by long-distance training runs, especially cross-country, together with long sessions on outcrops – six to eight hours at a stretch.

Before setting off to do a route, he should make a study of the weather forecasts. At Chamonix there is a special centre which gives forecasts for the following twenty-four hours (usually very reliable) and further outlooks of a more general sort. This allows you to go up to a hut in poor weather if the forecast for the next day is good. If you intend doing a route which will take several days, it is worth taking a barometric altimeter.

It is also quite essential, especially on certain routes, to wear a helmet. This affords the only effective protection against a fractured skull brought about by stonefalls or by a climbing fall.

EQUIPMENT

Since the golden age, equipment has enormously improved.

Nylon ropes are much stronger, particularly because of their elasticity, and much less rigid, even when wet, than hemp or manilla ropes. Moreover, they do not rot – although this does not mean that they do not wear; a rope will lose elasticity and strength even when it is not being used. This is why, each time that you set off for a climb, you should say to yourself that your rope may have to hold a falling climber. If this climber is the second, and provided that the rope between leader and second is as taut as it should be, then there will be no sudden strain on the rope (which will only have to take the weight of the second – nothing much for a climbing rope). If on the other hand the rope is not taut, and especially if it is the leader and not the second who falls, the rope will have to absorb a considerable strain and stop the fall. For this reason, you should never hesitate to throw away an old rope or one you are uncertain about. After all, there is no way in which a climber can check the amount of wear on his rope or its condition, so it is better to change it too soon rather than a little too late. This is true for 11 millimetre rope used for climbing, for 9 millimetre rope used double for abseiling, and for slings and abseil loops.

While on the route, it is essential not to walk on the rope, especially in crampons; do not let the rope drag on the ground or pass over sharp edges.

There have been changes in roping-up as well. At one time you tied the rope round the climber; nowadays the rope is tied to a harness, like a parachute harness, which fits round the climber, so that although a fall is still not an enjoyable experience, the dangers both of the fall itself and of the

Abseiling down.

aftermath (the latter often as dangerous as the fall) are considerably diminished.

Ice axes, crampons, hammers, pitons and carabiners are now fortunately stronger and lighter because of special sorts of steel and new alloys. But naturally they still need looking after; the adze and the pick of an ice axe need sharpening, and so do crampon points, otherwise they will act less efficiently when they are really needed – in difficult situations.

Boots are not necessarily much better from the point of view of the leather, but their performance in hard climbing and in modern techniques is much improved due particularly to Vibram soles, developed in 1937 by a Milanese climber, Vitale Bramani. He made a careful study of the ways in which one could prevent the occurrence of accidents like one he had seen on the Piz Badile, which had cost the lives of three climbers, an accident caused by the fact that at the time espadrilles were used for hard climbing; one took off one's heavy nailed boots and left them on the glacier to be picked up on the way back.

The crampons must fit the boots tightly. A slightly loose crampon, a loose or worn strap, an ill-fitting boot, badly proofed or with the stitching torn, or even a broken bootlace, can all lead to a fall or to a bivouac under poor conditions and even in a storm lead to a disaster; so can the loss of one's goggles or gloves, or even the wearing of a pair of gloves with holes in.

On snow routes, when you set out in the dark when it is very cold and keep crampons on all day, it is useful to have overboots which protect the boots and prevent cold feet.

Rucksacks, formerly pear-shaped, are now cylindrical, but so-called 'improvements' should not make them heavier or more complex. Clothes are also greatly improved, especially protective clothing: duvet jackets against the cold, 'cagoules' against rain, snow and wind – these should always be in the bottom of a climber's rucksack, along with a pair of gloves or mittens, a pair of goggles, spare bootlaces, a small first-aid kit, a few metres of abseil cord, or better still tape which will fit cracks better than cord, an altimeter and a map (if only to allow the novice to place the peaks around him), and a compass.

And finally, the equipment: rope, ice axe, pitons, etc., all in good condition, should be selected for each route accordingly.

THE RULES OF THE GAME

In mountaineering, as in any sport, certain rules must be borne in mind:

Bad weather – You should keep an eye on things like unexpected storms, high winds, unpredictable cloud, freezing cold, potential avalanche slopes, falling seracs, snow bridges which can become very fragile at certain times, verglas on the face, thick mist or simply nightfall; all of them are as important as dry rock or good cramponning snow. Naturally, you should set off only in good weather, but you should never undertake any route unless you are certain of being able to reverse it from the summit in poor weather. It is no good counting on sunshine and ignoring the possibility of bad weather, and it is wrong to say that 'the Alps are killers'. Rocks and avalanches fall because gravity acts in the mountains. Barometers and thermometers rise and fall according to another law of physics. The climber should understand these laws and take note of them.

Nervous tension – Because of the astonishing profusion of peaks, with their faces and ridges, and because of the number of ski-lifts, it is possible to do a number of routes in a very short time, since the approaches can be very short. I myself have done the traverse of the Grépon and the Brenva route on Mont Blanc in two days: 6.15 am, the first cable-car up from Chamonix; 6.30, Plan de l'Aiguille; 10.30, top of the Grépon (with an hour's rest on the summit); 2.00 pm, Plan de l'Aiguille; down to Chamonix for a quick shower and to get some more equipment; 4.00 pm, téléphériques to the Aiguille to Midi and then to the Helbronner (arrive at 5.15); 7.00 pm, Col de la Fourche, and the Brenva the next day. This is no sort of record; they are classic routes done in guidebook times. It was just that the weather was good and we had to make the most of it. On the other hand I feel that there is a danger in the lack of an approach, which can provide some mental relaxation; in the two days described above, or indeed in any period of good weather, it is possible because of technical expertise, equipment and téléphériques, to do so many routes one after another that there is no relaxation from strain, and this can perhaps lead to accidents.

On another occasion, I did the South Face of the Aiguille du Midi twice in one day; here again, I offer it not as a record, but as another example. 6.15 am, start from Chamonix by the first cable-car, with an American friend, Henry Candle, an habitué of Yosemite and an excellent climber; 10.30, on the summit in guidebook time (all the pitons in place). Just as we got to the téléphérique station, I heard somebody calling me: Ricardo Cassin: 'I couldn't let you know before, but I've kept my promise, and here I am to do the South Face with you!' And so I set off again, delighted to be climbing with Cassin. And it is no exaggeration to say that I would have had time to do the South Face a third time that same day.

On the traditional sort of climb, or on climbs as they used to be done, the mind could relax during the approach. On the other hand, during that day on the Grépon-Brenva expedition, my mind could not wander and I had very little time to think of anything else but the climb itself, where concentration is essential. One must be wary of getting over-tired or of losing concentration, because either of these can lead to an accident.

Commitment – The climber is a man who goes where his eyes lead him – and comes back.

Climbing is a sport, but climbing in the mountains, like ocean-racing or crossing a desert, takes place in rather different conditions from those of the common run of sports. A runner, a boxer or a rugby-player, however serious he is, can always retire from the field if he is overcome by an access of fatigue, having pushed himself too far or started off too fast, or if there is a sudden downpour. If necessary, he can push himself to the limit, drop exhausted in his tracks and be carried off to rest immediately. But a climb is not a sort of game which can be stopped at any time. Even if you are at the limits of endurance, if your feet feel like lead, if your head is swimming with exhaustion; even if nothing but an extreme effort of will keeps you going, even if lightning is flashing across the sky, you cannot sit down and say: 'Pax, I've had enough, I'm giving up.' And even when you do

On the summit ridge of Mont Maudit.

get to the top, the route is still not finished, as we saw on Annapurna and elsewhere. This is undoubtedly the hardest of rules to accept, but it is nevertheless an attraction: on every ascent the climber must risk his whole self.

ENTHUSIASM AND CLEAR THINKING

For alpinism, two things are needed: enthusiasm and clear thinking.

The first comes in at every turn. Carrying a heavy rucksack, sleeping fitfully in a hut, feeling too hot then too cold, probably hungry, undoubtedly thirsty, knowing as you set off that you cannot call a halt to the climb if you are tired, or the weather turns bad, being dependent on a companion who may be going less well than you are – turning away, in short, from your comfortable habits; this is really what is meant by enthusiasm. And enthusiasm is a most worthwhile emotion, especially in a generation which is forgetting the use of its muscles and its individual intelligence, and forgetting the sense of fulfilment and peace that can come from tiredness. Climbing and walking do not involve some unnatural process; on the contrary, they are the natural functions for which each of us has received, at birth, the necessary apparatus, and, properly indulged in, they will procure us a healthy enjoyment.

Quite as necessary as enthusiasm is clear thinking; the two qualities may appear contradictory, but are in fact complementary.

Clear thinking is a question of knowing one's own limits, while trying of course to extend them, and of accepting them, so that each climb is adapted to one's own capabilities and to those of the rope as a whole. During the climb, it means being able to make an honest assessment of the situation, not so easily done since it means being able to stand back and evaluate, uninfluenced by one's emotions or one's most ardent ambitions, the difficulties (or indeed dangers) remaining on the climb, as compared with the strength (mental and physical) of the party, so that an intelligent decision can be made whether to go on or turn back. This is an extraordinary and very rewarding self-examination, requiring exact analysis: prudence can often be confused with a sort of cowardice and a stubborn refusal to be turned back could be simply pig-headedness.

FREE AND ARTIFICIAL CLIMBING

Pitons should be used only in two very specific situations: firstly for belaying, secondly for artificial climbing and then only when all free climbing possibilities have been exhausted. Yet there are certain climbers who, having chosen a route beyond their abilities, bang in pitons in places where ten, twenty or even forty years ago, other climbers managed without artificial aids. Of course everybody is free to climb as he likes, but it is preferable that routes should be done correctly and well.

Last summer, I had the pleasure of climbing the Amone Slab, a large slab, 400 metres high, above the village of La Fouly in the Swiss Val Ferret. This is a slab which, without

On the Géant Glacier (opposite page).

being vertical or even particularly steep, is almost entirely smooth for its 400 metres length. The rock is compact, with no cracks and very few holds. The La Fouly guides have concreted in belay-pitons about every 40 metres.

But in between the belay-pitons, each pitch gives delightful free climbing, very difficult and very exposed. Because of the very compact rock with few grooves or cracks, it would be impossible to peg, and so this route will remain as unspoilt as it is now.

Another day I spent on the Sarre Roof, in the Aosta valley, an ideal climb for a wet day – which it was – because it is sheltered for all except the last few metres: it is an overhang 32 metres high and 25 metres or so in width; it may not be horizontal but it is very attractive, except that it is only just above the road and the railway. Even so, it is a useful training-ground, since all the pitons are put in vertically upwards and half of it is done on expansion bolts. Everything is in place, but the climb is strenuous and amusing.

But there is always something a little laborious about artificial climbing, whereas free climbing is lighter and less cumbersome, and therefore more satisfying. And in the latter, too, we have the satisfaction of route-finding, which brings us into closer contact with nature, with rock, ice and snow and leads us to find the best line, to search out the holds and to progress as if by instinct from pitch to pitch. And this satisfaction, this use of instinct, becomes more and more elusive as everything, including our leisure-time, is more strictly organised.

THE CHOICE OF ROUTES

The mountaineer's goal is not only to do interesting routes, but also to derive from them a deeper and less obvious satisfaction, that of becoming an alpinist; this is why the routes given here represent an evolution, though this does not necessarily imply progressive difficulty.

On the one hand, in the Mont Blanc range, there is a very great variety of routes:
Rock routes: Petits Charmoz, Aiguille du Peigne, Drus, Aiguille du Fou. Snow and ice routes: Petite Verte, Midi-Plan, Mont Blanc, the Couturier Couloir.
Mixed routes: Tour Ronde, Dolent, North Ridge of Mont Maudit, Arête de la Tour Ronde, Mont Blanc by the Innominata Ridge.
Routes where, from a single walk-up, one can do several quite different peaks: Rochefort-Géant, Courtes-Ravenel-Mummery.
Traverses from hut to hut over a summit, the descent usually following the ordinary routes: North-East Face of the Courtes, traverse of Mont Blanc, the Jorasses by the Hirondelles Ridge.
Series of routes done from one hut, which avoid the necessity for several hut-walks and also enable the climber to experience high-altitude life for days together: Midi-Plan and the Requin by the Chapeau à Cornes, the Tour Ronde and the Rochefort-Géant, the Aiguilles Dorées and the Chardonnet.

Generally speaking, the recommended routes are selected so that the would-be alpinist can get to know the different sides of the range, its general structure and the lay-out of valleys and peaks.

Moreover, each route offers the climber both technical variety and enjoyment. This explains why the sequence of climbs is based not only on the idea of technical difficulty (in itself so variable) but also on other criteria; thus although each route has its place in the series, it can rarely be directly compared with what precedes or follows. Nevertheless, each route has its place in the whole and all are there for a reason.

Again, just as the range as a whole has such a great variety of routes, each route has a variety of contrasting features: the approach: the Torino Hut, the Gonella Hut, the Plan de l'Aiguille, the Durier Hut; the altitude: the Aiguille de l'M, the Aiguille du Fou, Mont Blanc by the Frêney; the steepness: North or South Face of the Aiguille du Midi; whether the difficulty is continuous or not: the Grépon, the Mer de Glace Face and the Knubel Crack; whether the route is easy to find or not: the Grand Montets ridge on the Verte, the Couturier Couloir; whether the route is popular or not: the North Ridge of the Dolent, the Peuterey Ridge, the Aiguille du Midi and the Dent du Géant; the length of the route, which can take from three hours to two days.

Naturally, other factors have been taken into account, such as the quality of the rock or snow, whether a climb is principally strenuous (those Chamonix cracks), or principally delicate (slabs, traverses); whether or not there are good belays and protection; whether the climb is exposed; which way it faces (north, south, east, west); whether it is easy to reverse if the weather turns bad; whether the descent is long or short, obvious or awkward to find and complicated; the quality of the granite which varies according to the different peaks, the Chamonix Aiguilles, the Jorasses, the Peuterey, the Gugliermina: its colour, its smell, its friction, the way it reflects the light; and then there are all sorts of other variables, which can change from minute to minute and which affect each climber differently, according to his individual temperament.

But beyond these different factors, these subtle but important considerations, there is one necessary proviso to be made from the technical point of view: for every route, you should never be climbing at your limit, so that you will always have a margin of safety; and you must learn through experience to judge this margin of safety accurately, just as you should be able to judge accurately these resources which you, like all of us, have deep within you and which you can call on in an emergency. The only thing is that these resources must not be taken for granted; they vary too far according to the mental resilience of each individual. This is why you must never commit yourself until you are absolutely certain that you can get back, either over the summit or by turning back, even if the weather turns bad.

Finally, the times given are precise; you must stick to them and it is essential not to confuse two ways of calculating them. For example, a normal time for the traverse of the Grépon is 3–3½ hours from the C. P. Terrace. If in fine weather you stop to take photographs or to wait for a better light, or sit for an hour or two or more on the summit because it is comfortable, and in this way spend an extra three hours on the traverse, this, from the technical point of view, is unimportant. If on the other hand you spend three hours more than the guidebook time because you thought yourself technically capable of doing this particular route but have in fact had to struggle, to stop and rest, or because you got lost and got off-route, or because you spent too long sorting out the rope at the Mummery Crack or the Grand Gendarme, if in short you have spent your extra three hours on climbing and not on contemplation, then you have chosen a route that is too difficult for you and should do some hard thinking. It is in this sense that each route can be regarded as a test.

Of course, no climb is simply a time-trial; far from it, a climb should represent a new and complete freedom. You have escaped from the city, and then, once you set out on the mountain path, you go as you please. I myself must have stopped innumerable times, simply because it was so beautiful, or have waited for a better light on such-and-such a face, or have broken into a run to catch the sunrise, or have waited in the evening to watch the sunset. At other times I have hurried up at night from the Montenvers to the shoulder of the Drus in two hours to take part in a rescue, or else sat for half an afternoon looking at the soaring lines of the South-West Pillar and the sunlight playing on the granite.

Alpinism is freedom, but this freedom cannot exist if the climber does not play the game correctly, for his own sake above all. This is true of the times; it is also true for the pitons used. What is the point of doing the Walker, or even the South Face of the Midi, if to do so you have to use twice the number of pitons necessary and more than were used on the first ascent? After all, you hope to become an alpinist. It has been said that part of the appeal of alpinism as a sport lies in the fact that it takes place not in a stadium, but out in the wilds and without an audience. This is no doubt true. On the other hand, a stadium means a judge, and an audience which can pick out and punish any mistakes or errors. To use more pitons than necessary proves that you are out of your depth, that you are ignoring the rules and cheating, and that you deserve to be eliminated if you do it again. You, the climber, must be the judge. No doubt, it is admirable to rise above yourself in poor weather, but it is not so admirable to climb repeatedly and inelegantly beyond your capability.

It is above all essential that the climber should not have to force himself, for any reason, whether he is on a III or a VI; he will not be able to keep it up and will undoubtedly come to harm. He should on the contrary be as it were 'inspired', at ease physically and mentally, always perfectly balanced, possessing expertise and common sense; his movements should be imaginative, his daring should be calculated; he should be elated, cheerful rather than gloomy, serene, light-hearted and well-balanced rather than ecstatic or dogged; he should move rhythmically and intelligently, anticipating well ahead, flexible, receptive to the quality of the rock, the placing of the holds and to the consistency of the snow; all this on an instinctive, unforced level, and coming from a direct communion between the climber himself, the face, the sky and the winds.

Becoming an alpinist involves climbing well, but, even more, it involves improving this sense of communion with every route, understanding the high mountains better, integrating oneself more and more with the snow and the rock.

KEEPING TO TIME

Generally speaking, doing a route takes two days: the walk up to the hut on the first day, and the route itself the second. Try to get to the hut early, at least early enough to sort out the start of the path or the climb that you will be taking the next day. For certain routes, it is a good idea to go and have a look at the bergschrund.

From the hut itself, and also from the route and particularly from the summit, check on the descent, because a pitch is often difficult to recognise when seen from a different angle or from the other side. If the descent does not follow the same route as the climb, check it even more carefully: marks in the snow or on the rock, landmarks, shoulders, gendarmes, brèches, ways round series of crevasses or round a large crevasse with no snow bridge cutting across a whole glacier, or ways through a continuous line of seracs.

You will normally leave the hut very early, often in the middle of the night, especially for snow routes. This is primarily for safety reasons. At night, because of the cold, the snow is firm and pleasant to walk on and above all, safe; but as soon as the sun is up, its rays will melt the snow progressively all day, so that it will become soft and loose. The result is that snow bridges become unsafe enough to break under the weight of a climber, and that the snow on some slopes grows heavier with the heat and can avalanche; moreover the stones frozen into the snow can fall as soon as they are released by melting. Setting off early and keeping to the guidebook times are both essential safety rules.

GRADINGS

It has always been possible, and fairly easy, to say of a snow or ice slope that it is at an angle of, say, 53°, which is a precise and exact piece of information for the man who wants to climb it (it is up to him to visualise the snow or ice conditions, taking into account temperature, exposure and angle); but giving any sort of grading for difficulty on rock alone posed much greater problems. At one time, it was usual to say of a pitch (slab, crack, chimney, groove, overhang) that it was easy, or was a 'crux', while adding certain details: difficult, quite difficult, dangerous, very difficult. Slab or groove pitches demanding balance-climbing were always said to be difficult and delicate, while cracks and chimneys (the Chamonix variety especially which need considerable strength) were almost always said to be difficult and strenuous. These adjectives were very vague and allowed only the most superficial of comparisons; they tended to produce surprises, sometimes unpleasant ones, and to result in accidents: difficult, very difficult, delicate, strenuous—as compared with what?

It was the climbers in the Eastern Alps who first thought of using a system of gradings of difficulty in six degrees (from I, the easiest, to VI, the most difficult, with an upper and lower grade, superior and inferior, for each). This was perfectly understandable; in these ranges, especially in the Dolomites, the climbs are almost exclusively rock.

For the Western Alps, things seemed rather more difficult; the climbs are often mixed (rock, snow and ice), the altitudes are greater and this in itself adds to the difficulties, and moreover the Western Alps are predominantly granite where the Dolomites are limestone. Lucien Devies, however, always on the watch for new ideas in the climbing world and for ways of improving the technical descriptions in the Vallot guides of which he was joint editor, put forward proposals, with Armand Charlet and the Italian climbers Piero Zanetti, Giusto Gervasutti and Gabrielle Boccalatte, who knew both the Dolomites and the Mont Blanc range, for a system of numerical gradings for the Western Alps, which incorporated a novel and original idea: that of giving a sample graded list of climbs which would act as a reference for the grading of other climbs.

Most climbers immediately realised the value of the gradings and of the graded list, but there were some who were shocked and accused Devies of reducing the mountains to a mere catalogue of numbers; they felt that the aura and the beauty of the Grépon or the Drus would be lost if they were to be prosaically described as routes of grade III or IV. This attributed to the gradings an importance which had never been claimed for them; their aim was simply practical, to give better guidance to climbers. And it is essential to remember that, even so, numerical gradings have their limits; after all, the difficulty of any route as a whole involves more than the intrinsic difficulty of any particular pitch (which is in any case always graded for dry rock, to allow for some precision); whether the face is accessible or involves a long walk; how long or short the walk up is, and whether it is easy or awkward to find; the height or vertical height of the climb itself; its orientation, whether south-facing and therefore sunny, or north-facing and therefore in the shade; whether there are plenty of good stances, that is platforms or ledges, between pitches; whether the descent is easy or difficult. And other things must be taken into account, too, which make up the whole atmosphere of the climb: its reputation, its general structure (convex and open, or concave and shut in), whether it attracts cloud, whether it is exposed to wind or sheltered. It would therefore be very unwise to confuse the numerical grading of a climb with its value, to say nothing of its beauty and interest; the concepts are totally different and supplement each other.

It might be possible to accuse the grading system of removing some of the mystery of the mountains. But everyone is, after all, perfectly free to make enquiries or not as to the geography of the Grépon or as to the different ways of getting to the summit. And in any case, not all problems are solved by a map, a compass, a description with grading and a sketch; it is one of the attractions of the sport that there are other factors such as the night temperature which will ensure whether the snow freezes or not, the way the rising sun looks (pale, bright, or indeed invisible), whether the clouds are ominous or encouraging, whether visibility is good or limited for a couple of hours to only a few metres — so many things! Nothing can ever wholly remove mystery from the mountains.

Another accusation against numerical gradings made by some, and which arises from the foregoing, is this: that the gradings lead to an unfortunate tendency on the part of the climber to say: 'I'm not interested in that route, it's only a IV.' Alpinists do of course have their faults, and these can include arrogance or vanity, but I have never in fact heard that particular remark. On the other hand, if there are two routes for a given summit, one a IV and the other a V, there seems nothing to prevent a good climber used to grade V from choosing it rather than the IV. And quite often, because he is looking at some other time for a different sort of pleasure or because he has different responsibilities, he will come back and do the IV route, with some less able friends.

I have often said myself: 'This is an interesting route, with excellent views and with four pitches of V, three of them delightful.' I do not imply by this any self-satisfaction or scorn of other people's efforts, but simply that a climber will enjoy them.

As for artificial climbing, at first it was graded according to the same VI degrees, but, rightly, a different system of grading has evolved:

Free climbing: Six degrees. I represents a degree of difficulty where hands are barely necessary, and is intermediate between walking and climbing, whereas VI represents the limits of human capability.

Artificial climbing: Four degrees. A1 is easy artificial, for example placing pitons on an easy-angled but holdless slab, with one crack across it so that pegging is no problem. Often this sort of artificial is easier than free climbing of VI, V or even IV. A4 is very difficult artificial; it implies that pegging is hazardous, that the rock is either poor or very compact with few cracks or holes, and that the climber is awkwardly placed for banging in pitons, under a roof, for instance, or horizontally under a traverse, or at the back of an overhung dièdre. The pitons themselves are uncertain. They are to be used for climbing and not for belays, which means that they will hold the weight of a climber but not of a falling climber.

Finally it is easier and more exact to grade a pitch (slab, crack, chimney, overhang), rather than a whole route which is made up of a number of pitches which may or may not be of the same standard. Take for example the East (or Mer de Glace) Face of the Grépon; it is composed of a series of pitches mostly of grade IV; the route comes out at the Balfour Brèche under the summit block of the Grépon, which is climbed by the Knubel Crack, V sup. Thus, from the gradings, the climber knows that the most difficult pitch comes at the top of the climb, after some 800 metres of climbing. If the same pitch, still graded as V sup., appeared at the beginning of a route, it would probably weigh less heavy in the scales when the decision to do the route is taken; the gradings have the advantage of delineating the problem clearly.

The grading of pitches is established by a consensus of climbers capable of doing the most difficult pitches. It is interesting to note that without prior consultation, climbers very often grade the same pitch at the same standard of difficulty.

The Mer de Glace. The Grandes Jorasses and the Aiguille du Géant in the background, the Chamonix Aiguilles on the right.

ROUTES ARRANGED BY SUMMIT

ADOLPHE REY (PIC)
Salluard Route   148

AIGUILLES (CHAMONIX)
Traverse   200

AMONE SLAB   38

ARGENTIÈRE (AIGUILLE D')
Ordinary Route   60
North Face   162

BIONNASSAY (AIGUILLE DE)
North-West Face   126

BLAITIÈRE (AIGUILLE DE)
Blaitière-Ciseaux-Fou Traverse   96
West Face   174

BOSSONS (GLACIER DES)   31

BRENVA (AIGUILLE DE LA)
East Face   166

CAPUCIN (GRAND)
East Face   212

CHARDONNET (AIGUILLE DU)
Forbes Arête   82
North Spur   144

CHARMOZ (GRANDS)
Charmoz-Grépon Traverse   90

CHARMOZ (PETITS)
Traverse   40

COURTES (LES)
North-East Face   84
Courtes-Ravanel-Mummery Traverse   104
Central North-North-East Spur   184
North Face   222

CROCODILE (DENT DU)
East Ridge   168

CROUX (AIGUILLE)
South Face   46
South-East Face   112

DIABLE (AIGUILLES DU)
Traverse   140

DORÉES (AIGUILLES)
Traverse   78

DROITES (LES)
North Spur   196
North Face   234

DRUS (LES)
Petit Dru-Grand Dru Traverse   108
North Face   192
Bonatti Pillar   218
West Face — American Direct   232

ÉCANDIES (LES)
Traverse   80

FOU (AIGUILLE DU)
South Face   220

GÉANT (DENT DU)
Ordinary Route   92
South Face   146

GLIÈRE (CHAPELLE DE LA)
South Ridge   33

GRÉPON (AIGUILLE DU)
Grands Charmoz-Grépon Traverse   90
Pic de Roc-Grépon Traverse   160

GUGLIERMINA (POINTE)
South-West Face   208

INDEX (AIGUILLE DE L')
South-East Ridge   32

INNOMINATA (POINTE DE L')
South Ridge   46

JORASSES (GRANDES)
Ordinary Route   70
Hirondelles Ridge   164
Rochefort-Jorasses Traverse   178
Pointe Croz — Central Spur   228
Walker Spur   230

JORASSES (PETITES)
South Ridge   106
West Face   204

LACHENAL (POINTE)
South-South-East Face   138

M (AIGUILLE DE L')
North-North-East Ridge   58
Ménégaux and Couzy Routes   120

MIAGE (DÔMES DE)
Traverse   48

MIDI (AIGUILLE DU)
Arête des Cosmiques (South-South-West Ridge)   56
Midi-Plan Traverse   64
Eperon des Cosmiques   138
South Face   142
Frendo Spur   156

MINARET (LE)
South-East Spur and South Face Direct   152

MOINE (AIGUILLE DU)
South Ridge   54
East Face   132

MONT BLANC
Ordinary Route   72
Aiguilles Grises Route   86

Traverse	126
Brenva Spur	144
Innominata Ridge	194
Route Major	214
Peuterey Ridge	224
Central Pillar of Frêney	236

MONT BLANC DU TACUL

Ordinary Route	56
Gervasutti Couloir	150
Boccalatte Pillar	176
Gervasutti Pillar	206

MONT DOLENT

North Ridge	118

MONT MAUDIT

Tour Ronde Ridge	130
Crétier Route	172

MUMMERY (AIGUILLE)

Courtes-Ravanel-Mummery Traverse	104

PAIN DE SUCRE D'ENVERS DU PLAN

North Face	124

PEIGNE (AIGUILLE DU)

Ordinary Route	88
Papillons Ridge (West Ridge proper) West Face,	
North-West Pillar, North-West Face, North Ridge	134
Vaucher Route	154

PÈLERINS (AIGUILLE DES)

Grütter Ridge	76
Carmichael Route	88

PEUTEREY (AIGUILLE NOIRE DE)

South Ridge	182
West Face	198

PERSÉVÉRANCE (AIGUILLE DE LA)

North-East Ridge	36

PLAN (AIGUILLE DU)

Midi-Plan Traverse	64
Ryan-Lochmatter Ridge	122
North Face	170

PLANPRAZ (CLOCHERS AND CLOCHETONS)

Traverse	30

PORTALET (PETIT CLOCHER DU)

East Face and South-East Ridge	158

POUCE (AIGUILLE DU)

South Face – Voie des Dalles	37

RAVANEL (AIGUILLE)

Courtes-Ravanel-Mummery Traverse	104

REQUIN (DENT DU)

South-East Ridge	68
East Face	116
North Face	188

ROCHEFORT (AIGUILLE DE)

Traverse of the Ridges	92
Rochefort-Jorasses Traverse	178

SARRE ROOF

	39

TACUL (PYRAMIDE DU)

East Ridge	62

TACUL (TRIDENT DU)

Lépiney Route	102

TOUR (AIGUILLE DU)

Table de Roc Ridge	52

TOUR NOIR (LE)

Traverse	50

TOUR RONDE (LA)

South-East Ridge	44
North Face	98

TRÉLATÊTE (AIGUILLE DE)

Traverse	100

TRIOLET

North Face	210

VERTE (AIGUILLE)

Whymper Couloir	110
Grands Montets Ridge	180
Sans Nom Ridge	186
Couturier Couloir	190
Nant Blanc Face	216

VERTE (PETITE AIGUILLE)

Ordinary Route	42

Orientation

The directions *right* and *left* assume that the climber is following the direction described in the guide. On the other hand, the phrases *right bank* and *left bank* refer to the direction of flow, i.e. looking downwards along the river, glacier or couloir.

The reader should note that the different heights given for the Aiguille du Midi are deliberate and correspond either to the start (route 21, with a bivouac on the summit) or to the finish (routes 17, 53, 55, 62).

Gradings

(NB. Not to be confused with English and USA gradings; cf translators' note on right)

F	facile	D	difficile
PD	peu difficile	TD	très difficile
AD	assez difficile	ED	extrêmement difficile

Abbreviations

hrs:	hours	N:	North	W:	West
min:	minute	S:	South	E:	East
m:	metres				

Diagrams

———— :	route described
· · · · · · · · :	any concealed section of the route described
- - - - - - :	any variant of the route described
—·—·—·— :	other routes

Translators' note

We have followed common British and American usage in naming routes and features, despite apparent inconsistencies (*Fissure Brown* on the Blaitière, as opposed to *Knubel Crack* on the Grépon):

Certain continental terms in wide use among American and British alpinists have been taken as understood without need of definition: bergschrund, brèche, couloir, dièdre, gendarme, névé, rognon, serac.

In the gradings the symbols *inf.* and *sup.* denote pitches *low* and *high* in their category. Verbal gradings are not translated to avoid any confusion with American and English rock-climbing grades.

JHMT CHT

THE HUNDRED FINEST ROUTES

1. **CLOCHER AND CLOCHETONS DE PLANPRAZ**   30
Traverse

2. **GLACIER DES BOSSONS**   31
Introduction to ice-climbing

3. **AIGUILLE DE L'INDEX**   32
South-East Ridge

4. **CHAPELLE DE LA GLIÈRE**   33
South Ridge

5. **AIGUILLE DE LA PERSÉVÉRANCE**   36
North-East Ridge

6. **AIGUILLE DU POUCE**   37
South Face – Voie des Dalles

7. **AMONE SLAB**   38

8. **SARRE ROOF**   39

9. **PETITS CHARMOZ**   40
Traverse

10. **PETITE AIGUILLE VERTE**   42
Ordinary Route

11. **TOUR RONDE-VALLÉE BLANCHE**   44
South-East Ridge

12. **AIGUILLE CROUX**   46
South Face

POINTE DE L'INNOMINATA
South Ridge

13. **DÔMES DE MIAGE**   48
Traverse

14. **TOUR NOIR**   50
Traverse

15. **AIGUILLE DU TOUR**   52
Table de Roc Ridge

16. **AIGUILLE DU MOINE**   54
South Ridge

17. **MONT BLANC DU TACUL**   56
Ordinary Route
AIGUILLE DU MIDI
Arête des Cosmiques (South-South-West Ridge)

18. **AIGUILLE DE L'M**   58
North-North-East Ridge

19. **AIGUILLE D'ARGENTIÉRE**   60
Ordinary Route

20. **PYRAMIDES DU TACUL**   62
East Ridge

21. **AIGUILLE DU MIDI – AIGUILLE DU PLAN**   64
Traverse

22. **DENT DU REQUIN**   68
South-East Ridge or Chapeau à Cornes Ridge

23. **GRANDES JORASSES**   70
Ordinary Route

24. **MONT BLANC**   72
Ordinary Route

25. **AIGUILLE DES PÈLERINS**   76
Grütter Ridge

26. **AIGUILLES DORÉES**   78
Traverse

27. **LES ÉCANDIES**   80
Traverse

28. **AIGUILLE DU CHARDONNET**   82
Forbes Arête

29. **LES COURTES**   84
North-East Face

30. **MONT BLANC**   86
Aiguilles Grises Route

31. **AIGUILLE DU PEIGNE**   88
Ordinary Route
AIGUILLES DES PÈLERINS
Carmichael Route

32. **GRANDS CHARMOZ – GREPON**   90
Traverse

33. **AIGUILLE DE ROCHEFORT**   92
Traverse of the Ridges
DENT DU GÉANT
Ordinary Route

34. **AIGUILLE DE BLAITIERE**
LES CISEAUX – AIGUILLE DU FOU   96
Traverse

35. **TOUR RONDE**   98
North Face

36. **AIGUILLES DE TRÉLATÊTE**   100
Traverse

37. **TRIDENT DU TACUL**   102
Lépiney Route

38. **LES COURTES – AIG. RAVANEL – MUMMERY**   104
Traverse

39. **PETITES JORASSES**   106
South Ridge

40. **PETIT DRU – GRAND DRU**   108
Traverse

41. **AIGUILLE VERTE**   110
Whymper Couloir

42. **AIGUILLE CROUX**   112
South-East Face

43. **AIGUILLE DU CHARDONNET**   114
North Spur

44. **DENT DU REQUIN**   116
East Face

45. **MONT DOLENT**   118
North Ridge

46. **AIGUILLE DE L'M**   120
Ménégaux and Couzy Routes

47. **AIGUILLE DU PLAN**   122
Ryan-Lochmatter Ridge

48. **PAIN DE SUCRE D'ENVERS DU PLAN**   124
North Face

49. **AIGUILLE DE BIONNASSAY**   126
North-West Face
     MONT BLANC
Traverse

50. **MONT MAUDIT**   130
Tour Ronde Ridge

51. **AIGUILLE DU MOINE**   132
East Face

52. **AIGUILLE DU PEIGNE**   134
Papillons Ridge (West Ridge proper), West Face,
North-West Pillar, North-West Face, North Ridge

53. **POINTE LACHENAL**   138
South-South-East Face
     AIGUILLE DU MIDI
Eperon des Cosmiques

54. **AIG. DU DIABLE – MONT BLANC DU TACUL**   140
Traverse

55. **AIGUILLE DU MIDI**   142
South Face

56. **MONT BLANC**   144
Brenva Spur

57. **DENT DU GÉANT**   146
South Face

58. **PIC ADOLPHE REY**   148
Salluard Route

59. **MONT BLANC DU TACUL**   150
Gervasutti Couloir

60. **LE MINARET**   152
South-East Spur and South Face Direct

61. **AIGUILLE DU PEIGNE**   154
Vaucher Route

62. **AIGUILLE DU MIDI**   156
Frendo Spur

63. **PETIT CLOCHER DU PORTALET**   158
East Face and South-East Ridge

64. **PIC DE ROC – GRÉPON**   160
Traverse

65. **AIGUILLE D'ARGENTIÈRE**   162
North Face

66. **GRANDES JORASSES**   164
Hirondelles Ridge

67. **AIGUILLE DE LA BRENVA**   166
East Face

68. **DENT DU CROCODILE**   168
East Ridge

69. **AIGUILLE DU PLAN**   170
North Face

70. **MONT MAUDIT**   172
Crétier Route

71. **AIGUILLE DE BLAITIÈRE**   174
West Face

72. **MONT BLANC DU TACUL**   176
Boccalatte Pillar

73. **ROCHEFORT RIDGES – GRANDES JORASSES**   178
Traverse

74. **AIGUILLE VERTE**   180
Grands Montets Ridge

75. **AIGUILLE NOIRE DE PEUTEREY**   182
South Ridge

76. **LES COURTES**   184
Central North-North-East Spur

77. **AIGUILLE VERTE**   186
Sans Nom Ridge

78. **DENT DU REQUIN**   188
North Face

79. **AIGUILLE VERTE**   190
Couturier Couloir

80. **PETIT DRU**   192
North Face

81. **MONT BLANC**   194
Innominata Ridge

82. **LES DROITES**   196
North Spur

83. **AIGUILLE NOIRE DE PEUTEREY**   198
West Face

84. **CHAMONIX AIGUILLES**   200
Aiguille du Midi-Grépon Traverse

85. **PETITES JORASSES**   204
West Face

86. **MONT BLANC DU TACUL**   206
Gervasutti Pillar

87. **POINTE GUGLIERMINA**   208
South-East Face

88. **AIGUILLE DU TRIOLET**   210
North Face

89. **GRAND CAPUCIN**   212
East Face

90. **MONT BLANC**   214
Route Major

91. **AIGUILLE VERTE**   216
Nant Blanc Face

92. **PETIT DRU**   218
Bonatti Pillar

93. **AIGUILLE DU FOU**   220
South Face

94. **LES COURTES**   222
North Face

95. **MONT BLANC**   224
Peuterey Ridge

96. **GRANDES JORASSES**   228
Pointe Croz – Central Spur

97. **GRANDES JORASSES**   230
Walker Spur

98. **PETIT DRU**   232
West Face – American Direct

99. **LES DROITES**   234
North Face

100. **MONT BLANC**   236
Central Pillar of Frêney

FROM THE AIGUILLES ROUGES TO THE FRENEY PILLAR

A hundred routes are not very many for a range with as many possibilities as this, but they would be a fine enough list of achievements for a young climber. The first climbs are not in the Mont Blanc range itself but in the surrounding area, and particularly in the Aiguilles Rouges; these have a magnificent view over the great range and are particularly useful, either for training or for pleasant climbing when bad weather or fresh snow put high altitude routes out of condition.

As for the range itself, the routes are chosen not just for their gradings, but by taking into account a variety of factors, difficulty and grading included, which contribute to their quality. To check the impartiality of my choice, I have called upon a number of climbers of different age groups and very often, without prior consultation and without even knowing each other, they have made the same choices as myself, having either done the routes in question themselves, or having wanted to do them.

But what is essential in the choice of routes is that it has been made to follow a sequence; for every climber, whatever his status, beginner or expert mountaineer, the routes are at each standard the finest corresponding to the technical expertise and experience he may have at that stage in his career.

The choice is in any case independent of fashion and it has this additional and final advantage: that it should take the climber all over this range, and make him acquainted with all its lavish variety.

On the Arête des Cosmiques.

1. CLOCHER AND CLOCHETONS DE PLANPRAZ 2428m
Traverse

The Clocher and the Clochetons (Belfry and Bell-towers) are in the Aiguilles Rouges chain opposite the Mont Blanc range, on the crest of the ridge between the Chamonix valley and the barren slopes of the La Diosaz valley. The climb, which takes in the traverse of the Clocher, the Petit Clocher and the three Clochetons, and comes back over the Petit Clocher, the N Ridge (IV) and the Layback Flake (V) on the Clocher involves a number of different pitches: slabs, cracks and chimneys need particular techniques: there is balance climbing and chimney climbing, along with practice in abseiling and the possibility of doing a Tyrolean traverse. The rock on the Clocher and Clochetons is midway between the limestone of many training crags and the Mont Blanc granite. The holds are sometimes sharp, but more often rounded with use. The chimney on the third Clocheton, although very short, is an excellent example of the sort of chimneys and cracks typical of the Chamonix area such as one finds on the Aiguilles.

● **Grade**: AD with pitches of IV (IV sup. if the N Ridge is climbed and V with the Layback Flake).
● **Time**: 2–5 hrs depending upon the route chosen.
● **Equipment**: Abseil rope.
● **Starting point**: Planpraz (1999m). The Clocher and the Clochetons can be seen from the téléphérique station and the path is marked. The approach is short and takes one hour to reach the col west of the Clocher where the rucksacks are left. For fun, and for practice too, it is interesting to bivouac on the Planpraz plateau.
● **Route**

Clocher: From the col W of the Clocher, climb the W Face of the Clocher up steep easy flakes for about 10m, then, when the face becomes smooth and vertical, traverse horizontally right to reach the SW Ridge (belay). Turn the SW Ridge, traverse horizontally for 5m onto the S Face and then climb straight up a thin crack to reach and climb a wider crack with rounded edges (III, strenuous) or the slab on its right (III, delicate) to the summit. Descent: abseil (there is a ring in place on the starting platform).

Clochetons: Between the Clocher and the Clochetons is the Petit Clocher. To reach the Clochetons, one must either avoid this (by descending into the little gully on the N), or, better, traverse it: climb the S Ridge and descend the E Ridge (several moves of III).

First Clocheton: (SW, 2407m). Climb the steep 20m slab to the S (III sup.). Abseil down the E Face.

Second Clocheton: (Central, 2412m). From the brèche between the first two Clochetons traverse left (descending slightly) to climb a vertical wall 5–6m high on the NW side (IV), moving right to reach a large platform. This platform can also be reached from the summit platform of the first Clocheton, which is at the same height, by a Tyrolean traverse. For the traverse the rope is fixed to a rock spike on the First Clocheton and to a large iron ring in place on the platform of the Central Clocheton. From the platform make a short exposed ascent (III) to reach the narrow sloping summit. To descend, abseil down the partly overhanging SE flank, passing the rope round the summit of the Clocheton itself (delicate start).

Third Clocheton: (NE 2411m). Climb a short chimney, fairly difficult at the start (IV), on the W side, slightly right of a point directly below the summit, to reach a platform. From here gain the summit by the E Face on the right. Abseil down the W side putting the rope round a large piton in place.

Return to the brèche between the First Clocheton and the Petit Clocher. From here traverse back over the Petit Clocher to reach the foot of the N Ridge of the Clocher. If you are feeling fit, climb the ridge, a delicate and exposed pitch (IV sup.) on friction holds, followed by a layback. It is also possible, after abseiling down, to climb back up the Clocher by a strenuous layback (V) along a detached flake situated above the small flakes on the W Face (where the ordinary route traverses to the right).

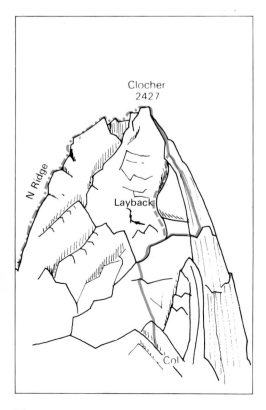

Layback on the Clocher de Planpraz.

2. GLACIER DES BOSSONS
Introduction to ice-climbing

This can scarcely be called a route, but it is a very useful initiation into ice-climbing and provides a very enjoyable expedition. First, an important piece of advice: it is essential to take great care, as the ice is very smooth and if you slip you will find it difficult to brake.

In some years but not others, it is possible to climb the glacier as far as the Pyramides (1895m); if it is impossible, you should spend more time lower down on the glacier and practice more intensively. In any case, you will find a day on the Bossons Glacier useful, whether you are a novice, or a mountaineer more experienced on snow and ice who wants a few hours at the beginning of a holiday to get used to crampons and to redevelop the different balance required for ice-climbing.

Either the same day if you are fit, or preferably later on, from the chalet des Pyramides (1895m) you can walk along the Montagne de la Côte (the old road to Mont Blanc) and follow the path to Mont Corbeau (2334m) and the Gîte à Balmat (2530m). This gives a magnificent view of the Bossons and Taconnaz Glaciers, and over the great glacier coming down from Mont Blanc. You can then walk down over the Bossons Glacier towards the Junction and come back by the Pierre à l'Echelle path and the Plan de l'Aiguille téléphérique. This route can also be done the other way round, and in either case it will help you to develop a technique of route-finding on a glacier.

● **Starting point**: Les Bossons. At about

the height of the ski-jump, a path goes off to the right and leads to the foot of the glacier — a very fine landscape formed by the bowl between the moraines.

● **Equipment**: Select crampons with short, well-sharpened points; on ice crampons with long points give you the feeling of standing on stilts and the points exert considerable leverage. On the other hand crampons with long points are very good on snow. It is better, besides, to have 12-point crampons, that is with front points.

So far as axes are concerned, you should have two, for inevitably axes which give a good belay cut badly because they stick, and those which cut well belay badly. The axe has also to act as a walking-stick, and it is important that the pick is sharp, otherwise the axe will slip. All this should show you the absolute necessity of keeping your equipment always in an excellent state of repair.

Carry a few ice-pitons and ice-screws and put them in to find out their potential.

● **Time**: 2–8 hrs depending on the route chosen.

● **Route**: Choose your own. Everyone can go where he likes, depending on his technique and upon possible danger from falling seracs.

In fact, it is a matter of gaining experience on the material 'ice', unfamiliar by comparison with rock with which beginners are made familiar on outcrops, on crevasses, on seracs and on névé snow, which can be found at the side of the glacier.

So on a first visit, on the level glacier or on gentle slopes, walk about in all directions, turn about, make changes of direction until you feel that you have acquired a new sense of balance, and that the crampons are as familiar as if they were part of the boot and the feet.

Then, still with crampons on, begin to jump about, landing with legs well bent.

Now try steeper and steeper slopes, but only short ones with a good run-out at the base, to learn why you stay in place, how and how far. Observe the usefulness of the axe, and then once you have become practised in your crampons repeat the same exercises but without your axe — this will make you balance properly on your feet.

Learn about and try out belaying methods on ice with ice-screws, always using a dynamic belay.

With your axe, learn to cut steps then to use the pick, first while stationary and then while moving in ascent and descent to synchronise and put rhythm into the sequence of movements.

Repeat the same exercises but without crampons, to make you take care over step-cutting; count how many cuts are needed to make a step, and try gradually to reduce them. Learn also how to cut ice-mushrooms and then how to abseil down ice.

During this apprenticeship, remember not to step on the ropes. The result will be an enjoyable, interesting and extremely valuable day.

Dynamic belay on ice (left).
Crampon technique (above).

3. AIGUILLE DE L'INDEX 2595m
South-East Ridge

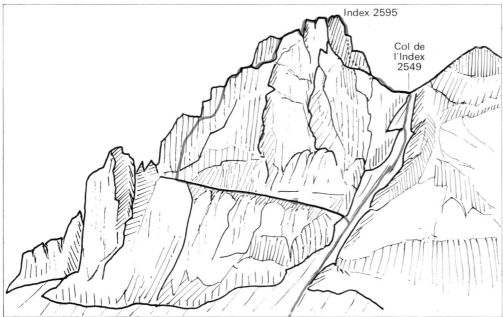

A very attractive little route with magnificent views. The Index is like the Clocher and Clochetons (and at a slightly higher level of difficulty the Chapelle de la Glière Ridge, the Aiguilles Crochues, the Aiguille de la Persévérance, the Aiguille de Praz-Torrent, the Perrons and so on) in being an intermediary route, not just a training route, but not yet quite a high-mountain route. And you come out on summits which are superb viewpoints. As well as their technical difficulty, the climbs in the Aiguilles Rouges are an excellent way of getting to know the Mont Blanc range, always in front of your eyes. You can see its changing contours all day, as the sun strikes and highlights one slope after another. In this way the young climber can learn the lay-out of the peaks and their different faces, and realise the effects of the sun for the snow-routes he will do later; conversely, the play of light and shadow brings out the faces and ridges which can be confusing otherwise. This is a very pleasant way of learning the geography of the range and the relative positions of the peaks (remember of course to bring a map), of discovering not only the climb itself but the feeling of high altitude, and of developing ambitions to become 'attuned' to it.

The SE Ridge of the Index has been gardened, so that the holds are good and there are good belay-points.

- **Grade:** AD.
- **Time:** 1–1½ hrs.
- **Equipment:** Abseil cord.
- **Starting point:** From the Index téléphérique.
- **Route:** From the Index téléphérique go across to the bottom of the couloir coming down from the Col de l'Index and go up towards the SE Ridge by a grassy ledge cutting across the E Face. Just before reaching the ridge climb a chimney (III) leading to the crest of the ridge. The line of ascent is now determined by the ridge itself to the summit; unclimbable steps are turned on the right (III with a move of IV).

Descent: On the Brévent side follow to the left (towards the S) a short descending ledge and return right along a longer ledge (towards the N), which leads to a small shoulder from which an abseil (on the NW side) leads to the Col de l'Index. Now descend the easy E couloir.

Abseil on the Index.

4. CHAPELLE DE LA GLIERE 2663m
South Ridge

This route bears some resemblance to the Index, being also on the Glière, but it is higher, longer and more difficult; it is also more imposing, since the narrow, steep ridge rears up suddenly out of the great scree-slopes. The route is to the W of the Index, and is reached by turning the base of the Index to get to the foot of the ridge. The climbing is very varied: cracks, dièdres, ridges and slabs (including a thin, exposed traverse); the route is of sustained difficulty and finishes with a fine pitch up to the Clocher de la Chapelle. Finally, since it involves some fifteen pitches, the route is useful training in rope-work and belaying.

● **Grade:** D with two moves of IV sup.
● **Time:** 2–3 hrs.
● **Equipment:** Abseil rope.
● **Starting point:** From the Index téléphérique.
● **Route:** From the upper téléphérique station go down and round the bottom of the SE Ridge of the Index and then to the couloir just before the Chapelle Ridge (20 min). Climb this couloir up smooth slabs for about 20m to reach the foot of a dièdre-crack. Climb this (IV) to the ridge and follow the ridge to the foot of a large 50 metre dièdre (IV, with a move of IV sup.). Climb this to get out again onto the ridge, follow the ridge to the foot of a 2 metre wall and climb this (IV sup.). You are now on the left-hand side of a great smooth slab. Traverse horizontally right across it (IV). An easy section now follows, cut by a small dièdre (IV) which leads to the brèche between the great S shoulder and the Chapelle itself. Climb this at first on the left-hand side, then up the ridge and the summit slab (IV, a move of IV sup.).

Descent: Abseil (starting from a sitting position). To return to the téléphérique station, follow the track which traverses (apart from short ascents and descents) roughly level with the Col de l'Index.

Chapelle de la Glière Ridge: the slab pitch (left).

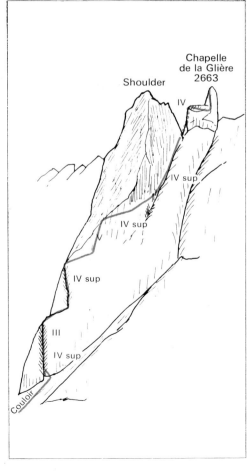

Slab on the Clocher de Planpraz (left)
Bossons Glacier (below)
The Mont Blanc range from the Aiguilles Rouges
(opposite page, above)
The North-East Ridge of the Aiguille de la Persévérance
(opposite page, below left)
The Aiguilles Rouges are often possible when there is
bad weather high up — (opposite page, below right)
ice on the Aiguille du Midi.

5. AIGUILLE DE LA PERSEVERANCE
North-East Ridge
2899m

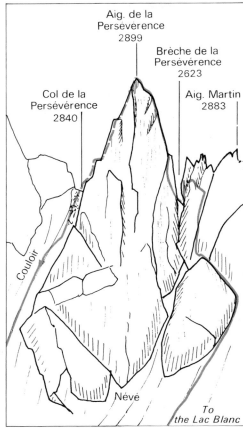

This is undoubtedly the finest summit of all the Aiguilles Rouges, and it reveals two other facets of climbing scarcely found on the preceding routes, which are popular and easy of access: the sense of isolation, and the technical difficulties of route-finding.

In the Mont Blanc range itself, the routes are determined by the natural geological features of the granite and by infrequent but obvious holds; not so on the Aiguilles Rouges, particularly on certain climbs like the NE Ridge of the Persévérance. Difficulties must be avoided rather than overcome, and you will need to develop an instinct for the rock; you will find it a help to remain constantly on the alert, searching, guessing, picking out both the route itself and the holds, which are often at irregular intervals, incut or concealed; they must be used in a certain way, for balance and for pulling up.

As well as technical difficulty, the NE Ridge of the Persévérance has interest and character; the stance in the brèche is impressive and so is the climb itself, since the ridge looks over both the sunny S Face and the cold, barren N Face.

- **1st Ascent:** A. and G. Charlet, 7 June 1925.
- **Grade:** D with three moves of IV sup.

- **Time:** 2 hrs from the brèche to the summit.
- **Starting point:** The simplest is from the Index téléphérique and from there to the hut at the Lac Blanc. The route can be done in the day, but I strongly recommend either a night at the Lac Blanc Hut or a bivouac beside the lake; the latter will give magnificent views of sunset and sunrise. It is also possible to set out from the Col des Montets or from Argentière by the path to L'Aiguillette; all these approaches are very fine.
- **Route** – *Outline:* Easy to find so far as the ridge itself is concerned. From the brèche after a detour left to avoid the big bulge the ridge itself, fairly broad and cut by dièdres, is followed. On the other hand, to reach the brèche it is necessary not to follow the couloir coming down from it, but to ascend the often snowy couloir on the right of the Aiguille Martin for about 150m to the point where a ledge rising to the left cuts across the Aiguille Martin. Follow this ledge and before it reaches the couloir from the Brèche de la Persévérance, climb straight up small pillars and chimneys to reach the small SW shoulder of the Aiguille Martin just above the Brèche. Gain a small platform and make a 10m abseil from a piton in place to reach the brèche, an imposing stance.

Description: From the brèche traverse horizontally left for 15m or so to reach a sort of secondary ridge which is followed for some 10m (III and IV) to a ledge on the right which leads back above the bulge overhanging the brèche. Follow a small couloir-dièdre with two cracks (IV sup.) to reach a small balcony-ledge. On the right traverse below an overhang (IV sup., very good hand-holds on the right at the start), and then climb a crack (IV) to reach a system of slabs and open grooves (IV) which lead to the summit.

Descent: Descend the W Ridge easily (one abseil) to reach the Col de la Persévérance, and from there descend slabs and then snow and scree on the south side.

The Aiguille de la Persévérance, with the North-East Ridge and Aiguille Martin on the right.

36

6. AIGUILLE DU POUCE 2873m
South Face – Voie des Dalles

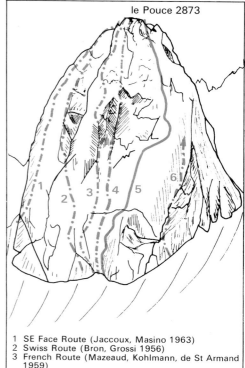

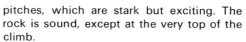

1 SE Face Route (Jaccoux, Masino 1963)
2 Swiss Route (Bron, Grossi 1956)
3 French Route (Mazeaud, Kohlmann, de St Armand 1959)
4 Direct Route (Cecchinel, Nominé 1971)
5 Voie des Dalles (Kintzelé, Mallon and Marutzi)
6 Right-hand Dièdre Route (Bron, Gauchat 1954)

The Pouce (Thumb) is in wild countryside on the Diosaz side of the long ridge-line (NNE-SSW) of the Aiguilles Rouges. The great bulk of the S Face is imposing, because of its height (450m), its dark-coloured rock, its monolithic rock-formations and its lines of overhangs. It constitutes an obvious problem, and as such has naturally appealed to some very good climbers. All the routes on it are hard, the most attractive being the Voie des Dalles or Slab Route. This is a climb of very sustained difficulty for the first 10 pitches, which are stark but exciting. The rock is sound, except at the very top of the climb.

- **1st Ascent:** B. Kintzelé, R. Mallon, J. Marutzi, 2 September 1967.
- **Vertical height:** about 450m.
- **Grade:** Very sustained TD, with two pitches of V sup.
- **Time:** 6–7 hrs.
- **Equipment:** Carabiners. The route requires 40 pitons or so, generally in place. Take several blade pitons and some American angles.
- **Starting point:** Planpraz and the Col du Lac Cornu.
- **Route – *Outline:*** Take a slightly slanting line across the great slabs (on the right-hand section of the face). Turn overhangs on the right, and higher up, after coming back left, climb a spur, a dièdre and couloir, keeping left to reach the summit.

Description: Start 20m right of the main dièdre on the S Face near the highest point of the snow up a small poorly marked dièdre blocked at 10m by a slightly overhanging step (I move of V). Traverse left below this step and climb up to a grassy niche (IV). Leave this by a detour left, then climb bearing slightly right (IV); one pitch of III leads to the grassy terraces at the foot of the great smooth slabs. Start up a slab on the right slightly below the highest point of the terraces. Traverse 4–5m across the slabs (IV sup., V). Follow then a somewhat grassy crack above and leave it on the right (15m, IV sup., V). Here there is a small platform. From there start on the right up a slight bulge which is climbed, always keeping right (V sup., VI), to reach a narrow crack in the open slab which continues as a dièdre. Climb this crack for 4 straight rope-lengths past two small overhangs (V, V sup., AI), tiny stances. After the fourth rope-length you will be 10m below the big overhangs. Traverse the slab right towards a detached block below a reddish-grey wall (V); good belay. Now avoid the overhang by two pitches on the SE side: make a descending move and traverse obliquely right (IV). Climb vertically up a small dièdre (IV), then traverse left (V). Belay on the terrace above the overhangs. It is also possible from the top of the small dièdre to climb the slabs very slightly to the right. Above follow the crest of the spur (two pitches, IV, one move of V) to grassy terraces. Continue up a fine grey dièdre which turns into a couloir (three rope-lengths, IV, III) and ends on the SE Ridge. A grassy terrace and then two rope-lengths up a chimney-couloir filled with big blocks lead to the summit (III, III sup.).

Aiguille du Pouce, South Face.

7. THE AMONE SLAB

● **Equipment:** Carabiners, 50m of rope. Stances are equipped with iron pitons.
● **Starting point:** From Martigny and then Orsières (Valais), go up the Swiss Val Ferret; one km before La Fouly, take a little road on the right, go through the hamlet of L'Amone and cross the bridge over the Dranse. You are now 5 mins away from the foot of the slab.

In the Swiss Val Ferret, a little below the village of La Fouly and opposite the little village of L'Amone, is a great slab, 400m high, framed by a marvellous landscape of forest and alpine meadows. The slab is of white limestone, and stands out gleaming in the sun; it is not surprising that young climbers in the valley have found it attractive.

It is not particularly steep, indeed it is at a quite gentle angle, but the rock is very compact and holdless. The climbing is difficult, never strenuous but always delicate. M. Darbellay and M. Vaucher have been responsible for cementing in belay-pitons. On the actual pitches there are only six pitons altogether, and no more can be used since the rock is remarkably compact and lacks cracks or holes. And this is no place for cheating and using unnecessary expansion bolts. The pitches are usually long (40 or even 45m), and this provides some very fine climbing. This is an exciting climb, very interesting technically; sheer strength is no good, and even on the pitches of IV it is a question of balance on friction footholds or on very small flakes.

This delightful climb has its dangerous side: in a storm it can become a waterfall. Water gushes out of the gully at the top and often brings away large stones. The climb should therefore be attempted only in settled good weather (remember that waterfall and stonefall can both be provoked by melting snow in spring).

● **Vertical height:** 400m.
● **Grade:** TD sup., very sustained, but not serious.
● **Time:** Ascent, 2–3 hrs; descent, ½ hr.

● **Route** – *Outline:* The route starts on the right and continues up the white streak coming down from the gully at the top.

Description: There are 16 pitches of which five are of 40m and two of 45m. From the path, traverse right and then climb obliquely up the right-hand side up rocks stained with rust. After two rope-lengths, reach a quartz ledge and then, after five more rope-lengths, a second ledge about halfway up the wall which allows an easy escape; from here there are nine more very fine pitches of which the upper five are climbed directly below the gully, then up the gully itself.

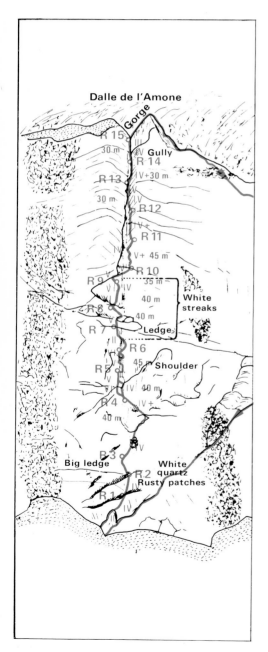

Free climbing on the Amone Slab.

8. THE SARRE ROOF

The Sarre Roof is excellent training and ideal for a wet day, since it is entirely sheltered from the rain. It consists of a roof, not quite horizontal but sloping outwards for 32m. It was done by some Aosta climbers and all the pitons are in place, including some bolts. It is strenuous practice for good climbers used to artificial.

The Roof is just above the road and the railway, just outside a tunnel in fact, so that the setting can scarcely be called idyllic, even if the Aosta valley itself is beautiful. But in spite of the rather disappointing setting, the climb itself is enjoyable, especially in wet weather when nothing else is possible anyway. The last few moves can be made easier by tying a rope to a tree above the overhang beforehand, and leaving it hanging with a loop in it.

Grade: If all the pitons had to be put in, the route would take several days and the grade would be A1, A2 and sometimes A3. However the pitons are in place and so the climb is only practice with pitons and étriers.

● **Time:** On average, 2 hrs per climber.

● **Equipment:** 40m ropes, about 50 carabiners, and a set of étriers for each climber.

● **Starting point:** From Sarre go up for about 2 km towards Courmayeur along the road directly beside the railway. To avoid a bend, the road disappears into a tunnel, the entrance to which is dominated by a great overhanging slab. At this level, going up, there is a parking place beside the road.

● **Route:** From the road go up a terraced slope. Cross the railway and go up a grassy slope to arrive below the roof. After 3m of vertical climbing, the line of pitons marks the route.

Artificial climbing on the Sarre Roof.

39

9. PETITS CHARMOZ 2867m
Traverse

This is a very pleasant route, a very good start for the would-be alpinist and also an interesting introduction to the Mont Blanc range. Moreover, whereas the ordinary routes on the Petits Charmoz and on the M are technically not very interesting, the traverse is much more so, for three main reasons: first of all, it starts up the Etala Chimneys, and then continues along the crest of the ridge, the first giving face-climbing and the second something very different and complementary; the Etala Chimneys are difficult, but they have their own personal character, jamming on granite, something very different from the normal outcrop climbing; finally, the stance on the Col de l'Etala is much more impressive than that on the Col de la Bûche, not only, subjectively, because it comes above the difficulties of the Chimneys so that you have a sense of achievement, but also because you are close to the high stark N Face of the

Grands Charmoz, which adds something to the plunging view down to the Mer de Glace and across the valley to the soaring Drus.

From the Col the traverse continues to follow the ridge overlooking both faces: the new one, and the Nantillons Face where you have climbed from. The climbing is easier, not so strenuous but very exposed. The stances are good. Finally, this is a very popular route and the rock is worn; if at any time the climber gets to a position where the holds are not rounded and polished, he can assume that he has made a mistake and is off-route.

● **1st Ascent:** (for the traverse): Mlle M. Pasteur, J. H. Wicks, C. Wilson, 5 July 1898.
● **Vertical height:** About 170m (between 2700 and 2867m).
● **Grade:** AD with two pitches of V. Beware of stonefall usually started by climbers in the Etala Chimneys and the couloir from the Col de La Bûche. Take care not to start any falls.
● **Time:** 2½ hrs from the Glacier to the summit. 1 hr from the summit to the glacier.
● **Equipment:** Leave axes at the foot of

the wall. Pitons are in place. Carry several carabiners.
● **Starting point:** You can start from the Montenvers (1913m) but it is better to start from the Plan de l'Aiguille (2310m). In the first place, the approach is half an hour shorter, and secondly, it is made by an ascending traverse below the Aiguilles — a fine setting because they are just above. This leads to the Nantillons moraine which gives an excellent view of the day's objective, the traverse of the Petits Charmoz. Before beginning a route, no matter which, it is pleasant, and moreover interesting and worthwhile to see it, to look carefully at it, to study it, to imagine the sequence of pitches, to plan out the descent, particularly if this follows a different line from the ascent, which will always be the case on a traverse.
● **Route** — *Outline:* This is best seen from the Nantillons moraine, because the Petits Charmoz are here just opposite. On their right are the Etala Chimneys leading to the col from which you move left to make the traverse and reach the summit. On the left is the Col de la Bûche by which you will descend. Further left is the Aiguille de l'M.

Description: From the Nantillons Glacier go up the Etala Couloir on snow and scree to a step crossed by chimneys and cracks. Climb the slab left of the right-hand crack-chimney for 3m (IV) and gain this crack-chimney which has a big chockstone; climb this and continue to a large terrace. Climb a second chimney for 8—10m (III) and leave it on the left by a sloping slab to continue up a

Aig. de l'M
2844

Petits Charmoz
2867

Col de l'Etala
2786

The 'Open Book'

Col de
la Bûche
2785

Etala
Chimneys

2700

Ladder

Nantillons Glacier

chimney for 4m (III) and reach a small platform. Climb easy ground and then a scree couloir to reach the Col de l'Etala (to the right S of the Col is the Doigt de l'Etala, and then the Grands Charmoz).

From the col go left (N) towards a small triangular wall; begin 4m left of the ridge, then climb the ridge and go back left to reach the foot of the dièdre, the 'open book'. Climb this (IV) and follow the jagged, nearly level crest on the Thendia side. Climb a short vertical step and regain the ridge, following it to the summit.

Descent: From the summit descend easy rock on the Aiguille de l'M side and then go through a 'letter-box' to the Nantillons side, where a system of cracks and short steps brings you back towards the ridge leading down to the Col de la Bûche.

From the Col it is worth climbing the Aiguille de l'M (20 min) to get a fine view of the valley. On the descent from the Col de la Bûche watch out for stonefall; never stop in the bed of the couloir; descend first the left bank then the right bank, to return to the left bank near the ladders. Finally instead of going back to the Plan de l'Aiguille, you can descend to the Montenvers. This completes the traverse properly; better still you arrive at the Montenvers at a good time, when the spires of the Drus are highlighted by the afternoon sun.

Petits Charmoz (opposite page), with the Col de l'Etala on the right and the Col de la Bûche on the left; The Col de l'Etala (right), with the Drus and the Aiguille Verte in background.

41

10. PETITE AIGUILLE VERTE 3508m
Ordinary Route

The Petite Verte is an excellent introduction not only to snow-climbing but also to mixed and high-altitude climbing. The Grands Montets téléphérique makes it not at all exhausting. From the Col des Grands Montets it takes only 1½ hrs — it is only 275m in vertical height — but even if it is short the climber should start training himself to walk rhythmically, whether upwards or downwards. Naturally, though, you can linger as long as you like on the summit, either to rest or to study the superb view; the only thing that might hurry the descent is the snow which will soften in the sun.

Technically the route, if short, is interesting on both ascent and descent; it involves a fairly steep snow-slope, crossing a bergschrund, and then, above the shoulder, a ridge on mixed terrain and an exiguous summit.

As for atmosphere, this is a route looking out over two distinct worlds, the peaceful green valley and the high mountains towards which you are climbing; this is the beginning of the high-altitude world. The Petite Verte is in fact the first spur on the difficult, elegant Grands Montets Ridge which goes up to the Aiguille Verte, a ridge which separates two wild and imposing sides, the Nant Blanc side to the right and the Argentière Glacier to the left, and above, soaring out of the line of granite towers and pillars, is the extraordinary summit dome of the Aiguille Verte.

You can do the climb by taking the first téléphérique up at 7 am, but I strongly advise you to bivouac on the rocks of the Aiguille des Grands Montets; this can be done in comfort, since all the equipment needed can be brought up by the téléphérique. But a bivouac will provide first of all unforgettable views: sunset and sunrise with their different lights, the excitements of a night out at 3300m; and secondly, a very useful training: before having to spend a night out on a long route, you will need some experience of bivouacs so that you will know how well you can stand up to conditions and especially to the cold.

It is also possible to give added interest to the route by doing some ice- or snow-climbing practice on the way down, or after finishing the route proper: cramponning, step-cutting, belaying on snow and ice, crossing the bergschrund. You could also practice dynamic belaying, with glissading on safe slopes just above the col.

Finally, you can finish off the day by doing some rock-climbing practice on the prepared pitches on the E Face of the Aiguille des Grands Montets, or on the little aiguilles W of the col, opposite the Drus and Mont Blanc.

● **1st descent:** J. E. and R. Charlet, with P. Charlet, September 1886.

● **Vertical height:** 275m (between 3233 and 3508m).

● **Grade:** A snow-climb with a fairly steep slope below the ridge.

● **Time:** 1—1½ hrs from the col to the summit.

● **Equipment:** Crampons.

● **Starting point:** The upper téléphérique station and the Col des Grands Montets (3233m).

● **Route** — *Outline:* The NW slope, then above the bergschrund up the ridge to the summit.

Description: From the Col des Grands Montets where you should put on crampons and rope up, climb the fine slope which is gentle to begin with (practice walking in crampons, holding the axe and rope management) and then steepens quite considerably. Climb the bergschrund on the right, which can sometimes be a little tricky, to reach the shoulder of the Petite Verte. Go up the ridge on mixed terrain with a slightly difficult move (III) to descend a big block forming a short wall 3—4m high and continue along the ridge to the very exposed summit. Do not stop at the big block as some parties do.

Return by the same route. Take care at the bergschrund and on the upper part of the snowslope, depending upon the condition of the snow.

Bergschrund on the Petite Aiguille Verte (opposite page).
Rock-climbing practice on the Col des Grands Montets
(right).
The Petite Aiguille Verte from the
Aiguille des Grands Montets, with the Aiguille Verte
and the Aiguille Sans Nom in the background (above).

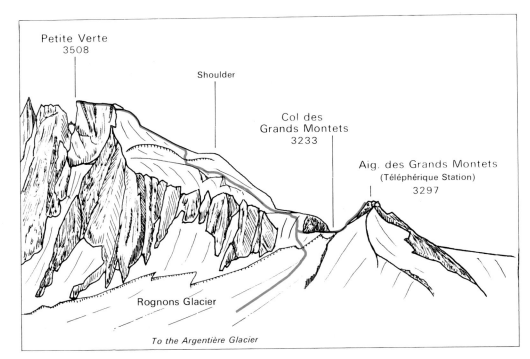

Petite Verte
3508

Shoulder

Col des
Grands Montets
3233

Aig. des Grands Montets
(Téléphérique Station)
3297

Rognons Glacier

To the Argentière Glacier

11. TOUR RONDE 3792m
VALLEE BLANCHE
South-East Ridge

The Tour Ronde is a delightful peak and an excellent viewpoint. The SE Ridge, a mixed snow and rock route, is not difficult technically. On the other hand, the rock is sometimes poor, and if, instead of following the SE Ridge from the bottom at the Col d'Entrèves, you decide to go direct and follow a system of couloirs from the glacier to halfway up the ridge or even to the top, you must be on the lookout for stonefalls, the Tour Ronde being a very popular peak. This danger is accentuated towards midday when snow and ice melt; this is often the time for the descent, and you should be particularly on your guard.

● **1st ascent**: J. H. Backhouse, T. H. Carson, D. W. Freshfield and C. C. Tucker, with D. Balleys and M. Payot, 22 July 1867.
● **Vertical height**: 650m from the Torino Hut to the summit (from 3300m to 3792m) counting the ascent to the Col des Flambeaux and the descent to the foot of the Aiguille de Toule.
● **Grade**: This is mainly an ice route, the rock sections on the ridge itself being II.
● **Time**: 2½–3 hrs from the Torino Hut to the summit.
● **Equipment**: Crampons.
● **Starting point**: It is possible to start from the Requin Hut (2516m), but this makes the route long; it is also possible to start from the Refuge des Cosmiques (3613m) at the Col du Midi, but the most logical starting point is the Torino Hut

(3371m). From this hut the evening views towards the Dent du Géant and the Peuterey Ridge of Mont Blanc are superb.

You should leave the hut very early, at least an hour before dawn, partly for safety reasons – the snow will be better – but above all for aesthetic reasons; the Tour Ronde is an ideal viewpoint for the sunrise over Mont Blanc. The view is very fine all day long, but it is only very early in the morning, because of the slanting light, that you can benefit from an extraordinary panorama and discover the architecture of the mountains and the layout of the ridges, which gradually emerge into the light and appear clear and detached one from the other. Later, on the other hand, when the sun is directly overhead, they are difficult to distinguish. But as well as purely aesthetic pleasure, you will experience a sense of participating in some great and moving event; climbing is something you can do anywhere, on outcrops, but seeing the sunrise, the return of the life-giving sun from its retreat, is an experience which will stand the climber in good stead when at the end of his holiday he goes back to the city.

● **Route** – *Outline:* From the hut continue below the frontier ridge on the French (N) side to the Col d'Entrèves, then follow the (SE) ridge of the Tour Ronde.

Description: From the Torino Hut (3371m) leave the Col du Géant on the right and cross the Col des Flambeaux (3407m) and descend towards the Combe Maudite to go

round the base of the N Spur of the Aiguille de Toule (about 3300m). Then climb towards the Col d'Entrèves and get onto the SE Ridge just below the col (1½ hrs). Follow the ridge keeping first on the French side and then on the Italian to avoid gendarmes. Go past an obvious snow-saddle called the Col Freshfield (3625m). From here climb direct towards the summit up a rocky and then a snowy slope (1½ hrs); 2½–3 hrs from the Torino Hut. Return by the same route.

Variant: The SE Ridge can be gained at several points especially just left of the summit tower. This gives a quicker route than the SE Ridge, but after climbing the bergschrund, the rock is loose with piles of big blocks and so fairly dangerous. Worse, this variation is often taken by fairly large parties.

At the summit of the Tour Ronde, it is pleasant to stay for a while, for the country is as awesome as it is beautiful. And here too, with the aid of a map, the beginner can understand the layout of this part of the massif.

Descent: Instead of returning to the Torino Hut it is interesting and useful practice, and so recommended, to descend to the Requin Hut and then down to the Montenvers along the Géant Glacier and the Mer de Glace. The view remains very fine and technically the descent is an excellent exercise as much in the upper part of the glacier in crossing crevasses by snow-bridges as in route finding down through the seracs. Finally this descent, crossing different country using different techniques, losing so much height on foot rather than using téléphériques, will add to the high mountain atmosphere and the sense of altitude given by this fine beginner's route.

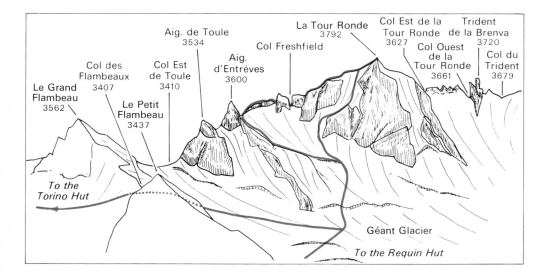

The Tour Ronde with the Grand Capucin on the right and the Vallée Blanche below (opposite page).

12. AIGUILLE CROUX 3251m
South Face
POINTE DE L'INNOMINATA 3730m
South Ridge

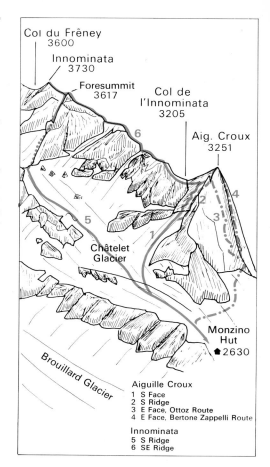

Col du Frêney 3600
Innominata 3730
Foresummit 3617
Col de l'Innominata 3205
Aig. Croux 3251
Châtelet Glacier
Monzino Hut 2630
Brouillard Glacier

Aiguille Croux
1 S Face
2 S Ridge
3 E Face, Ottoz Route
4 E Face, Bertone Zappelli Route

Innominata
5 S Ridge
6 SE Ridge

Whereas the French side of Mont Blanc is relatively simple in structure, with vast stretches of glacier which go up in a series of shoulders and ridges to the summit, the Italian side is definitely more complex. First of all there is the Brenva cirque with great granite pillars emerging from the ice here still a main feature, then the Peuterey Ridge, the Frêney face, the Innominata, the Brouillard Ridge with its extraordinary steep, even vertical rock-formation, and then further S and W the angle eases off and the glacier predominates once more.

I feel it a good idea for the young climber to get to know this side of Mont Blanc. I realise that he will not venture onto the routes at any very early date, but he needs to be acquainted with all the different aspects of the range, that playground of snow, ice and rock, and to appreciate the harmonies of granite and glacier. It is undoubtedly satisfying to study and to understand those great faces and those soaring ridges; both the novice and the tyro will thus feel themselves closer to the mystery of the mountains. And then it will also awake ambitions. Here you can look up – and a long way up – and say: 'When I am better, more experienced . . .'

Going up to the Aiguille Croux, the first bastion of the Innominata Ridge, is primarily a climb, naturally, but also a place for dreams. And the dreams start down below when from Courmayeur or from Entrèves you follow the foot of the Brenva Glacier, hidden under moraines but still omnipresent, then go along under the great faces of the Peuterey, and later when you go up to the Monzino Hut, with its still-living memories of the Gamba Hut, and walk into the shrine guarded by the Peuterey and the Brouillard. You remember the scenery and the names, of soaring mountains and of those who loved them; this too is a dimension of alpinism.

The Aiguille Croux by the S Face is an interesting climb but unfortunately rather short; it can therefore be finished by doing as a descent the traverse of the Col des Chasseurs (2750m). Alternatively, you can go up the traverse and should in that case spend the night at the Noire Hut, also a memorable experience. You can climb the Pointe de l'Innominata (3732m), a justly famous viewpoint, either by the SE Ridge (the ordinary route) which is easy, on poor rock but interesting early in the season when it is still snowed up, or alternatively by the S Ridge, a pleasant and enjoyable route first climbed in 1913 by P. Preuss and Ugo di

Vallepiana, followed by a descent by the SE Ridge. In that case you might do the following: up early to the Monzino Hut and then the Aiguille Croux that same day, followed by a night at the hut and the Pointe de l'Innominata the next day.

Finally, after having done your routes and got back to the Val Veni, instead of going back to Courmayeur you might go up to Lac Combal and even up to the Elizabetta Hut. This will make two days' climbing, as well as providing something even more worthwhile in terms of experience.

● **1st ascent:** Mlle Mazzuchi with J. and H. Croux, 25 August 1900.
● **Vertical height:** About 200m (from 3050 to 3257m).
● **Grade:** PD with a pitch of IV.
● **Time:** 3 hrs from the hut to the summit.
● **Equipment:** Carabiners, abseil rope.
● **Starting point:** The Monzino Hut (2600m) or perhaps the Noire Hut (2316m).
● **Route** – *Outline:* The route follows the great couloir of open slabs facing SW to gain a small well-marked brèche on the S Ridge and then takes the ridge to the fore-summit and then the summit. This brèche can also be reached by gaining the S Ridge lower down at the well-marked snow shoulder. This is a more interesting and elegant variation.

Description: From the Monzino Hut climb grass slopes and then the small Châtelet Glacier. Slant right up easy rock – there is a system of slabs and ledges – to the brèche on the S Ridge. You are now at the foot of the grande plaque' (Big Slab); climb this direct (IV) to reach a broad shoulder and then the summit. Instead of taking the slabs of the SW Face it is possible to climb the S Ridge from the snow shoulder without great difficulty (III).

Descent: Take the slabby couloir on the SW. One or two abseils.

Col des Chasseurs:
From the Noire Hut (2325m) climb right up to the col up scree, snow slopes and finally up a fairly steep, often snowy couloir. Preferably reach the S brèche (1 hr).

From the Monzino Hut traverse grass and scree slopes to reach the Frêney Glacier just opposite the col. Cross the very crevassed Frêney Glacier and then go up steep grassy rock slopes to one of the two brèches on the col, preferably the S brèche ($1\frac{1}{2}$ hrs).

Pointe de l'Innominata:
– By the S Ridge: From the Monzino Hut gain the little Châtelet Glacier and climb it keeping right. Climb a short rampart of polished wet slabs to reach very easy scree. Climb towards the S Ridge of the Innominata and gain this at the lower shoulder below the first gendarme. Continue up the ridge turning this on the right by slabs without losing height (III). Turn the next gendarme on the same side, first along a ledge and then up a chimney (III) which leads back to the ridge. The third gendarme is smaller and easy. Above trend left on the wall of the W Face for about 20m, then take a small loose secondary ridge to the fore-summit which is

gained slightly above the junction of the S and SE Ridges. Gain the summit by the sometimes snowy SE Ridge (45 min from the fore-summit; about 5 hrs from the hut).
– By the SE Ridge: From the Monzino Hut climb up the Châtelet Glacier and easy rock mixed with snow to the ridge which can be gained at several different places but is generally reached about a third of the way up ($2\frac{1}{4}$–$2\frac{1}{2}$ hrs). Follow the snowy rock of the crest easily, turn a gendarme to the right or to the left and reach the fore-summit, keeping on the Frêney side especially at the end ($1\frac{1}{4}$–2 hrs). Continue along the summit ridge to the summit proper (45 min; $4\frac{1}{2}$–$5\frac{1}{2}$ hrs from the hut).

The 'grande plaque' pitch on the South Ridge (opposite page).
From right to left (above): Aiguille Noire and Peuterey Ridge, Frêney Glacier, Aiguille Croux, Innominata Ridge, Brouillard Glacier and Ridge.

13. DOMES DE MIAGE 3673m
Traverse

This a very fine snow route, along the ridge between five summits: NE to SW they are the Points 2672m, 3673m, 3630m, 3666m and 3669m. Between Points 3673m and 3630m is the Col des Dômes (3564m).

You can do the climb SW − NE and start with the ascent of the Aiguille de la Bérangère, but this has the disadvantage of taking you back from the Col Infranchissable over the Trélatête Glacier late in the day when the snow is soft. This makes it wiser to do the route NE − SW. You will need to leave very early from the Trélatête Hotel (low, at 1970m), so that you will have an easy walk up the Trélatête Glacier to the Col Infranchissable (3349m).

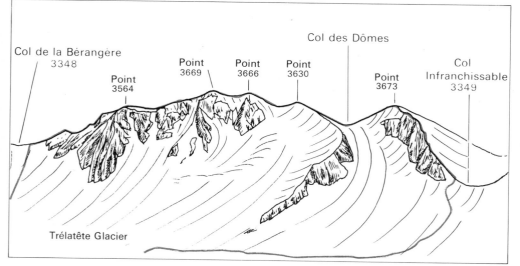

Col de la Bérangère 3348
Point 3564
Point 3669
Point 3666
Point 3630
Col des Dômes
Point 3673
Col Infranchissable 3349
Trélatête Glacier

Afterwards the climb to the first point is pleasant and easy, and so is the traverse along the ridge. Moreover if you do it this way round you will have an impression of height and exposure, since you will see no large mountains beyond the ridge.

- **1st ascent**: T. Coleman with F. Mollard and J. Jacquemont, 2 September 1858.
- **Vertical height**: 1700m from the Trélatête Hotel to the summit (from 1970 − 3670m).
- **Grade**: A fairly long snow ridge (beware of cornices).
- **Time**: 6−6½ hrs from the Trélatête Hotel to the summit; 3½−4 hrs from the summit to the hotel.
- **Equipment**: Crampons.
- **Starting point**: Trélatête Hotel (1970m).
- **Route − *Outline:*** The traverse proper of these tops is easily seen from both sides: from a distance, in the valley, from closer to as you go up the Trélatête Glacier; and finally, from the E summits (Points 3672 and 3673) you can see along the line of ridges. As well as studying the route, it is interesting to note the effects of winds and sun on the snow of a ridge.

Description: From the hotel follow the path which makes a rising traverse to the E and leads along the moraine to the glacier (45 mins). At the start of the Glacier keep rather to the left to avoid the crevasses and then make for the middle to pass the first icefall and gain the plateau of Trélagrande (1¼ hrs). Cross a zone of long transverse crevasses more on the right bank; when the glacier changes direction return and keep to the middle. Beyond a lightly crevassed area you reach a second crevasse barrier. There are two possibilities. The first is to continue in the direction of the Col Infranchissable; to do this, cross the barrier rather towards the right bank and gain the almost horizontal, long and monotonous slopes of the col (2−2½ hrs). Just before the col, strike sharply up fairly steep snow slopes and then return right towards the rocky frontier ridge to avoid a very crevassed zone. Gain the easy broken ridge and follow it; higher up it becomes snowy. The frontier ridge is gained slightly right of the first summit (3672m; 1 hr 20 min). Here the traverse proper of the Dômes de Miage begins. Follow the crest to the summit 3673m.

From here descend to the Col des Dômes and then continue always on the narrow corniced crest to Points 3630m, 3666m, and 3669m (45 min from the col). Start the descent down snow-slopes and shattered rock to the Col de la Bérangère, and from there easily to the Trélatête Hotel. The complete traverse takes about 10 hrs.

The second possibility is to join the ridge

in the middle. Instead of going up close to the Col Infranchissable, leave the glacier earlier (when the notch of the col appears, just after the last ice-fall, 3 hrs), and climb the great couloir, really a branch of the glacier, which is easy, gently-angled and only slightly crevassed. It leads to the Col des Dômes (1 hr 20 mins). From the col follow the ridge to the right to reach the summit 3673m (15 mins) where you get back to the line of the traverse proper.

Other possibilities: when the beginner has become more experienced, he will be able to come back to the Dômes de Miage, either climbing them on the N side — considerable glacier problems — or doing the traverse SW — NE from the Aiguille de la Bérangère to

sleep at the Durier Hut, and continuing the next day towards the Aiguille de Bionnassay and Mont Blanc. The whole makes a long and very fine expedition.

The ridge and the North Face of the Dômes de Miage (above), with the Col de Miage on the left, below, and the Col Infranchissable in the centre.
On the Dômes de Miage ridges (opposite page).

49

14. TOUR NOIR 3837m
Traverse

The Tour Noir is a fine peak on the frontier ridge between Switzerland to the E and France to the W; it therefore looks out over the Neuve Glacier and the Swiss Val Ferret on one side and the Améthystes Glacier low down on the other. At first very popular, then much neglected, it is now attracting a certain amount of attention especially now that the Grands Montets téléphérique has made access to the Argentière Hut so easy (1¾ hrs). Nevertheless for a variety of reasons it is worth doing. The view is magnificent and unusually wide, looking out as it does over the Mont Blanc range and also the Rhone valley, the Valais and the Oberland.

The best route is the Traverse: up the Améthystes Glacier to reach the Col Supérieur du Tour Noir (3690m), and then up the N Ridge; down the SE side by the ordinary route over the Javelle Ledges to the Col d'Argentière (3552m) and then down the Tour Noir Glacier to the hut.

You can also reach the Col Supérieur du Tour Noir from the Swiss Val Ferret and the Neuve Hut, but in that case the climb is longer and more difficult than the Argentière side. The same is true of the descent; by the Col d'Argentière on the Neuve side it crosses rather steep shattered rocks, a bergschrund which can be difficult and then the Neuve Glacier which is much crevassed; the whole route would therefore be longer and more difficult than that by the Tour Noir Glacier.

● **1st ascent:** SE Face (ordinary route), E. Javelle and F. F. Turner with J. Moser and F. Tournier, 3 August 1876. N Ridge, L. H. and Th. Aubert with M. Crettex, 23 July 1898.

● **Vertical height:** About 900m from the Argentière Hut to the Col Supérieur du Tour Noir; about 150m from the Col Supérieur to the summit (from 2771 to 3837m). From the Neuve Hut (2729m), the height is slightly greater.

● **Grade:** A mixed route in high mountain country with pitches of III. Beware of broken unstable rock.

● **Time:** 2½–3 hrs from the Argentière Hut to the Col Supérieur. 1 hr from the col to the summit. 2 hrs from the summit to the Argentière Hut.

● **Equipment:** Crampons.

● **Starting point:** Argentière Hut (2771m) or the Neuve Hut (2729m), also called the Dufour Hut.

● **Route – Outline:** The route is a N – S traverse: Col Supérieur du Tour Noir – Tour Noir – Col d'Argentière.

Description: From the Argentière Hut (2771m) take the path which follows the water pipe, then the moraine of the Améthystes Glacier and skirt the foot of the Arête du Jardin passing directly below the Y-couloir of the Arête de Flêche Rousse, then traverse right towards the couloir below the Col Supérieur. Climb this to gain the col (3690m) − 2½–3 hrs.

Climb the N Ridge of the Tour Noir on mixed ground rather than taking to the shattered and unstable rock of the W side. Keep as close as possible to the more impressive but easier crest of the ridge to reach the summit, 1 hr (3½–4 hrs from the hut).

Descent: This follows the ordinary route and the Javelle Ledges on the SE Flank. Reach the brèche between the two summits, and on the Neuve side descend the spur right (S) on big easy blocks. When the descent steepens, traverse right towards the Javelle Ledges. To do this gain a distinct rock ridge and then a slabby couloir-chimney. The Javelle Ledges traverse about 100m across the E Face in a slab zone. (do not descend too far onto the scree below the

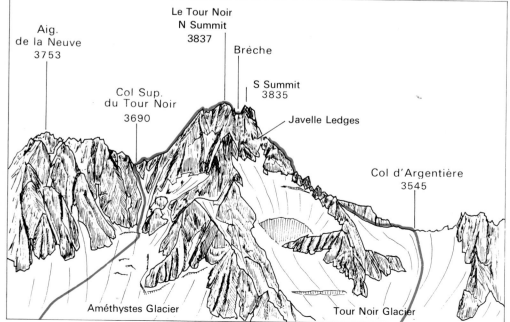

Aig. de la Neuve 3753

Col Sup. du Tour Noir 3690

Le Tour Noir N Summit 3837

Brèche

S Summit 3835

Javelle Ledges

Col d'Argentière 3545

Améthystes Glacier

Tour Noir Glacier

ledges). Ascending again slightly, reach the ridge leading to the Col d'Argentière. Follow this, then make for the Tour Noir Glacier leaving the col on the left. The glacier leads easily to the hut (1½–2 hrs).

On the Tour Noir Ridge (opposite page).
On the way up the Tour Noir with the Grand Combin and Mont Velan in the background (right).
The Tour Noir from the Courtes (above).

15. AIGUILLE DU TOUR 3542m
Table de Roc Ridge

The Aiguilles du Tour are two distinct peaks, the N Summit (3544m) and the S Summit (3542m), very close together but separated by a fairly deep brèche. They are above the Col de Balme on the frontier ridge between the Trient Glacier to the E (Switzerland), a wide snow plateau rising to the very foot of the Aiguilles, and the Tour Glacier to the W (France) over which they loom. Onto this glacier descend a long western ridge and the SSW Table Ridge, which broadens into a spur towards the bottom.

They stand out at the far NE end of the range forming a superb viewpoint and a fine climb for the novice. Both summits can be reached by the ordinary route, either directly from the Trient Hut (3170m) or from the Albert Premier Hut (2702m), the latter making for a rather longer approach but a very fine one, since it follows first one side (the Tour face), crosses a col and then follows the other, the Trient side.

They can also be traversed, by climbing up the N Ridge to the N Summit, down the ordinary route to the col (3544m) between the two summits, then up to the S Summit by the NE Ridge and down the ordinary route on the E. From the Albert Premier Hut, you get to the foot of the N Ridge of the Aiguille by going up the W slope of the Col du Midi des Grands then over the Trient side to turn the Aiguille du Pissoir.

Finally for anyone who has reached a good standard on outcrops and wants to get used to climbing on granite at high altitudes, it is possible to do the traverse from the Aiguille Purtscheller to the Aiguille du Tour by starting up the S Ridge of the Aiguille Purtscheller (AD with 2 pitches of IV). But this, though a fine climb, makes for a rather uneven route, inconsistent in style and difficulty.

This is why I would suggest as the best solution climbing the Aiguille du Tour by the Table de Roc Ridge; I have three reasons for this:

1. The huge granite table sticking out from the ridge at one end, standing like a table on one leg of rock and overhanging on three sides, is a natural curiosity and unique in the range. Climbing it is enjoyable and fairly easy; there are two ways up to it: to climb the fine long W Ridge, then traverse right to join the Table Ridge just below the Table, or alternatively, to climb the Table Ridge itself, which is a broad spur further down.

2. On the W Ridge and on the Table Ridge (except for the Table itself) the rock is sometimes poor. This makes it very good training; from the very beginning the novice needs to learn that even in the Mont Blanc range, famous as it is for its solid granite, he must always be on his guard. He will survive as a mountaineer only in so far as he is constantly on the alert on rock or snow, on the descent as well as on the ascent. It is essential therefore that he should remember that a hold may give way at any moment, even in a range like this where he might become over-confident. The Table Ridge will remind the climber that he should climb delicately and not with brute force, and that he should use his legs, and not arm-strength, to move upwards.

3. Lower down on the climb, on the spur before the ridge, the route is not very clear; you can go more or less anywhere, and the gradings are mostly III with no more than a few moves of IV. The route is therefore good and very safe training for route-finding. You should always anticipate difficulties accurately, and work out beforehand which way to go and the sequence of moves needed to avoid difficulties or dead ends. The Table Ridge offers an excellent opportunity for this, being at a relatively gentle angle and being wide without being enormous; there are no vertical pitches, not even any really steep ones, so that the climb is not too tiring and fairly easy to reverse if necessary. Moreover, to make a few mistakes is useful; it is the only way to gain experience, and it is much better to make your mistakes on short, easy routes than later when a mistake might have much more serious consequences.

● **1st ascent:** M. Dreyfus, A. and R. Duval, P. Henry and M. Ichac, 18 July 1926 (but they avoided the Table itself higher up on the right – a pity, since this is the most amusing part of the climb).

● **Vertical height:** About 440m (from 3100 to 3542m).

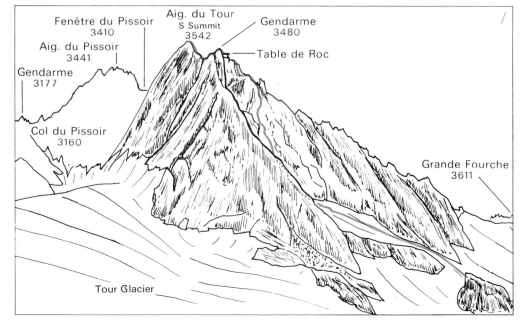

Fenêtre du Pissoir 3410
Aig. du Pissoir 3441
Gendarme 3177
Col du Pissoir 3160
Aig. du Tour S Summit 3542
Gendarme 3480
Table de Roc
Grande Fourche 3611
Tour Glacier

- **Grade:** AD
- **Time:** 4–5 hrs.
- **Equipment:** To reach the start crampons may be worn, but if you wish to avoid having to carry them, you can cut steps up the snow ridge to the rock.
- **Starting point:** The Albert Premier Hut (2702m); it is also possible to start from the Trient Hut (3170m), cross the Col du Tour or the Col Supérieur and reach the foot of the spur by crossing the Tour Glacier (1½ hrs).
- **Route** – *Outline:* The left side of the spur and then the Table Ridge.

Description: From the Albert Premier Hut (2702m) follow the route to the Col du Tour (a path, then the rocky outcrop on the glacier called the Signal Adams Reilly, then easy slopes to the SE just below the small glacier bay between the W Ridge on the left and the SW Spur on the right). Here make for the spur up steeper slopes; at the top of the névé (1½ hrs) begin to climb right towards a poorly-defined ridge. A succession of slabs, steps and short couloirs lead right while the spur narrows into a ridge and leads to the Table, which is climbed (III). Above, the ridge merges into the summit crest which to the right leads to the summit (2½–3½ hrs; 4–5 hrs from the hut).

Descent: From the summit descend the NE Ridge made of easy blocks, cross the bergschrund, gain the Trient Glacier, and cross the Col Supérieur du Tour (3289m) if you want to get back to the Albert Premier Hut.

Table de Roc on the Aiguille du Tour (right and opposite page).

16. AIGUILLE DU MOINE 3412m
South Ridge

Right in the middle of the range, not too high up between the big peaks and the glacial valleys, standing out distinct like a lighthouse, on the S Ridge of the Verte, and at a pivotal point looking over the meeting of four great glaciers, Talèfre, Leschaux, Géant, Mer de Glace, the Aiguille du Moine is a first-class viewpoint. There is an extraordinarily good view in all directions, but quite apart from the beauty of this vast panorama, the novice will find it interesting from the technical point of view; he will be able to get an idea of the lie of the land, the range as a whole, its orientation, its detail, ridges, couloirs and faces, study the routes — and make plans. He can for instance see the traverse of the Drus, the Sans Nom Ridge, the Whymper Couloir, the Chamonix Aiguilles, the Peuterey, the Brenva, the Aiguilles du Diable and particularly the N Face of the Grandes Jorasses near at hand;

he can see them clearly, but they are so huge they will preserve their aura. From the Moine, you can see what is meant by an Alpine career.

I advise you to go up by the S Ridge and down by the ordinary route. If you take the latter both up and down this can be monotonous, and would be poor training.

The S Ridge is varied and interesting, giving quite different impressions depending on whether you are following the W side looking down on the Mer de Glace, or the E side, sunny and peaceful, the same side as the ordinary route.

You can also start the S Ridge at its base right from the Moine névé, and follow its bristling towers and gendarmes and its brèches. This is the equivalent of the lower part of the ridge and joins up with the upper half taken by the so-called S Ridge route. The route as a whole would then be called the 'S Ridge intégrale'; this is a fine climb but not very appropriate for a beginner, since it is rather long (5–6 hrs) and sustained (several pitches of IV and IV sup.). On the other hand, it is very suitable for a climber more experienced in rock-climbing and rope-management.

Finally, on the descent by the ordinary route, you should watch carefully, think, anticipate the pitches and their series of cracks, dièdres and chimneys, and ledges leading to yet more cracks, dièdres and chimneys. Even if the climb presents no great difficulty, it offers interesting and complex route-finding problems.

- **1st ascent**: E. Bruhl and L. Valluet with A. Ravanel and F. Belin, 2 September 1928.
- **Vertical height**: About 725m from the hut to the summit (from 2687 to 3412m); about 450m from the top of the Moine névé to the summit.
- **Grade**: D with two pitches of IV.
- **Time**: 1 hr from the hut to the start. 3 hrs from the start to the summit. 2 hrs for the descent.
- **Equipment**: Carabiners. Leave axes at the bergschrund.
- **Starting point**: The Couvercle Hut (2678m). Arrive a little early at the hut to look at and take in the country — the Couvercle Hut is in one of the most beautiful cirques in the massif — as well as to find the short path up to the Moine.
- **Route** – *Outline*: From the top of the

Moine névé a diagonal line is taken left to the ridge, then the S Ridge itself is followed.

Description: From the Couvercle Hut follow the path to the Moine Glacier, more often called the Moine névé. Climb the névé to the foot of a large couloir. The ordinary route goes off right, and the S Ridge route left up an ascending diagonal line which is followed for about 200m. Then climb chimneys, dièdres, steps and easy ledges, at first straight up and then left, to join the S Ridge below a T-shaped gendarme. A large horizontal ledge on the Mer de Glace side, then an often icy pitch between the wall and a large flake leads to a dièdre-chimney (IV) which leads back onto the ridge. Follow this without difficulty to a short 4m wall which is climbed either directly up grooves on small sloping holds (a move of V sup.) or on the left by a crack (IV). The summit can easily be reached from here.

Descent: This consists of a series of cracks, chimneys and dièdres; each time these are broken or become too difficult, you can take

Aig. du Moine
3412

Ledges

Moine Glacier

To the Couvercle Hut

ledges joining up with other cracks and dièdres on the right or left, so allowing an easy descent. If you find yourself on rock unpolished by many climbers, then you have gone wrong.

From the summit descend directly for about 100m, traverse slightly left to the E across a sort of poorly-marked spur which comes down from the summit, then go back right to the W towards a large buttress standing out from the rest of the Face. Follow a ledge going down left and cross the great couloir to reach a platform. The descent now follows the left side of the large couloir taking two short dièdre-chimneys (III) and a series of short easy walls to a shoulder. A step with a couloir-chimney (III) leads to a track down a terraced grassy slope which makes left (E) and then comes back right, where two chimneys on the left bank of the couloir lead to the foot of the face and the Moine névé.

South Ridge of the Moine, with the Grandes Jorasses in the background (above).
The short wall pitch (opposite page).
Aiguille du Moine (left).

17. MONT BLANC DU TACUL 4248m
Ordinary Route
AIGUILLE DU MIDI 3800m
Arête des Cosmiques (South-South-West Ridge)

Since the building of the téléphérique up to the Aiguille du Midi, Mont Blanc du Tacul has become a convenient and interesting objective.

Mont Blanc du Tacul is a 4000m peak, and is useful from the technical point of view as well as offering a very fine climb; its slopes are very even, broken by clearly-defined rows of seracs and crevasses, all in infinitely varying shades of white, which bring out the special character of ice. The climber has the satisfaction of being on a major peak, on a N Face entirely made up of glacier, whose snow varies considerably in quality and in angle; he must sometimes traverse, sometimes climb direct, sometimes work his way through crevasses and sometimes climb seracs.

Finally, the summit gives a most impressive view over the world of the high peaks. Having done several climbs of around 3500m, the climber is now making the acquaintance of a quite new dimension. Because of the téléphérique, Mont Blanc du Tacul is a short route which can be done

easily in a morning, but it should not be underestimated; here wind, mist and changeable weather are to be feared, and in a storm it is disturbing to lose the route. Moreover this is a slope which can become dangerous after snowfall because of avalanche-danger, and which can stay dangerous until the snow has stabilised.

For the return to the Aiguille du Midi, you will find it much more pleasant all round not to follow the NE Ridge, banal and rather laborious, but to take the SSW Ridge or Arête des Cosmiques; you will have a view, very different from that from the Mont Blanc du Tacul itself, but just as magnificent, down to the right over the peaceful Vallée Blanche, and to the left over the towering peaks plunging down to the Bossons Glacier. Moreover you will also have a very interesting climb, from the technical point of view. It is, as it were, an excellent training for mixed climbing in the high mountains.

There is another advantage: not only is the climb an elegant way of getting back to the Aiguille du Midi, not only is it a way of doing

two climbs for the price of one relatively short approach march, but doing the climb after the Mont Blanc du Tacul, at about 11 am to midday, should be pleasant, since in theory the ropes heading directly for it, who will have started early by the first cable-car, will already have finished and the ridge should be deserted. But you should avoid looking up too often towards the summit, that is the concrete platform built for the tourists and the television mast, both unrelievedly ugly. I must also admit that this is a climb without a true summit, that is without a place where one can go no further upwards and where the climber and his companions can rest in silence and solitude.

Finally, and obviously, while the two climbs can be done together, they can also be done separately.

● **1st ascent:** Mont Blanc du Tacul, by one or several members of the Hudson-Kennedy party, 8 August 1855.

Aiguille du Midi, SSW Ridge, G. and M. Finch, 29 August 1911.

● **Vertical height:** 716m from the Col du Midi to Mont Blanc du Tacul (from 3532m to 4248m); 268m from the Col du Midi to the Aiguille du Midi (from 3532m to 3800m).

● **Grade:** Fairly steep snow-slopes on Mont Blanc du Tacul; AD with pitches of III and one of III sup. on the Arête des Cosmiques.

● **Time:** 2½–3 hrs from the Aiguille du Midi to Mont Blanc du Tacul. 1 hr from Mont Blanc du Tacul to the Col du Midi.

2–2½ hrs from the Col du Midi to the Aiguille du Midi by the Arête des Cosmiques.

● **Equipment:** Crampons (for Mont Blanc du Tacul) and abseil rope (for the Arête des Cosmiques).

● **Starting point:** Cosmiques Hut (3613m) or the upper Midi téléphérique station.

● **Route:**

Mont Blanc du Tacul – *Outline:* Diagonally across the main slope.

Description: From the upper téléphérique station descend the NE Ridge and turn right towards the Col du Midi (30 mins). Leave the col proper on the right to go across to Mont Blanc du Tacul which is climbed up the main slope, at first diagonally. Then either directly or turning the serac barriers and the crevasses, if they are uncrossable, on the right, go up again diagonally to the shoulder formed by the almost horizontal section of the W Ridge. Go back left to reach the summit of Mont Blanc du Tacul (2–2½ hrs depending on conditions). Return to the Col du Midi by the same route (1 hr).

Aiguille du Midi, SSW Ridge or Arête des Cosmiques – *Outline:* The ridge, turning the second gendarme on the right and the third on the left.

Description: From the col, turning the rock below the Cosmiques Hut (3613m), go up to the foot of the ridge where the old disused Simond Hut stands. Go straight up, slightly right of the ridge (snow and rock), to reach the first gendarme (3731m). Follow the snowy and then rocky crest of the ridge to the foot of a great tower. Turn this on the right (abseil). Continue along the ridge to the foot of a second tower which is left on the right. Descend a couloir, easy if snowed but slippery if icy (possible abseil), and then gain the final step along a horizontal snow ridge. Climb straight up for 6–7m (IV) to reach a chimney-couloir of snow or ice and then continue up a series of cracks (III) on the W flank to reach the last snow-shoulder and from there the téléphérique platform (2–2½ hrs).

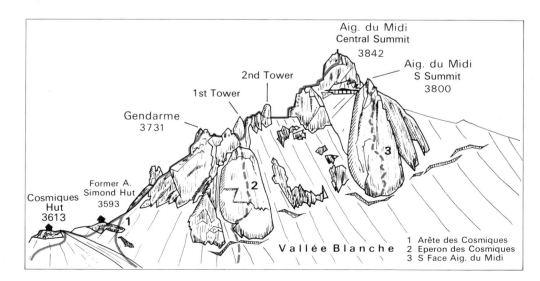

Mont Blanc du Tacul, Mont Maudit, Mont Blanc (opposite page).
The Aiguille du Midi with the Arête des Cosmiques on the left and the ordinary route on the right (above).

18. AIGUILLE DE L'M 2844m
North-North-East Ridge

Modest in altitude and height, the Aiguille de l'M is a small-scale route, but an enjoyable one and very interesting from the technical point of view. It has a pleasant atmosphere (something like an outcrop in the high mountains), especially so since, although it is in very fine surroundings, looking over the Mer de Glace and the Drus in particular, there is no glacier and no great rock-face near at hand. There are also no route-finding problems, the route being obvious and very popular. So it is relaxing and peaceful, and you can devote yourself to the actual climbing, to climbing for sheer pleasure and technical progress.

The climb is continuous with no breaks or scrambling sections. The difficulty is sustained and of a constant standard, but with continual technical variety. The NNE Ridge offers a fairly complete selection of the different types of rock-formation to be found along the Aiguilles: cracks, slabs, chimneys, walls, dièdres, ledges, grooves and even a 'letter-box'. You can get used to the feel of the granite and to its degree of friction on different sorts of hold, including pinch-grips.

This is therefore an excellent test-climb both for the novice, who can try out his competence in techniques for different types of climbing, and for the more experienced climber who, at the beginning of a season, wants to get back into practice and to assess his own fitness.

But above all, this is an ideal climb for times when other routes are out of condition, when the snow is down to 3000m, when the weather is doubtful or when you feel good weather may break at midday. To take advantage of the training aspect, this is a climb where you should concentrate on technique, especially in the slanting crack climbed by jamming, when the little bridging holds give out.

Finally, the descent, by the ordinary route, is easy and simple to find.

- **1st ascent:** Mme M. Damesme, F. Batier, M. Damesme, J. Morin, 25 August 1945.
- **Vertical height:** About 160m (from 2680 to 2844m).
- **Grade:** D with two moves of V.
- **Time:** 2 hrs.
- **Equipment:** Carabiners.
- **Starting point:** Plan de l'Aiguille téléphérique station (2310m).
- **Route** – *Outline:* When you have climbed the bottom section, the ridge is well-marked, fairly wide lower down and bounded on the left by the snow slope from the Col Blanc, narrow and compact in the middle when the climb goes to the right of the ridge, and smooth and exposed in the upper section.

Description: From the Plan de l'Aiguille take the path to the Nantillons Glacier and

Aig. de l'M 2844

Col Blanc

when you get to the glacier, instead of traversing almost horizontally as you would to go to the Petits Charmoz, descend obliquely before the curve right of the glacier around the base of the Pic Albert. Go up grassy slopes (a poor track), cross a small col between Pt 2503 to the NW and Pic Albert to the SE and then go up obliquely below the NNW Face of the M towards the bottom of the NNE Ridge. Turn this, that is to say go round onto the sunny side, and immediately you will see the whole ridge ahead. First study the general line, then go closer: the climb starts with a cracked slab, very steep for a metre and then less so (IV). Above, the slabs are cracked and a chimney is taken to reach a shoulder at the foot of a short wall (V) which leads to a large terrace. Climb a sloping crack (typical Chamonix crack, IV sup.) right of the ridge. To climb this use the smallest holds inside the crack as well as on its edge and do not get too far into the crack, so that you can use these bridging holds, quite adequate to hold you, to the best advantage. When there are no holds, you must resort to jamming feet and arms, the crack being too wide for normal hand-jamming. Remember that a foot-jam only holds if it is done properly and decisively. There is an excellent stance above the crack. Higher, climb a dièdre then make a short traverse left (IV) and go back to the ridge and follow it to a stance. Traverse horizontally left for 5m along a ledge which grows narrower and leads to the foot of a short system of vertical grooves (one move of V), then bear right and, through a 'letter-box', continue up large blocks (easy but unstable) and then up a short dièdre to reach the summit ridge (2 hrs).

Aiguille de L'M with the North-North-East Ridge on the skyline and the Ménégaux and Couzy routes facing, directly below the summit (opposite page).
On the North-North-East Ridge (right).

19. AIGUILLE D'ARGENTIERE 3900m
Ordinary Route

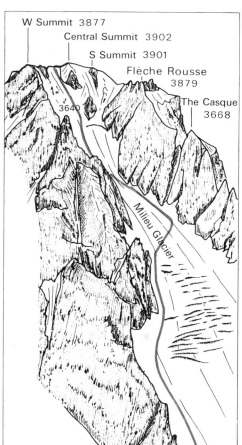

W Summit 3877

Central Summit 3902

S Summit 3901

Flèche Rousse 3879

The Casque 3668

3640

Milieu Glacier

The Aiguille d'Argentière is an outstanding and majestic peak at the northern end of the range, on the frontier ridge between Switzerland to the N and E, and France to the S and W.

From the summit on the Swiss side, a huge spur goes down towards the Saleina Glacier between the magnificent N Face, an open glacier, and the E side, mixed terrain, concave and very desolate. On the French side there are two long parallel rockridges, the Jardin Ridge and the Straton Ridge, which separate three fine glaciers, also parallel, the Chardonnet Glacier, the Milieu Glacier and the Améthystes Glacier, all of which go down to the Argentière Glacier.

The Aiguille d'Argentière is invisible from the valleys, but its French side is now well-known because of the Grands Montets téléphérique, from the top of which you can see the Milieu Glacier which comes down from the summit itself and makes two sweeping turns between the rock-ridges, with their warm tints and their massed pinnacles and towers. This is a very well-proportioned landscape, and luckily this is the way followed by the ordinary route; luckily, because as you go upwards you feel you are penetrating deeper and deeper into an inner sanctum of snow and rock. This is an elegant route, of no great difficulty, except for the final section which is sometimes iced at the end of the season. But the route, an excellent introduction to the high mountains, should only be undertaken in good conditions.

● **1st ascent:** Aiguille d'Argentière by the N Ridge, A. A. Reilly, and E. Whymper, with M. Croz and H. Charlet, 15 July 1864.

Glacier du Milieu (first done in descent by L. Declé and Y. A. Hutchinson with A. Imseng and L. Lanier, 14 August 1880), in ascent by V. Attinger and A. Dubois with F. Biselx and M. Joris, 17 July 1895.

● **Vertical height:** 950m from the foot of the glacier to the summit; 1130m. from the hut to the summit (from 2771m to 3900m).

● **Grade:** An easy glacier walk on crampons to the bergschrund; higher up the last steeper slope presents no problem if it is snow; on the other hand it can be tricky if icy, particularly on the descent. In this case it is better either to stop on the ascent at the bergschrund, or to descend from the summit by the Flèche Rousse Ridge or NW Ridge.

● **Time:** 4 hours from the Argentière Hut to the summit. The time for leaving the hut depends upon the descent of the upper slope. If it is to be in good condition you should make the descent before the sun has softened the snow too much — remember that the slope faces SW. So it is necessary to leave the hut very early and to keep to time. In order not to lose time looking for the path, you are recommended the evening before to reconnoitre the path leading to the glacier (20 min).

● **Equipment:** Crampons.

● **Starting point:** The Argentière Hut (2771m) three hours away from the Croix de Lognan or $1\frac{1}{4}$ hrs from the upper station of the Grands Montets téléphérique.

● **Route** – *Outline:* The route is easily seen from the Grands Montets: the Milieu Glacier between the two ridges.

Description: From the Argentière Hut take the path going off to the left which leads to the moraine. Go up this to the Milieu Glacier (20 min). Go up the glacier diagonally left towards the fine big gendarme on the SW Ridge, then go along beside the base of this ridge to a small plateau where you return to the centre to cross the bergschrund and climb straight up the long slope, to come out on the summit ridge about 100m from the main summit.

Descent: Choose the time for this according to the sun and the condition of the snow — avoid being too late. At the foot of the glacier you should watch out for stonefall. Cross it diagonally to gain the moraine directly, or else descend directly, or perhaps over on the right, towards the moraine of the right bank and turn finally the foot of the glacier.

Aiguille d'Argentière, with the Milieu Glacier coming down between the Jardin Ridge and the Straton Ridge (opposite page).
Portrait of Michel Croz (above).

20. PYRAMIDE DU TACUL 3468m
East Ridge

The Pyramide du Tacul is no very great summit, but its ascent by the E Ridge is very pleasant and easily accessible, and so it is very popular. Without the téléphérique on the Aiguille du Midi and Col du Géant it would be much less so, not unnaturally since the walk up would be disproportionately long in relation to the climb itself.

The best way to go, for a well-planned route, is: Aiguille du Midi (3840m), Pyramide (3468m), Col des Flambeaux (3407m) and Col du Géant (3365m). This avoids, after the climb, the long and arduous climb back up to the Aiguille du Midi and gives a walk through very fine country, very varied, across the top of the Vallée Blanche. The Pyramide route is very safe, not very tiring, on good grey granite, at a relatively easy angle, and the face itself is only 200m high. The pitches are pleasant if fairly long and exposed; the most difficult and impressive of them is the overhang.

The descent is useful practice; it is done largely in abseils. For training, the novice should try to speed up not the descent itself but his rope-management — while remaining extremely cautious; after all it is caution that saves time and avoids the abseiling accidents which are only too numerous.

● **1st ascent**: E. Croux, L. Grivel and A. Ottoz, 29 July 1940.
● **Vertical height**: About 250m (from 3220 to 3468m).
● **Grade**: Fairly sustained D.
● **Time**: 40 mins from the Aiguille du Midi to the start; 2 hrs from the start to the summit. 1–1½ hrs for the descent. 1½ hrs from the start to the Col du Géant.
● **Equipment**: Abseil rope.
● **Starting point**: Aiguille du Midi (3840m) or the Col du Géant (3365m).
● **Route** – *Outline:* Elegant, defined by the ridge. However, the foot of the ridge, just above the glacier, consists of smooth slabs which are turned on the left, so that the means of access to the rock depends on the state of the glacier. Above, ledges lead right to the ridge which is followed to the summit.

Description: Climb the glacier left of the ridge for about 50m (watch out for falling

seracs) and traverse right to reach the area of small terraces. From here climb up diagonally right to reach the ridge. (Instead of using the glacier left of the ridge, it is possible to reach the same point by taking a system of couloir-chimneys [III] situated to the right, to the N of the slabs at the foot of the ridge, but the rock is not very sound.)

Go up easy steps and a short dièdre sloping right for about 50m and then return left to climb a crack (IV). Continue on the left of the crest of the ridge up a crack to arrive at a slanting dièdre leading back to the right (III). You are now at the foot of the crux pitch formed by an overhang. Climb the cracked slab, at first slightly left and then right (IV), turn the overhang on the left (IV) and climb a short dièdre (IV). You now arrive at a zone of terraces, sometimes snowy. Belay with a long sling to prevent the rope jamming.

The step above has two cracks; take the one on the right which leads back to the crest of the spur on sloping slabs. Climb to the right, then left, then right again (IV) and ascend cracks and big easy blocks to reach the summit (III). 2 hrs from the start.

Descent: — By the N Face, the ordinary route. First descend the last two rope-lengths of the ascent route, and then go left to mixed ground on the N Face with two or three abseils, depending upon the conditions, to reach the snow slope and then the glacier.
— By the E Ridge, down the ascent route:

Climb down for two rope-lengths, then abseil 30m and climb to the top of the step with the two parallel cracks. Abseil down the one that would have been on the left going upwards, and reach terraces above the overhang. From here a series of 4 abseils brings you back to the start.

East Face of Mont Blanc du Tacul with its pillars and couloirs; the Vallée Blanche below, above the Pyramide (opposite page, below).
A crack in the sloping slabs above the overhang (opposite page, above).
Cracked slab and overhang pitch (above).

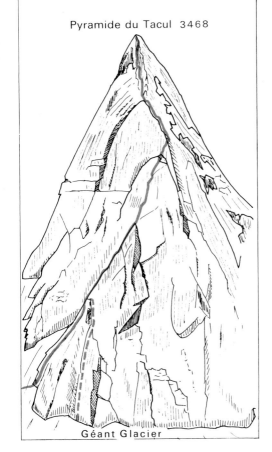

Pyramide du Tacul 3468

Géant Glacier

21. AIGUILLE DU MIDI — AIGUILLE DU PLAN 3842–3673m
Traverse

This is a superb snow-route along a ridge varying from the narrow and delicate, like filigree-work, to something broader and corniced, where one is aware of the effects of the battling winds, and with a rock section which has a starker atmosphere. The whole traverse is on the frontier between two worlds: that of the valley to the left, where you see the awakening life and bustle of a new day, and that of the high mountains on the right, peaceful, unchanging, eternal.

It is a very popular route, which makes it feel less remote, but the ridge is long and you can get away from the little specks that are climbers queuing for pitches.

In general, the way is marked all along, so there are no route-finding problems. On the other hand, you need to be constantly on the alert as you change from one side of the ridge to the other; the character of the route changes, and so do the angle and the quality of the snow, while a fall could be difficult to halt.

On the traverse on the NW side and then up to the Rognon du Plan, you may be exposed to stonefall, perhaps started by other parties. From the Col Supérieur du Plan (rucksacks can be left here), you go up to the Aiguille du Plan; in contrast with the snowscapes you have just crossed, this looks out onto a wild, rough landscape of granite pillars and aiguilles. The Aiguille du Plan is in a strategic position, at the intersection of four ridges, and this explains why it offers a panorama which is not only of great beauty, but is also extensive and interesting.

You then come back to the col to go down to the Requin Hut by the Envers du Plan Glacier, a very tortuous glacier where crossing some crevasses and seracs can be awkward, alarming and sometimes strenuous, but always interesting.

Do not stop at the foot of the Requin couloir; there is danger of stonefall. However, spend some time studying it, because you will use it the following day, coming down from the Dent du Requin. A little further down, study the little cirque at the start of the Chapeau à Cornes Ridge.

Watch out for snow- and rock-falls, where the route turns east over glaciated rock and then traverses snow-slopes to the moraine leading to the hut.

- **1st ascent:** G. W. Young with J. Knubel, 10 August 1907.
- **Vertical height:** About 1400m, mostly in descent, from the Aiguille du Midi to the Requin Hut (from 3800 to 2516m).
- **Grade:** Some sections of the ridge are very narrow or very corniced. The rock sections are II with several moves of III.
- **Time:** 3–4 hrs from the Aiguille du Midi

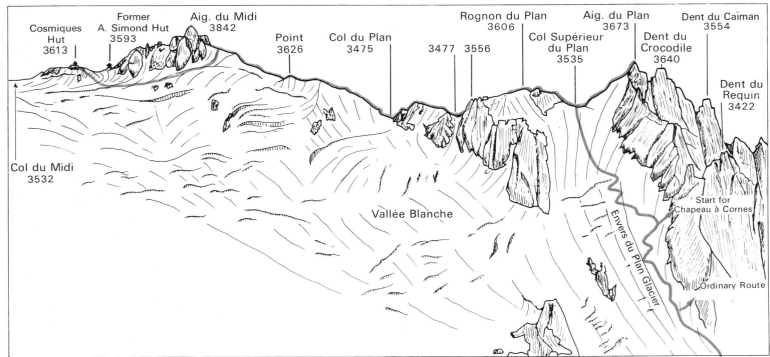

to the Aiguille du Plan. 1½–2 hrs from the Aiguille du Plan to the Requin Hut.

● **Equipment:** Crampons. Do not forget to take an abseil rope if you intend to follow the programme I propose and climb the Dent du Requin the next day.

● **Starting points:** There are three possibilities: — the Cosmiques Hut (3613m), a traditional, friendly and very typical hut.
— the Aiguille du Midi (3800m) [this is really a bivouac, with no guardian or dormitory] — sometimes it is possible to sleep in one of the rooms of the téléphérique station. The evening before, when everyone has gone down with the last cabin, you can enjoy sitting on the summit of the Aiguille and seeing sunset and nightfall. The next day, leave the hut or the Aiguille at daybreak.
— Chamonix itself taking the first cabin at 6 am to the Aiguille du Midi. There is no time for you to break yourself in gently, and you will have a very strong feeling of contrast.

Going up the Aiguille du Plan, with the Rognon du Plan at the bottom and Mont Blanc and Mont Blanc du Tacul above (opposite page). Summit of the Aiguille du Plan (above). Midi-Plan Ridge, with the Géant Glacier below (right).

You leave Chamonix and then almost immediately you are at 3800m. At the door of the cabin you are directed into a tunnel, over a foot-bridge, into another tunnel, and then all of a sudden, everything changes. It is a revelation. From a snow balcony in the sky, the rising sun before you, there is a view not only of the entire ridge along which you will go, but also of an otherworld, beautiful, widespread before you, its effect enhanced because you have just emerged from the tunnel. And this too is almost symbolic: behind you, the city, a grey sombre prison; before you, light, beauty and freedom. You are overcome with wonder, even if the whole route is perfectly familiar, even if this is the tenth or the hundredth visit.

● **Route** — *Outline:* The ridge, with a detour to the left and then to the right to turn the rocks of the Rognon.

Description: From the tunnel of the Aiguille du Midi descend and follow the snow ridge going ENE which widens for a little and then narrows near Point 3626m and make a fairly steep descent to gain the rocks at 3518m which precede the thin ridge of the Col du Plan (3475m).

Climb the rocks on the Chamonix side and then the snow couloir which leads to the Rognon du Plan (3606m). Follow briefly the rocky flat crest and then descend right on the Envers du Plan side by a system of easy couloir-dièdres and ledges which lead back to the snow. Make a horizontal traverse just below the rock to gain the Col Supérieur du Plan (3535m). Go up the snow ridge and then up easy rocks which lead to the Aiguille du Plan (3673m, 3–4 hrs).

Return to the Col Supérieur by the ascent route and from there descend the great snow slope and then, below the bergschrund, the Envers du Plan Glacier whose crevasses and seracs compel sometimes quite long detours. At the foot of the wall of the Requin turn left and N. Climb a rocky step by a system of descending ledges, return to the snow and then descend the moraine leading to the Requin Hut (2516m, 1½–2 hrs).

Sun, snow, and the rope (opposite page, below).
Beginning of the Midi-Plan Ridge (opposite page, above).
The Midi-Plan Ridge from the Vallée Blanche side (above).
On the ridge before the descent to the
Col Supérieur du Plan, with the Aiguille du Triolet in the background (above).

22. DENT DU REQUIN 3422m
South-East Ridge

The Dent du Requin is a very fine aiguille, and the Chapeau à Cornes Ridge a delightful route. It joins the ordinary route at the shoulder, where it becomes interesting, and the combination of the two routes makes for a very homogeneous route of quite considerable vertical height (500m).

On the technical side, this is a fairly sustained route where you will need some route-finding ability and where keeping to time is essential, since the way down is much more complex, for instance, than on the Aiguille du Midi. This means that the descent by the ordinary route will be both excellent training and a good test to assess the climber's route-finding ability, his anticipation of difficulties, his sense of the linking of ledges, chimneys and other ledges, etc.

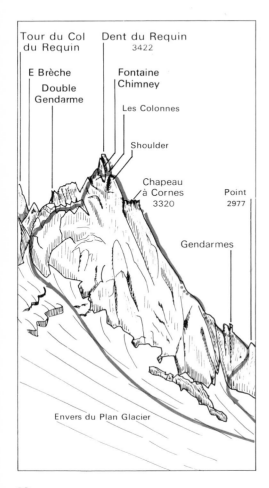

Moreover, curiosity being one of the qualities indispensable in the mountaineer, you should be on the alert for any clues (while remembering that some may themselves result from error): worn rock, holds rounded in the old days by nailed boots. Except on the few short and more delicate pitches where it is better and safer to climb separately, you should move together in a controlled way, not speeding up after a difficulty but waiting until your companion has got over it too; carrying coils carefully, without letting the rope drag, and putting it behind spikes where possible. Remember that a fall can easily take place when you are moving together on easy ground; you should be ready to stop any fall immediately.

● **1st ascent:** ordinary route, G. Hastings, A. F. Mummery, J. Norman Collie and W. C. Slingsby, 25 July 1893. Chapeau a Cornes Ridge, R. C. Mayor, C. D. Robertson, G. W. Young, with J. Knubel and a porter, 3 August 1906.

● **Vertical height:** About 400m from the hut to the start; about 500m from the start to the summit (from 2516 to 3422m).

● **Grade:** AD with pitches of IV.

● **Time:** 1¼ hrs from the hut to the start; 3 hrs from the start to the summit; 2½ hrs from the summit to the hut.

● **Equipment:** Abseil rope.

● **Starting point:** Requin Hut (2516m).

● **Route** – *Outline:* The Chapeau à Cornes Ridge is reached up its S flank and then climbed mainly on its E side. Above the Shoulder the summit block and the Nose are turned by the Colonnes (Columns) on the right.

Description: Follow the route up the Envers du Plan Glacier until level with a small cirque which is at about 2900m in the SE Ridge of the Dent du Requin and which is dominated by a pair of well-defined gendarmes (1 hr). Cross the bergschrund, climb smooth, wet rocks (IV) and then climb ledges diagonally right to dièdres which lead to the ridge well below the gendarmes, between the two lowest small points on the ridge (marked 2977m). Turn the one above on the right, continue along the crest, again on the right turn the two well-marked gendarmes (the second of which is a fairly massive tower) and return to the ridge up a couloir-chimney (IV) which leads to the brèche just beyond the tower. Continue along the ridge to the Chapeau à Cornes (3320m) which is reached by dièdres to the right (or by a 'letter-box' if you prefer). From here go up right to gain the Shoulder where the ordinary route is joined for its interesting section (2 hrs). Here you are in a good position to study the rest of the route, both the ascent by the Colonnes (parallel cracks) right of the Requin Nose, and the descent by the Fontaine Chimney on the left.

Leave the rucksacks and axes and start climbing again; first descend to the right to reach the ledges which lead back to a short couloir, and go up this for several metres to continue the traverse to the Colonnes. An easy chimney and then a

crack lead to a good platform on the right. Continue above up a crack (III sup.) slightly on the left and then a traverse below an overhang leads to a second platform. An enclosed chimney slightly right, a third platform and another open chimney take you to a series of crack-chimneys leading to a shoulder. By a short chimney on the right (N), a series of flakes and a final pull-up, you then arrive on the summit block (1 hr; 4¾ hrs from the hut).

Descent: Descend the flakes to get level with the Fontaine Chimney W of the summit. Two 20m abseils (pitons in place) lead to the traverse and from there to the Shoulder (where you can pick up your sacks and axes).

On the W side gain ledges cut by short walls which lead to the couloir of the Col du Requin. Do not go into the couloir, there is stonefall danger; descend the steps on the left bank, cross the bergschrund and reach the glacier.

The Colonnes on the Requin (opposite page). The Dent du Requin with left to right: the Chapeau à Cornes Ridge, the East Face, the Mayer-Dibona Ridge, the North Face; in the background the Aiguille du Midi, with the Grand Gendarme on the Envers du Plan and the Pain de Sucre (above).

23. GRANDES JORASSES 4208m
Ordinary Route

The Grandes Jorasses, because of their altitude, their height above the valley and their appearance, are an important summit in the Mont Blanc range, or rather, more precisely, a series of summits since the summit ridge, covering about a km at over 4000m, includes the Pointe Young (3996m), the Pointe Marguerite (4066m), the Pointe Hélène (4045m), the Pointe Croz (4110m), the W Summit or Pointe Whymper (4184m) and the E Summit or Pointe Walker (4208m). The N side, very high and steep, rises from the Leschaux Glacier and the Mont Mallet Glacier, and it is on this side that we find some of the greatest routes in the Alps. The S side is easier of access because of the Planpincieux Glacier and the Grandes Jorasses Glacier coming up from the Italian Val Ferret. To the E, separated from each other by sharp ridges, are the two little glaciers, Pra Sec and Tronchey, and the huge Frébouzie Glacier which comes up to the foot of the E Face; this is steep and very difficult, not very attractive, framed by the Tronchey Ridge to the left and the Hirondelles Ridge on the right.

In 1865, three-quarters of a century after the first ascent of Mont Blanc, the Grandes Jorasses were still unclimbed. It was Whymper, with his guides M. Croz, Ch. Almer and F. Biener, who climbed them. However, they had done the ascent only 'to obtain a view of the upper part of the Aiguille Verte', and so stopped at the W Summit (4184m), now known as the Pointe Whymper, lower by 36m than the summit, which they did not bother to climb. Anyway, 'the weather was boisterous in the upper regions' and 'storm-clouds enveloped us in misty spray. The mists lasted longer than [Whymper's] patience', although this did not prevent his doing the first ascent of the Aiguille Verte five days later. For the moment the descent was problem enough, steep and indeed 'very dangerous'. Moreover, no sooner had the rasher members of the party suggested trying a glissade than the crust slipped away into an avalanche (no doubt a case of wind-slab slipping away and leaving the underlying ice bare), and carried away the whole party. 'Luckily the slope eased off at one place', and one after another the men 'cleverly jumped aside out of the moving snow'. And this is how the strongest rope of the time could well have vanished on the Jorasses. One last word on this exploit: its extraordinary times. 24 June, 1.30, departure from Courmayeur; 5.30, arrival at the rocks where the hut now is; 8.00, at the seracs under the Rocher du Reposoir; 13.00, the W Summit; 20.45 (on the same day), arrival in Courmayeur. Quite apart from their strength and skill, we are amazed by the mountain sense of these men, under the 'dextrous leading' of Michel Croz.

Finally, on 30 June 1868, H. Walker with M. Anderegg and J. Jaun with J. Grange, reached the E Summit, the highest (4208m), which was to become known as the Pointe Walker.

● **1st ascent:** H. Walker, with M. Anderegg, J. Jaun and J. Grange, 30 June 1868. (They left the Whymper route at about 3850m to traverse E and reach the summit directly).

● **Vertical height:** 1400m (from the hut at 2804m to the summit at 4208m).

● **Grade:** A mixed route, mainly ice with some steep slopes, large open bergschrunds; however this is not a difficult route, but a 'grande course', long with some complex route-finding, an interesting route where bad weather and mist can be testing.

Two sections can present objective dangers, stonefall, icefall and snow slides: the crossing of the Planpincieux Glacier (sometimes called the Whymper Couloir) high up right of the Rocher du Reposoir, and the last traverse, below the seracs across the upper Grandes Jorasses Glacier.

● **Time:** 6 hrs. Leave the hut very early, in darkness and using head-torches, to keep the approach pleasant and reduce the objective dangers.

● **Equipment:** Crampons.

● **Starting point:** The Grandes Jorasses Hut (2804m) also known as the Boccalatte

Pointe Croz 4110

Pointe Whymper 4184

Pointe Walker 4208

Rocher du Reposoir

Jorasses Glacier

Rognon de la Bouteille

Planpincieux Glacier

Boccalatte Hut 2804

Hut, which can be reached in three hours from Planpincieux on the Val Ferret road.

● **Route** – *Outline:* First go S-N straight up the Planpincieux Glacier to the Rocher du Reposoir, then SW-NE by a series of traverses right (to the E) and direct ascents.

Description: From the Grandes Jorasses Hut (2804m) go N up rock slopes above the hut to gain the Planpincieux Glacier. Go up this glacier alongside the long rock—rognon known as The Bottle (La Bouteille, a local name due to its shape seen from below), which separates the Planpincieux Glacier to the W from the Grandes Jorasses Glacier to the E, towards the Rocher du Reposoir, an obvious snowy rock spine (which separates the same two glaciers between 3400 and 3700m), which is climbed on its E flank. Then cross the glacier right (Whymper Couloir) to reach, up a short slanting couloir, the lower rocks of the Pointe Whymper. Climb these for about 100m and leave them to move right onto a snow plateau on the glacier when you come level with it.

From here, depending on the conditions, there are two possibilities: either follow the glacier on the right towards the E shoulder and then take a mixed rock and snow rib to the summit ridge and follow this to the summit slightly to the right, or climb first up the easy rock ridge of the Pointe Whymper and then up the slopes of the Pointe Walker.

The first (the Walker Route) is exposed to serac falls and snow slides at the start of the traverse. The second (the Whymper Route) is safer, particularly on the descent and in mist; it is very popular.

The Reposoir Ridge on the Grandes Jorasses (opposite page).
The South-West side of the Grandes Jorasses (above).

24. MONT BLANC 4807m
Ordinary Route

It has been said that the ascent of Mont Blanc is long, laborious and not very interesting. This is quite untrue, and I am inclined to think that the Bosses Ridge is one of the finest snow-routes in existence. But this depends on two things; on starting early in the morning and on the climber's being really fit, so that the walk is a pleasure rather than a labour. It is the case that on Mont Blanc, more so perhaps than on any other peak, there is a ritual based on the sun, and provided this ritual is followed, the climb can be done in ideal conditions, with more ease and less exhaustion and thus with greater enjoyment and pleasure.

But in any case, on Mont Blanc and on this route in particular, you will never regret starting too early — always regret starting too late — and this for certain technical reasons: walking is easier when the snow is firm than when it has become sticky and slippery because of the heat of the sun; you are moreover more comfortable if you are breathing cool air — and this is particularly noticeable on Mont Blanc — than if the air is warm and sultry. So climbing the Bosses Ridge at 5–6 am is easier than at midday.

And there are aesthetic as well as technical reasons for an early start; Mont Blanc itself and the summits of the range are more beautiful in a slanting light than blazing under a sun directly overhead. This means that if the beauty of the view is to be an incentive, you should leave the Aiguille du Goûter Hut in the middle of the night, at 1.00 am at the latest. In this way, the most potentially laborious part of the climb, the walk up the Dôme, is done at night, and the climb as a whole is a climb up to the sun.

At the Vallot Hut you can leave a fair amount of equipment before tackling the summit ridge and coming back by the Grands Mulets Route; this will show you a new and attractive side of the mountain.

The ascent of Mont Blanc presents no technical difficulties, except that of walking in crampons; on the other hand, you need to be acclimatised for walking at high altitudes. You should also have a fairly wide experience in the Alps, for the ascent of Mont Blanc, perfectly simple in good weather, can be unpleasant in high winds and alarming in mist, and can lead to positive disaster in storm. It is essential to know when to turn back. You are advised to carry in your rucksack a duvet jacket, a long cagoule, a balaclava and a spare pair of gloves — hoping you do not need them.

If you are caught by bad weather or mist on the summit, the only thing to do is to go back down the Bosses Ridge to the Vallot Hut, and then if possible down the Grands Mulets route.

Finally, whether the weather is good or bad, spare a thought for the pioneers who first did the route nearly two centuries ago.

- **1st ascent:** J. Balmat and M. Paccard, 8 August 1786 (by the Ancien Passage between the Rochers Rouges).
- **Vertical height:** 1421m from the Eagle's Nest to the Goûter Hut (from 2396m to 3863m); 944m from the hut to the summit (from 3817 to 4807m); 2500m from the summit to the Plan de l'Aiguille.
- **Grade:** The Bosses Ridge requires the ability to walk in crampons, but the main difficulty comes from the altitude.
- **Time:** 4–5 hrs from the Eagle's Nest to the Goûter Hut. 4–5 hrs to the top from the hut. 3–5 hrs from the summit to the Plan de l'Aiguille.
- **Equipment:** Crampons; overboots which insulate the boots and protect the feet much better than gaiters which only protect the legs.
- **Starting point:** Aiguille du Goûter Hut (3817m).
- **Route** – *Outline:* From the Tête Rousse the whole of the ascent of the Aiguille is perfectly visible. So look at it, study the route and understand its rationale. Notice that the traverse of the couloir is the tricky section. From the Aiguille you can see the vast snowfields of the Dôme and distinguish the line dictated by the terrain: a detour right along the crest of the Aiguille, then a long diagonal section to the left and back right. Finally from the Dôme you can see straight up to the summit ridge, and it is interesting in view of the numerous steps and curves of the ridge, almost continuously fringed with cornices, to work out which route you would follow if it was unclimbed.

Description: From the Eagle's Nest follow the path which goes up NE in zig-zags towards the Désert de Pierre Ronde, climbs up below the crest of the Rognes, then changing direction goes right, to the SE, and ascends the spur coming down from the Aiguille du Goûter. Traverse across to the Tête Rousse Hut (3167m). From the Tête Rousse go left to make a big zig-zag which leads back right before the traverse of the 'Couloir' — watch out for stonefall — which comes down from the Aiguille, and then climbs first obliquely and then directly the ridge at the top of which is the Goûter Hut (3817m), 4–5 hrs.

The ascent to the Goûter Hut (3817m) is already quite good enough as an ascent. You should realise that the ascent of Mont Blanc is a route lasting two days.

From the Goûter Hut, first follow the

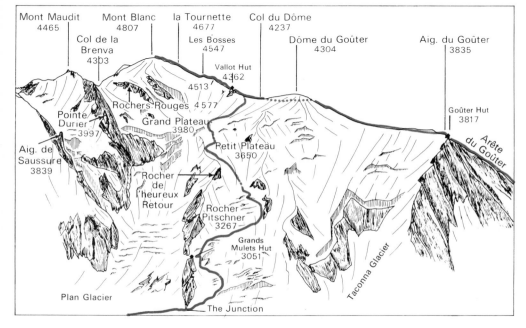

almost horizontal ridge on the right, and then go up obliquely left towards the Dôme du Goûter and leave the summit on the left to reach the Col du Dôme (4237m, 2 hrs) and then the Vallot Hut (4362m, 30 mins). From here, climb the W Ridge, going over the Grande Bosse (4513m) and the Petite Bosse (4547m), then gain the Rochers de la Tournette (4677m) and continue to the summit along the narrowing ridge (1½ hrs; 4–5 hrs from the Dôme du Goûter).

Descent: Follow the ascent route down to the Vallot Hut and the Col du Dôme. At the Col turn sharp right to reach the Grand Plateau (about 4000m).

Spare a thought for J. Balmat, forgotten by the other guides during their attempt, making as night fell, alone, the first bivouac in the high mountains.

Then turning the big crevasses, generally on the right, descend the fairly steep slope called the Grandes Montées, which leads to the Petit Plateau (about 3650m). Lose height down the steepish slope, the Petites Montées or Côte du Cerisier, and then, keeping well away from the walls of the Dôme du Goûter, traverse diagonally across to the Grands Mulets rock and the hut (3051m). From the Grand Plateau to the bottom of the Côte du Cerisier the route is not sheltered from falling seracs and snow-slides can come off the slopes of the Dôme du Goûter on the left-hand side of the route. The descent continues at first straight down, and then right to reach the junction and the level section of the Bossons Glacier, which leads to the Glaciers Path and to the Plan de l'Aiguille.

Mont Blanc, with the Bosses Ridge and the Dôme du Goûter on the right, and the Mur de la Côte, the Rochers Rouges and the Col de la Brenva on the left.

1. The Grands Mulets Hut (3051m).
2. Sunset from the Goûter Hut (3817m).
3. Bosses Ridge (4547m).
4. Vallot Hut (4362m) and the Bosses Ridge.
5. Arriving at the Aiguille du Goûter Hut.
6. First sunlight on the Bosses Ridge.
7. Arriving on the summit of Mont Blanc.
8. The great North face of the Dôme du Goûter; on the right, on the skyline, the Aiguille du Goûter route coming up to the Col du Dôme where the Grands Mulets route also finishes.

2

1

3

4

5

74

7

8

25. AIGUILLE DES PELERINS 3318m
Grütter Ridge

The Aiguille des Pèlerins is halfway between the summit of the Aiguille du Plan and the bastions of the Aiguille du Peigne. While the view from the summit is not particularly extensive, it is most striking; you are in the middle of the Aiguilles, that unmatched chain of great granite rock-faces and glaciers outlined against the sky.

From the Plan de l'Aiguille up the Pèlerins Glacier, an approach-march in crampons leads easily and quite quickly to rocks at the bottom of the climb. The ordinary route, easy and technically not very interesting, is passed on the right (but will be used on the descent, so that it is worth studying it on the way past), and the route follows the Grütter Ridge, where the climbing makes pleasant and and extremely useful training. This Grütter Ridge is just the fourth in a series of steps on the long SW Ridge of the Aiguille des Pèlerins, which separates the Pèlerins Glacier from the Peigne Couloir. The SW Ridge can be climbed as a whole, but this has two disadvantages: firstly the route is then long and inconsistent in standard (the first part being difficult, the second and third easy) and can be escaped from at any point — an advantage of course on a day when the weather is dubious; secondly, it avoids the walk in crampons up the Pèlerins Glacier which, without being particularly steep, is nevertheless excellent training at this stage for the future alpinist.

● **1st ascent:** R. Aubert and M. Grütter, 21 July 1935.

● **Vertical height:** 900m of which the ridge itself accounts for 200m (from 3100 to 3318m).

● **Time:** 1½—2 hrs from the Plan de l'Aiguille to the start. 3 hrs from the start to

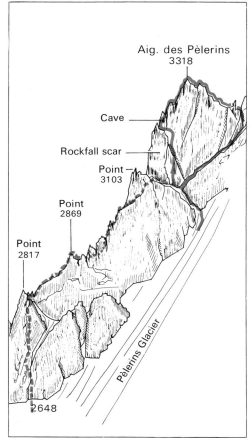

the summit. 2 hrs from the summit back to the Plan.

● **Grade:** D with a pitch of V.

● **Equipment:** Crampons, which are left with axes at the start at the top of the glacier. 5 or 6 carabiners. At several places slings are useful for protection.

● **Starting point:** Plan de l'Aiguille (2310m). The route can be done easily in the day if you take the first cabin up, because the Pèlerins Glacier faces W and so the slope is good for cramponning until 9 am.

● **Route** – *Outline:* At the top of the glacier a ledge goes diagonally up to the brèche just right of Gendarme 3103m. This brèche is at the foot of the ridge of which you climb not the crest, but the broader right-hand (S) side, crossed by cracks and chimneys. On the left there is the area which produced a rockfall in 1963, and after about 80m the crest is gained and followed to the summit with several detours, mostly to the right.

Description: From the Plan de l'Aiguille (2310m), follow the moraine leading to the Peigne névé (2648m) and the Pèlerins Glacier. Put on crampons and after turning the foot of the SE Ridge go up the glacier nearly to the top to where there is a large schist ledge on the left leading diagonally up to the brèche between Gendarme 3103m and the fourth step of the W Ridge. Follow this ledge, crossing the couloir-chimney of the ordinary route which goes up slightly right at right-angles to the ledge, and follow a succession of crack-chimneys for 4 rope-lengths (IV, fairly continuous) on the right of the rockfall area and so right of the original line.

Above, two easy rope-lengths and a traverse left lead to the ridge above the rock-fall area. Take a crack (III) slightly right of the ridge and gain a window formed by a block — view of the Peigne — then follow the ridge (III) to reach a cave (crumbling rock), traverse left for 2 metres, gain a cracked slab just below the ridge and return to the ridge at the foot of the groove pitch formed by two parallel cracks running up the ridge (IV, 2 moves of V). Go up by a series of steps to the square and the brèche where the Carmichael Route (NW Face of the Aiguille des Pèlerins) finishes. Continue up the crest of the ridge keeping to the left (N) side and climb a step (IV sup.) just before the summit, 3 hrs.

Descent: By the ordinary route. Follow the ESE Ridge which goes down towards the Col des Pèlerins. Turn the gendarme on the left (N) and halfway between the gendarme and the col rejoin by a system of couloir-chimneys with short slightly sloping steps the schist ledge on which the axes and crampons were left. From here descend the snow-slope of the Pèlerins Glacier. This descent is good practice. Only put crampons on if the slope is ice (which sometimes happens at the end of the season), and not if it is snow.

South-West Ridge of the Aiguille des Pèlerins, with the Aiguille du Peigne on the left, the Pèlerins Glacier on the right, and Aiguille de Blaitière behind (opposite page).
The big step on the Grütter Ridge (below centre).
The square Gendarme (below right).
The summit ridge (below left).

26. AIGUILLES DOREES 3435–3518m
Traverse

The Aiguilles Dorées are at the NE end of the Mont Blanc range; they are all in Switzerland and rise out of the Trient plateau to the N and the Plines and Saleina Glaciers to the S. The ridge they make up is 1·3 km long and is a series of summits and brèches of which the most important are (E–W): the Tête Crettex (3410m), the Aiguille Javelle (3435m), the Trident (3436m), the Col Copt (3410m), the Tête Biselx (3509m), the Aiguilles Penchées (3505m) and the Aiguille de la Varappe (3518m). The traverse E–W is in fact the most interesting, especially from the Albert Premier Hut. Taken this way, the crossing of the Trient Plateau is done early in the morning on firm snow, and the two most difficult stretches of the climb, the ascent of the Javelle and the crossing of the Col Copt, will come at the beginning. This is not a great route, but it is a long and serious one on mixed terrain, where good route-finding is very important and will avoid time-wasting delays from mistakes.

It is also a very varied route: there are pitches of pure rock-climbing, on the Aiguille Javelle for example (grade IV), which is an excellent test because it can either be climbed on technique – in which case it is not tiring – or by brute force and sheer arm-strength; there are also snow-pitches, which may be iced, like the top of the Col Copt, or else there is a whole series of ledges, chimneys, traverses, cracks and gendarmes to be avoided either on one side of the ridge or on the other. All this will help to train the novice as an alpinist.

- **1st E–W traverse:** Mlle Heiner with M. Crettex, 31 August 1898.
- **Vertical height:** 348m from the Trient Hut to the Aiguille de la Varappe, the highest (from 3170 to 3518m); but this is an inadequate assessment, since for the whole expedition the route follows a long ridge with a series of ascents and descents at a mean height of 3500m.
- **Grade:** D.
- **Time:** 2–2½ hrs from the hut to the Aiguille Javelle. 4–5 hrs from the Javelle to the Aiguilles Penchées. 2½ hrs from the Aiguilles Penchees to the hut. In all 8½–10 hrs.
- **Equipment:** Abseil rope; axes useful at the Col Copt.
- **Starting point:** The Trient Hut (3170m). It is also possible to set out from the Albert Premier Hut (2702m) and cross the Col du Tour, which lengthens the climb by some 2 hours.

- **Route** – *Outline:* The route follows the line of the crest but turns several sections on the right or on the left.

Description: From the Trient Hut descend to the Col d'Orny and go up a short snow couloir to the Brèche Crettex (W of the Col Droit). Go along to a second deep brèche between flakes; descend a short couloir for 3–4 metres, traverse W and reach a big ledge. Make a rising traverse across slabs and small ledges up the SE side of the Tête Crettex to reach the summit (3419m). Descend the summit block by easy ledges on the S side and reach the foot of the Aiguille Javelle. Climb a crack on the S side which widens into an 'open book', without getting too far inside at the start, bridge up facing E to the point where the right fist can be jammed, then swing round to reach a good hold on the left and pull up (IV). Climb the block above using a good foothold on the Trient side (IV) and reach the summit from there by an easy crack (3435m). Abseil down. Follow ledges on the Saleina side passing below a brèche, traverse below the Trident to a large platform and reach the summit by climbing a short step. Now follow the ridge to the Col Copt (3410m). If the slope is snow go up it on the right of a step to gain the horizontal ridge; if it is ice follow cracks on the left splitting the rock step. Follow the snow ridge, climb a large deep chimney, pass a small niche and traverse right to reach the Tête Biselx (3509m).

Descend slabs on the W Face (III) to the Brèche Biselx, then the narrow chimney from this brèche (III) on the Saleina side on its left to a ledge which turns the Pointe Fynn. Return to the ridge by a sort of 'letter-box' and follow it to the Brèche des Aiguilles Penchées. It is also possible, if more difficult, to turn the Pte Fynn to the right on iced rocks. Ascend diagonally across the N Face of the Aiguilles Penchées to rejoin the ridge between the E and Central Summits. Turn the last to the N and continue along the ridge to the W Summit (about 3505m) which is climbed by a crack. Continue along the sharp but easy ridge, turning to the N a group of pointed gendarmes, and reach a large ledge of broken rock on the Saleina side which leads to the foot of the two summit-blocks of the Aiguille de la Varappe.

A narrow strenuous chimney (IV) leads to the main E summit (3518m). The W Summit (3516m) is reached on the N side by climbing a sort of slanting gallery.

Continue along the W Ridge of the W Summit for 50m and then follow the NW ridge on the right which is steep but with good holds. Pass a step, return to the right on the N side. Continue along the ridge by short cracks and chimneys to another step

of yellow rock. Climb this on the left and then slant right along chimneys and couloirs to just above the bergschrund right of the NW Ridge. Cross the bergschrund, usually by an abseil, to reach the Trient plateau.

In dry years, because of stonefall danger, it is safer but more difficult to slant left at the foot of the yellow step on the ridge towards the Fenêtre de Saleina to an easy slanting chimney ending in a narrow couloir. Go up this couloir turning a step on the Trient side, continue on the Saleina side and descend to the Trient plateau skirting the rocks. Crossing the bergschrund requires the arrangement of an abseil of about 20 metres.

The Aiguilles Dorées from the South (opposite page). The first three Points and the Col Copt on the Aiguilles Dorées from the Trient side (right).

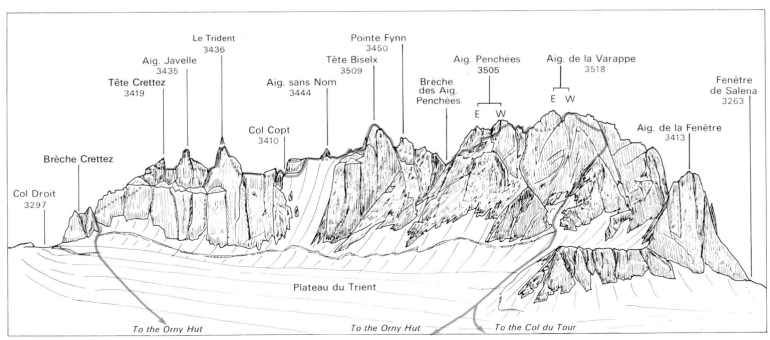

Col Droit 3297

Brèche Crettez

Tête Crettez 3419

Aig. Javelle 3435

Le Trident 3436

Col Copt 3410

Aig. sans Nom 3444

Tête Biselx 3509

Pointe Fynn 3450

Brèche des Aig. Penchées

Aig. Penchées 3505

E   W

Aig. de la Varappe 3518

E   W

Aig. de la Fenêtre 3413

Fenêtre de Salena 3263

Plateau du Trient

To the Orny Hut   *To the Orny Hut*   *To the Col du Tour*

27. LES ECANDIES 2873m
Traverse

The Ecandies Ridge can be divided into two: the southern part first, with its group of four towers above the Col des Ecandies, followed by a bristling ridge up to the S Summit which looks down on the Central Brèche — this is the more interesting section. The northern section beyond the brèche is made up of broader towers and rock flakes up to the highest point at 2873m. If it were higher and surrounded by glaciers, the traverse of the Ecandies as a whole would be a formidable enterprise.

Even so, placed as it is at the head of the Val d'Arpette in pleasant surroundings, done after an easy descent from the hut or a longer but even easier walk up from Champex, the route is not severe and, while quite difficult, is interesting. In fact this traverse is an enjoyable experience. The granite is excellent, the stances are good and well-protected; but you must remember to remain on the alert, especially on traversing pitches.

● **1st ascent:** This interesting traverse is made up of a combination of different routes done by a number of climbers.
● **Vertical height:** This is almost negligeable, since the route consists of an almost level ridge between the Col des Ecandies (2796m) and the Point S (2850m).
● **Grade:** D with two moves of V.
● **Time:** 1 hr from the Trient hut to the Col

des Ecandies. 3 hrs from Champex. 2½ hrs from the Col de la Forclaz. 3–4 hrs from the Col des Ecandies to the central brèche. If you want to go to the summit 2873m, you should add 2 hrs.
● **Equipment:** Carabiners, abseil rope.
● **Starting point:** Trient Hut (3170m). Champex (1466m). Col de la Forclaz (1532m).
● **Route** – *Outline:* This follows the crest going over the towers; if these are turned the traverse no longer has much interest.

Description: From the col go straight up for 15m then obliquely right to gain the brèche between the first and second gendarmes, from which the first is easily reached. From the brèche descend slightly on the Trient side and gain the brèche between the second and third gendarmes by a small chimney. Climb the second gendarme by its N Ridge (IV — abseil in descent); climb the third either by taking the ridge for about 3m, or on the Trient side, and then going on to the Arpette side to a chimney (III) which leads to the summit. Abseil 15m to the brèche between the third and fourth gendarmes. The fourth gendarme, which is not on the ridge itself but to the NW, is climbed up its SE wall. Return to the brèche and follow the easy ridge to a vertical flake 5–6m high, the Rasoir. Reach

the large summit by a flake (IV). Descend the ridge by a slab, continue along the ridge and then follow a ledge on the Trient side and return to the ridge above a short step. Climb a wall left of a large block. Climb the following gendarme up its W ridge (V) by laying away. Continue along the ridge, cross a gap by a sensational but not very difficult step across (the Saut d'Ange, Angel's Step), and turn on the Trient side a large tower to reach the brèche between this tower (which can be climbed by cracks, IV sup.) and a slabby buttress 25m high, which forms the crux of the traverse. Two possibilities for this: the first is to climb it on the Trient side. Climb a large overhanging block (good handholds), a short dièdre for 4m and, after a traverse 2m left, a slab by a thin flake. Then take two cracks to reach a little brèche (am move of V). The second takes you on the Arpette side. Traverse horizontally across a slab for 4m, then climb a short crack (IV) to a platform. Gain the brèche up a ledge ascending right and then a chimney.

Traverse horizontally for 3m and climb a crack slanting right to left below the summit. Follow the ridge and small ledges to the highest point of the middle section. Descend to the central brèche by a chimney on the E side (bridging, a crack on the right, or an abseil) and ledges. From here it is

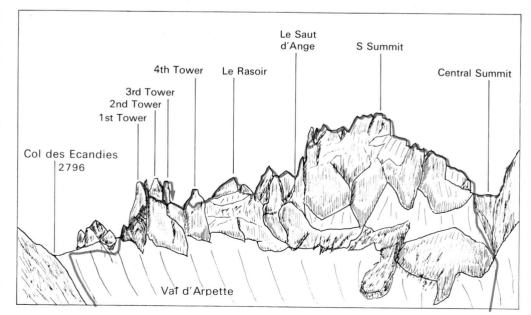

possible to descend easily to the Val d'Arpette. It is also possible to continue the traverse. To do this climb the wall overlooking the brèche to the N first by a detached gendarme, a niche of red rocks and a jammed block, then slant up cracks (IV) to a ridge on the Arpette side coming down from the first gendarme.

Climb rock steps to a couloir between the first tower and a small gendarme. Climb the first tower easily and then gain the brèche preceding the second gendarme up the steep wall bounding the couloir. Reach a small ledge overlooking the brèche between the second and third gendarmes. Descend to this and then climb the third gendarme.

To do this climb a ledge and slabs on the right, returning left towards the ridge at a notch formed by a large detached block. Climb the step directly with the aid of a shoulder (IV sup.). From the preceding notch traverse left across a slab (delicate); a flake and a crack then lead to a platform (IV). The ridge becomes easier, crossing a broad gently-angled slab. The last large step is climbed on the Arpette side by a crack (III), followed by several metres of descent and a dièdre (III). After grassy ledges and a chimney-dièdre the summit 2873m is reached without difficulty.

The Julien Dupuis Hut (opposite page).
The Ecandies Ridge from the Arpette side (above).

28. AIGUILLE DU CHARDONNET
Forbes Arête   3824m

The Aiguille du Chardonnet is a major summit in the range, and stands, majestic, at its NE corner; the Forbes Arête has a well-deserved reputation for beauty and has the further advantage, for my present purposes, of having an undoubted technical interest.

On this route, all members of the party should be of the same standard; this is because the ridge itself is a series of ascents and descents and unless the order of the rope is to be constantly changing, the second should be as competent as the leader to come down without needing a belay from above.

The most difficult pitch is usually the 'Bosse' (nose), a snow ridge steepening to a nose, very steep and very exposed because of the snow ridge descending sheer beneath one's feet and because this pitch is high up on the face. Up to this point you will have walked pleasantly up a glacier and then over comfortable slopes; here, all of a sudden, you are on a shoulder 50m high at an angle of about 53°, very rounded and with no features to act as reassurance.

When the snow is good, this pitch is no more than striking; when it is iced up — which it often is at the end of a season — you will need to cut steps and move very cautiously.

Higher up, the moments when you emerge onto the ridge and then traverse it are quite enchanting. There is a superb view, and the great N faces of the Argentière cirque are particularly impressive — they will awaken dreams and ambitions.

On the Aiguille du Chardonnet especially, the summit is no more than a first stage, for the descent, which follows the ordinary route, facing NW and often in shadow, has a number of steep couloir pitches often covered with ice or verglas.

● **1st ascent:** L. H. and Th. Aubert with M. Crettex, 30 July 1899.

● **Vertical height:** 600m (from about 3200 to 3824m).

● **Grade:** Mostly ice work at the Bosse, on the ridge and on the descent.

● **Time:** Leave the hut very early to arrive at the foot of the face at daybreak. 3–4 hrs from the bergschrund to the summit.

● **Equipment:** Crampons. An abseil rope can be useful if the descent is in bad condition, particularly at the bergschrund.

● **Starting point:** The Albert Premier Hut (2702m) or the Trient Hut (3170m). You gain an hour by starting from the latter.

● **Route** — *Outline:* From the Albert Premier Hut or from the Col du Tour coming from the Trient Hut there is a fine view of the route as a whole, which can easily be seen to fall into three sections:

— the approach to the ridge: by the glacier route between the Aiguille Forbes on the left to the E and the rocky rognon on the W to the right, then up the Bosse and the upper slope.

— the ridge proper, oriented E–W.

— the descent route right of the summit on the NW side.

Description: From the Albert Premier Hut do not descend onto the glacier to try and traverse straight towards the Aiguille Forbes, but on the contrary follow the path and the route to the Col du Tour. When you arrive at the foot of the last slope up to the

col, make a slightly rising traverse right and go over the large glacier hump. Then continue the traverse horizontally towards the Aiguille Forbes to climb the glacier branch which goes up between the Aiguille on the left and the rock rognon on the right, avoiding several crevasses. On the level section following, go up diagonally right towards the snow ridge which rises above the rognon. This ridge leads to the 'Bosse', an ice bulge about 50m high at an angle of 53°. Above gain the ridge at a brèche up less steep slopes and over a small bergschrund right of the gendarme at 3703m.

From here follow the ridge, climbing the first gendarme on the S side (III) and making several descents and ascents. Watch out for cornices. Pass the last gendarme on the left, and an easy chimney leads to the summit.

Descent: By the N side and the W Ridge. From the summit descend the snow W Ridge and gain the large snow couloir descending on the Argentière side. Take the centre of the couloir to reach mixed terrain. When this steepens traverse left to descend a short couloir, often icy (perhaps needing an abseil), which leads to the saddle. Traverse the saddle obliquely right to reach the col above the Aiguille Adams Reilly. Now descend the steep snow slope on the Albert Premier side and cross a bergschrund, sometimes very open, towards the rock rognon. Continue the descent leaving the rognon on the left to reach the Tour Glacier. Because of the state of the glacier, it is better now to go back up to the Col du Tour route, rather than cross straight to the Albert Premier Hut.

The 'Bosse' leading to the ridge (opposite page). The Aiguille du Chardonnet from the Tour Glacier; the Forbes Arête on the left, the ordinary route on the right and the North Spur coming down from the summit (above).

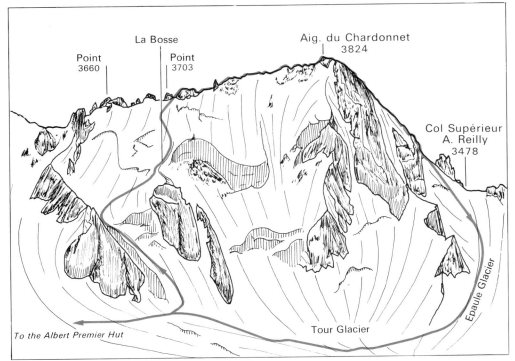

29. LES COURTES 3856m
North-East Face

This is a very fine introduction to the big snow-routes, for while the face is neither very steep nor very difficult — provided of course that it is done in good conditions — it is of impressive height (about 800m from the bergschrund) and it has an imposing situation, following as it does the crest of the mighty barrier of rock pillars, hanging glaciers and couloirs which, from the Verte to the Mont Dolent, tower above the remote cirque of the Argentière Glacier. This sense of awe you will already feel the evening before, in the Argentière Hut. However, this rather overpowering impression is mitigated firstly by the orientation of the face, which becomes more welcoming as soon as it is struck by the rising sun (and you should already be high up by that time) and secondly by its popularity, shown by other ropes and by the steps of other parties.

The line of the route depends, as do all snow-routes, on the conditions. You should join the summit ridge of the Courtes E of the summit.

Finally, the interest of the climb is not only technical but lies in the fact that it is a traverse: ascent by one side, descent by another, since the descent goes down the Talèfre side to the Couvercle Hut.
- **1st ascent**: P. Chevalier and G. Labour, 12 August 1930.
- **Vertical height**: 800m (from about 3000 to 3856m).
- **Grade**: The first major snow-route up an impressive wall.
- **Time**: 5–6 hrs from the hut to the summit.
- **Equipment**: Crampons.
- **Starting point**: The Argentière Hut (2771m); start very early to be already on the ridge at sunrise.
- **Route** – *Outline*: The great, fairly even slope seen from the hut lying to the E of the summit of the Courtes, bounded at mid-height on the left by a rock spur.

Description: From the Argentière Hut (2771m) cross the glacier towards the foot of this spur and just before reaching it, ascend the slope on the right of the spur.

Climb the bergschrund usually at the runnel and go directly up the slope to reach the snow ridge slightly on the left — above the rocks — then follow the ridge (which merges into the slope) right to the summit ridge and then along this to the summit (5–6 hrs).

Descent: The easiest route is the E Ridge. Always keep a look-out for stonefall between the Col des Cristaux and the bergschrund.

It is also possible to descend the W Ridge. For one thing this increases the feeling of a traverse because of the complete change of country, and for another, this route is more difficult and so technically interesting, particularly at two points: the traverse below the Tour des Courtes, and then the long slope between this traverse and the bergschrund. This long slope is grooved with runnels which are often tricky to cross. It is therefore necessary to plan the route well in advance to avoid as many runnels as possible or at least cross them at the easiest point where they are shallow. A necessary condition for this descent is that the slope should not be liable to avalanche.

The north side of the Courtes with the Grandes Jorasses in the background (below).
The North East slope of the Courtes (opposite page).

30. MONT BLANC 4807m
The Aiguilles Grises Route

This route could seem technically rather monotonous, but its atmosphere more than makes up for this; it is set in unusually remote surroundings, and this even from as low down as the walk up to the Dôme (or Gonella) Hut. The range may include noisy and over-popular routes like the NNE Ridge of the M, the Papillons Ridge or the S Face of the Aiguille du Midi, but here the climber will find true solitude.

You leave the peaceful Val Veni with its bright, rustling larches and its rippling river the Doire, then come to Lac Combal, the picture of peace, almost pastoral, and climb up deeper and deeper into the glacial valley, a straight barren gorge where life seems dead and where the silence is broken only by rumblings, crashes or creakings from a snowfall, or from stone-falls coming down from the ridges of Mont Blanc or the Trélatête, or from the movement of a huge block on the moraine, over-balancing because of the imperceptible advance of the glacier and falling forward to jam itself among other rocks at the bottom of a crevasse.

The Miage Glacier, which you climb and which is almost flat, seems to move and stretch under its covering of stone trails, flung down by the neighbouring glaciers and their finely curving moraines. This landscape of stone and ice, barren and elemental, emerging as it does straight out of the summery pastoral Val Veni, accentuates the impression of remoteness and out-landishness, and also of mystery, for from this glacier and from the Dôme Hut further up lights can be seen at nightfall, whether from roads or villages, as they can from the Goûter, or Torino, or Monzino Huts . . . This total absence of familiar and homely lights suggests a quite different silence, purer and harder, almost a geological silence, which gives a new dimension to these places.

The next day, on the ascent itself, the climber's impressions change gradually, step by step, as he changes direction or gains height and emerges from the shadows of the lower slopes: there are changes as you leave the hut path to set off for the glacier, as you leave the Dôme Glacier to climb the Aiguilles Grises Ridge to the N, as you leave this last to follow the Bionnassay Ridge which goes E, and then find the Mont Blanc Ridge and the sun. The day I did this route, the whole aura of mystery was enhanced by that curious atmospheric phenomenon, fairly rare in this range, the Brocken Spectre. At six in the morning the sun, still very low but coming over Mont Blanc, reached us as we climbed the Bosses Ridge and threw our shadows, surrounded by a halo, onto the light, early morning mists formed by a change of temperature in the basin of the Bionnassay Glacier which we had come from, in front of the S Ridge of the Aiguille de Bionnassay. Although scientifically this phenomenon is perfectly normal, it was nevertheless an eery sight, huge and mysterious, and very fleeting since the mists quickly melted away.

This route is usually called 'Mont Blanc by the Aiguilles Grises', in spite of not taking the long Aiguilles Grises Ridge proper, but following the same line a little lower down on the W bank of the Dôme Glacier. It is an easy route, convenient and easy to find, especially on the descent if you go down to Courmayeur. At the end of the season the glacier can be heavily crevassed and in that case it is better to follow the Aiguilles Grises Ridge itself; this is an easy climb which can make the long ascent more amusing, but has the disadvantage of making it even longer and of altering its character and destroying its unity.

● **1st ascent:** L. and J. Bonin and A. Ratti (Pope Pius XI), with J. Gadin and A. Proment, 1 August 1890 (in descent).

● **Vertical height:** About 1100m from Lac Combal to the hut; 1825m from the hut to the summit of Mont Blanc (from 3072 to 4807m).

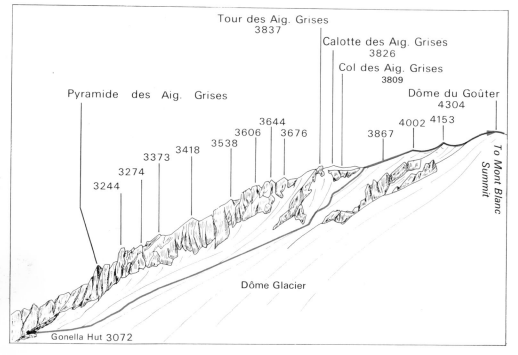

Tour des Aig. Grises 3837
Calotte des Aig. Grises 3826
Col des Aig. Grises 3809
Dôme du Goûter 4304
Pyramide des Aig. Grises
3644
3606 3676
4002 4153
3867
3538
3418
3373
3274
3244
To Mont Blanc Summit
Dôme Glacier
Gonella Hut 3072

- **Grade:** A long glacier expedition.
- **Time:** 3½ hrs from Lac Combal to the hut. 6–7 hrs from the hut to the summit.
- **Equipment:** Crampons.
- **Starting point:** The Dôme Hut, also known as the Gonella Hut (3072m).
- **Route** – *Outline:* A line S-N on the Dôme Glacier parallel to the Aiguilles Grises Ridge, then roughly W—E up the Bionnassay Ridge, the Dôme du Goûter and the Bosses Ridge.

Description: From the Dôme Hut traverse to the glacier, joining it at a level area. Go up the left-hand side of the glacier then towards its centre to pass the foot of the spur of the Tour des Aiguilles Grises and continue up the western glacier bay. From here there are two possibilities: either gain the Aiguilles Grises Ridge at the Col des Aiguilles Grises (3809m) and from there follow the ridge to the shoulder (4002m) of the Bionnassay Ridge above point 3867m; or, and this though more direct is less attractive, gain the Bionnassay Ridge a little higher near Point 4002m.

On the ridge you change direction, making towards the E and the summit of Mont Blanc along the airy Bionnassay Ridge, which is corniced in places, and then by the right (S) flank of the Dôme du Goûter, the Col du Goûter and the fine Bosses Ridge (6–7 hrs).

The South-West side of Mont Blanc: on the left the ridge coming down to the Dôme du Goûter and the Aiguille de Bionnassay, at the bottom the Bionnassay and Dôme Glaciers (above).
Mists and spectres on the Aiguilles Grises Ridge, from the Bosses Ridge on Mont Blanc (opposite page, right).
View looking down from the Bosses Ridge to the Aiguilles Grises Route (opposite page, left).

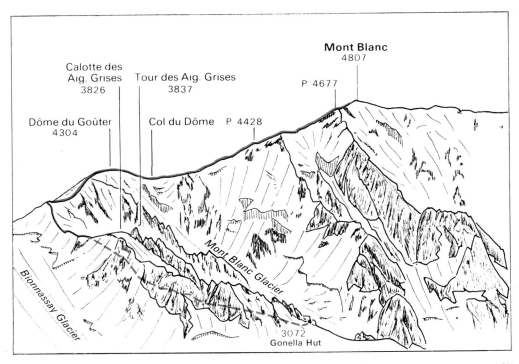

31. AIGUILLE DU PEIGNE 3192m
Ordinary Route
AIGUILLE DES PELERINS 3318m
Carmichael Route

This route becomes more difficult the nearer you get to the second summit, that of the Aiguille des Pèlerins. Not in fact technically of a very high standard (D), it is long, 800m or so in vertical height, and because it is a very cunning route, always following the best line — the climber should be aware of this important aspect — it requires more thought and intuition than do more difficult routes to find the best, and easiest, line. It will often be necessary to make a choice. An important element in the training of a mountaineer is training in the art of studying and making use of the structure of the terrain; later, this will be an essential art and will save time and give safety and pleasure on big routes, on the N Spur of the Droites, for instance. The ability to work out pitches beforehand and estimate their standard and angle without seeing them in profile, and without being overawed, is a most useful one.

This route, in fact, involves a skilful series of traverses whose line is dictated by the rock structure and which lead first to the summit of the Peigne, then down it and up to the Aiguille des Pèlerins; it is indeed a zigzag route, entirely changing direction a dozen times: the climber will therefore have to make decisions, and this will be good for him on several counts. For all these reasons, the route is here placed after the ascent of the Aiguille des Pèlerins by the Grütter Route; the latter may perhaps be technically a little more difficult, but it is on the one hand much shorter and poses few route-finding problems, and on the other hand the descent follows the ordinary route, goes down the same side as the ascent-route and soon rejoins it. However, the climber will find it very useful to have done the Aiguille des Pèlerins already — especially by the Grütter Ridge — and to know the descent, very useful for this long and interesting climb, crossing face after face, ridge after ridge, to reach the summit of two very fine aiguilles.

The route proper begins straight away, after an hour's walk to the Peigne névé; but the ascents of the Papillons Couloir and even of the face of the Peigne to the brèche at 3043m are still reminiscent of an approach-march; very often the party will be able to move together carrying coils. It is as if the climbing only really began on the ridge. If the Peigne were the only objective, the route would be very short; continuing it up the Aiguille des Pèlerins by the Carmichael Route means a good climb, and two summits after one approach-march.

You can leave rucksacks at the 'salle à manger' (dining-room) to be picked up again after the ascent of the Peigne.

- **1st ascent:** *Aiguille du Peigne.* G. Liégeard and R. O'Gorman with J. Ravanel and J. Couttet, 23 July 1906. *Aiguille des Pèlerins, Carmichael Route:* Misses E. and Y. Carmichael, with A. and G. Charlet, 10 September 1925.
- **Vertical height:** About 600m from the start to the summit of the Aiguille du Peigne (from 2600 to 3192m); a descent of about 150m from the summit of the Peigne to the trifurcation; about 250m from the trifurcation to the summit of the Aiguille des Pèlerins (from 3070 to 3318m).
- **Grade:** Aiguille du Peigne, AD with a pitch of IV. Aiguille des Pèlerins, Carmichael Route, D with pitches of IV sup.
- **Time:** 4 hrs from the start to the summit of the Aiguille du Peigne. 3–4 hrs from the Aiguille du Peigne to the summit of the Aiguille des Pèlerins.
- **Equipment:** Abseil rope. Carry one axe per party for the descent of the Pèlerins Glacier.
- **Starting point:** Plan de l'Aiguille. The route can well be done in the day but since the Carmichael Route faces W it is not advisable to climb it very early. Besides the technical aspect, the climbing is pleasant after the ascent of the Peigne, facing S and so quickly warmed by the sun.
- **Route** — *Outline:* A set of zigzags dictated by the terrain; an ascent of the SW couloir

Aig. du Peigne
1 Ordinary Route
2 Papillons Ridge
3 NW Pillar
4 W Face

Aig. des Pèlerins
5 Carmichael Route
6 Ordinary Route (descent)
7 Grütter Ridge

Aig. des Pèlerins
3318

Col du Peigne
3121

Aig. du Peigne
3192

Brèche
3043

Point
3009

Trifurcation

Névé du Peigne

(Couloir des Papillons) to the brèche W of the gendarme 3009; an ascent to the brèche 3043 on the SW Ridge; an ascent of the SW Ridge which is very soon left to rejoin on the right the ordinary route on the Peigne. This goes up the S Face beside the ESE Ridge to reach the battlemented summit ridge from which the Peigne gets its name, which is followed to the summit. A descent of the ordinary route level with the SW Ridge and then a traverse of the Peigne Couloir leads to the start of the Carmichael Route. This is followed by a diagonal ascent towards the SW Ridge of the Pèlerins and then an ascent of the upper part of the SW Ridge.

Description: From the Plan de l'Aiguille gain the Peigne névé. Go up this just on the left and take a ledge on the left and then a little brèche to reach the SW couloir which lies on the left, on the Chamonix side of the ridge-spur of gendarme 3009. This is also called the Papillons Couloir because higher up it comes close to the Papillons Ridge at the point where this ridge abuts on the wall of the Peigne. Climb easy steps to where the couloir steepens a little, traverse slightly right, ascend directly and then go back left at the point where the Papillons Ridge ends. Continue by a long easy ascending ledge towards gendarme 3009 which is left on the right to go up right to brèche 3043 by an ascending ledge and steps of bad rock at the base of the NW and W faces of the Peigne (2 hrs).

From the brèche it is possible either to descend along the ledge leading to the trifurcation of the Peigne Couloir and from there ascend steps on the left of the couloir between the SW Ridge and the couloir to a level area, the 'dining room', or to climb the bottom of the SW Ridge up the edge (IV and V) or below on the right and after two rope-lengths bear right to gain the 'dining room', where the sacks can be left.

Go up obliquely right towards the ESE Ridge and before reaching it, when level with the Col du Peigne (3121 m), go over to the very open chimney which ascends to the right, and climb it (IV) to arrive on the summit ridge at a little brèche. Follow the summit ridge on the crest or to the right. Abseil 4 m to descend into the last brèche and gain the summit (2 hrs). From the summit descend the Chamonix side for about 10 m to gain a sort of very open niche from where an abseil of 20 m is made to a large terrace. (For the routes to come, examine the Lépiney Crack going diagonally up the slab on the left.) Descend the less steep but sharp SW Ridge for 10 m or so, and go onto the Pèlerins side; then return and descend on the right a series of dièdres and chimneys which lead back to a step on the SW Ridge which is descended by a short

abseil (fixed rope for 7–8 m) – then return on the Pèlerins side to the 'dining room'.

Descend easy steps to the Peigne Couloir and at a great block in the bed of the couloir about 100 m below the Col du Peigne, go right on the Pèlerins side to reach terraces and gain the foot of a deep chimney. Do not climb the chimney but the spur on the left – the first rope-length is steep (III), the second less so and leads left to a terrace. From here go up easily towards the ridge, but 10 m below it traverse right to get into a system of slanting cracks (IV) which lead right to the brèche of the SW (Grütter) Ridge of the Aiguille des Pèlerins. At the end of the second rope-length go left for 5–6 m by a jamming crack towards a large block. Continue for two rope-lengths up a system of slanting cracks (IV) which lead to a small névé, and from there to the brèche where you join the SW (Grütter) Ridge. Continue up this to the summit (2 hrs; 7–8 hrs from the Plan de l'Aiguille).

Summit of the Aiguille des Pèlerins (opposite page).
The Aiguille des Pèlerins and the Aiguille du Peigne
from the téléphérique (above).

32. GRANDS CHARMOZ — GREPON
Traverse
3445–3482m

This is a very fine classic route and very typical of the Aiguilles; a fine glacier section, fairly steep and varied, leads to large faces of good red granite and up to a bristling, exposed ridge which is followed first on one side then on the other, depending on the structure of the rock and the cunning of the original party, and which gives at every moment a sense of discovery.

The traverse is also an excellent route on which to test your technique: the Mummery Crack is a very good example. If you can climb it effortlessly, without a foot slipping because it has been inefficiently jammed, then you have made very good and promising progress.

Even better for this purpose than the Mummery Crack is the Râteau de Chèvre; this can be climbed either as a chimney, the method favoured by climbers with more strength than skill and who arrive at the top fairly exhausted, or by jamming and bridging, the method favoured by the more technical climber who wants to save his strength and is not afraid of exposure.

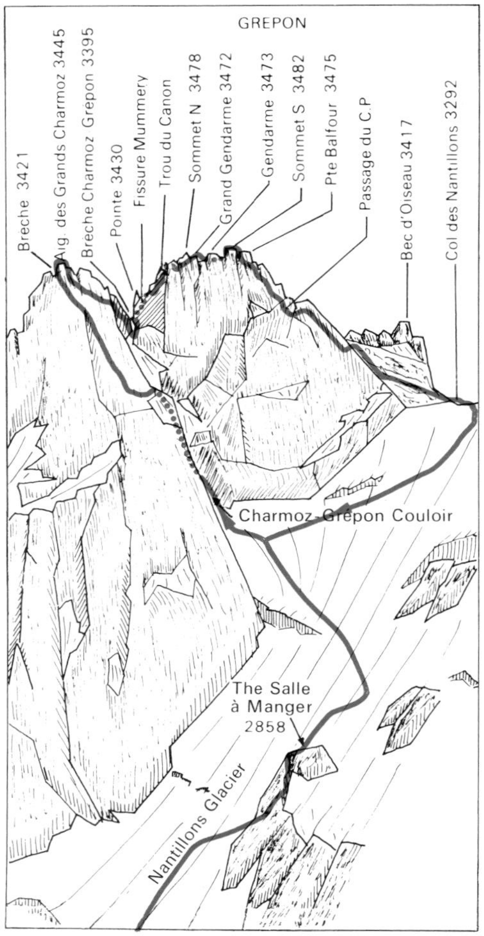

Finally, the climb becomes progressively more difficult as it goes on; the delicate pitches are principally on the Charmoz, the strenuous ones on the Grépon.

● **1st ascent:** Traverse of the Grands Charmoz, T. Jose with F. Simond and P. Burnet, 10 September 1887 (but on 15 July 1880 A. F. Mummery with A. Burgener and B. Venetz had reached brèche 3421 and climbed the NW point, gendarme 3431 and Point 3435); traverse of the Grépon, A. F. Mummery with A. Burgener and B. Venetz, 5 August 1881.

● **Vertical height:** About 900m from the Plan de l'Aiguille to the bergschrund; about 300–400m from the bergschrund to the crest of the Grands Charmoz and the Grépon. In all 1280m (from 2202 to 3482m).

● **Grade:** AD sup., to the Grands Charmoz (with short but fine pitches of III and IV). D for the traverse of the Grépon.

● **Time:** 4 hrs from the Plan de l'Aiguille to the Grands Charmoz. 3 hrs from the Grands Charmoz to the Grépon. 3 hrs from the Grépon to the Plan de l'Aiguille.

● **Equipment:** Crampons (to be left with the axes at the bottom of the Charmoz-Grépon Couloir). Take one axe per party. Abseil rope.

● **Starting point:** Plan de l'Aiguille Hut. Plan de l'Aiguille (2202m).

● **Route** – *Outline:* There are several points it is useful to study from a distance in advance, so as to appreciate the point of the detours in the description. There is the Charmoz-Grépon Couloir, which is the general line of approach but whose bed is avoided as much as possible. Then there is the traverse to the slanting line of chimneys leading to the brèche 3421m. On the ridge of the Charmoz, as on that of the Grépon, the route is dictated by natural features. While descending the Charmoz keep an eye on the ascent-route for the Grépon. Then there are the two diagonal lines from the Grépon to the Col des Nantillons.

Description: Go up the lower part of the Nantillons Glacier and then traverse right to reach the rocks of the Nantillons Rognon (go quickly, falling seracs). At first go up to the right and then go left to gain the crest and follow it to the top of the rognon ('salle à manger' not protected from falling seracs). Go up the glacier at first directly and then on the left (a section overlooked by the serac barrier and so exposed to avalanches) to reach the Charmoz-Grépon Couloir. Climb the bergschrund on the right of the couloir and cross the couloir quickly to the left to reach a zone of snow and scree. Ascend to the right towards the edge of the couloir and then either climb the couloir or traverse left and climb cracks for two rope-lengths to reach the large terraces where a slanting line left is taken to the foot of the wall of the Charmoz proper, to a slightly slanting groove right of a buttress. This is formed by a succession of chimneys or deep dièdres which lead to the brèche 3421m. The first is closed by an overhang avoided on the right (III) and leads to a deep chimney (III), then a slab on the right (III). Return left by an easy chimney which leads to the foot of two chimneys. Climb the right-hand one which is very deep, with two jammed blocks, often icy (Burgener Chimney, III sup.). At the top go through a 'letter-box' to reach a platform of large blocks whence chimneys lead to the brèche 3421m in three rope-lengths. Here the route changes its character completely;

Diagram labels
GREPON

Brèche 3421
Aig. des Grands Charmoz 3445
Brèche Charmoz Grepon 3395
Pointe 3430
Fissure Mummery
Trou du Canon
Sommet N 3478
Grand Gendarme 3472
Gendarme 3473
Sommet S 3482
Pte Balfour 3475
Passage du C P
Bec d'Oiseau 3417
Col des Nantillons 3292

Charmoz-Grépon Couloir

The Salle à Manger 2858

Nantillons Glacier

you come out into the sun and follow a ridge.

First climb the gendarme 3431 m either directly by lassoing the top or with a shoulder, or by the slab on the Nantillons side (IV). Now either climb Point 3435 m or turn it by a delicate step on the E side. Turn the Carrée by a 4m traverse on the Nantillons side (IV) and reach the platform overlooked by the Bâton Wicks, then abseil down a chimney to the brèche beyond.

Turn the next gendarme and reach the brèche 3429m. Climb the two following gendarmes and the summit tower (3445m). Return easily, passing below Point 3430 to the top of the Charmoz-Grépon Couloir and climb a dièdre, 'the Open Book' (IV), which leads to the Charmoz-Grépon col. Go onto the Mer de Glace side and go along a ledge for 20m, climb rock steps for 30m and arrive at a little brèche on the N Ridge of the Grépon which marks the top of the Charmoz-Grépon Couloir (right-hand branch) and from which there is a good view of the Mummery Crack.

Make a slight descent and a delicate traverse (IV) — take care not to descend too far as this makes the Mummery Crack longer — gain the crack at a level section and climb it (IV) by jamming the arms and the right foot. Above on the left return to the Mer de Glace side through the 'Trou du Canon'. Ascend obliquely left and climb a chimney pulling over an overhanging block (III). Pass through a narrow 'letter-box' onto the Nantillons side to climb the 'Râteau de Chèvre', either up the inside or on the out-

side (IV). Pass the foot of the N summit and gain the top of the Grand Gendarme (III). Abseil down to the brèche; do not abseil straight down but along the left (Nantillons) ridge of the Grand Gendarme after passing the rope behind the upper left-hand corner of the ridge. Continue along a ledge on the Nantillons side, up a short wall, along a level ridge, and make a descent of 2m on the Mer de Glace side to reach the 'Vire à Bicyclettes' below the gendarme 3473m. A short chimney leads to the brèche; then continue on the Nantillons side through a 'letter-box' to reach a platform and climb the final crack (IV). For your own satisfaction and to appreciate the skill of Venetz in 1881 on the first ascent, it is worth doing the crack which bears his name. This is the crack which is easily seen from the 'Vire à Bicyclettes' and which leads direct to the summit (IV).

Descent: From the summit abseil 20m down the E side left of the Knubel Crack and gain the Brèche Balfour along a flake (still on the abseil). Return to the Nantillons side and descend a slanting line of ledges and easy chimneys to reach a shoulder with a view down to the CP Terrace at the top of a step which is descended by abseil (pitons in place). Traverse horizontally right for 5–6m (still on the abseil) and then descend à cheval the top of a large jammed block forming a bridge across the brèche. Climb a short 2m wall to reach the CP Terrace. The descent continues diagonally, passing the Grépon-Bec d'Oiseau Brèche, and leads to the col and the Nantillons Glacier.

Traversing into the Mummery Crack (opposite page). The Grands Charmoz on the right, the Grépon on the left (above).

33. AIGUILLE DE ROCHEFORT 4001m
Traverse of the Ridges
DENT DU GÉANT 4013m
Ordinary Route

Each of these routes is magnificent and the novice could perfectly well have done them individually earlier in his career. But I felt it better to put them together, since they complement each other so superbly. The Dent is beautiful from any direction but especially from the Col du Géant, which is the best starting point and will certainly inspire you to climb it, but the nearer you get to it, among the broken rocks at its base, the more it seems diminished. Moreover in the early morning, the W Face where the Ordinary Route goes is still in the shadow and cold, so that the climb becomes more laborious and less harmonious than it should be, and you seem to be climbing at a disadvantage. It is therefore better not to stop, but to go on first of all along the Rochefort Ridges, which have better snow in the early morning, and whose curving crests are highlighted in all their beauty by the morning sunlight.

After a halt on the Aiguille de Rochefort to admire the magnificent view, you come back by the same route to the foot of the Dent; this has several advantages, and one disadvantage.

If you start from the Col du Géant you have easy access, by téléphérique, and can if you need do the route all in one day. From the technical point of view the double traverse over the narrow crenellated ridge with its towers, its cornices and its steepnesses, is wholly useful; ascents become descents on the return and vice versa. From the aesthetic point of view, the ridges are so lovely that nothing is lost whether in detail or in distance, and moreover, going E – W, on the way back, the Dent, dazzling above the snow ridges, is more attractive than ever.

You get back to the foot of the Dent at about 10.00, when the rock is already warm and when the rays of the sun are about to strike the W Face and make the climb pleasant and enjoyable.

On the other hand, psychologically, this traverse there and back has a certain lack of elegance for the climber; the fine ordinary route, popular in earlier times, remains: Requin or Leschaux Hut (the latter involving crossing the bergschrund), Mont Mallet, Aiguille de Rochefort and Rochefort Ridges, Dent du Géant.

● **1st ascent**: *Aiguille de Rochefort*: J. Eccles with M.-C. Payot and A. Payot, 14 August 1873, coming from the Mont Mallet. 1st traverse of the Rochefort Ridges, E. Allegra with L. Croux, P. Dayne and Al. Brocherel, 18 July 1900 (E–W).

Dent du Géant: Alessandro, Alfonso, Carradino and Gaudenzio Sella with Jean-Josephe, Baptiste and Daniel Maquignaz, 29 July 1882. The Maquignaz brothers had beforehand spent four days planting pitons and fixing ropes. Strangely enough the party stopped on the SW summit (4009m). The ascent of the NE summit, no more than 26m away and 4m higher (4013m) was done on 20 August in the same year by W. W. Graham with A. Payot and A. Cupelin.

● **Vertical height**: 636m from the Col du

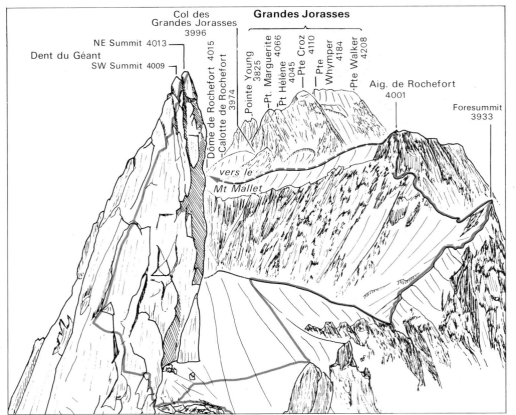

Col des Grandes Jorasses 3996

Grandes Jorasses

NE Summit 4013

Dent du Géant

SW Summit 4009

Dôme de Rochefort 4015

Calotte de Rochefort 3974

Pointe Young 3825

Pt. Marguerite 4066

Pt Hélène 4045

Pte Croz 4110

Pte Whymper 4184

Pte Walker 4208

Aig. de Rochefort 4001

Foresummit 3933

vers le Mt Mallet

Géant to the Aiguille de Rochefort (from 3365 to 4001m); about 180m from the 'dining room' to the Dent (from 3830 to 4013m).

● **Grade:** A narrow snow-ridge with cornices to the Aiguille de Rochefort. AD rock to the Dent du Géant. If the fixed ropes are one day removed from the Aiguille du Géant, it will regain its original integrity and the ascent will be difficult and magnificent.

● **Time:** 2 hrs from the col to the 'dining room'. 1–2 hrs from the 'dining room' to the Aiguille de Rochefort. 1 hr from the 'dining room' to the Dent du Géant.

● **Equipment:** Crampons, which are left with the sacks at the 'dining room' at the foot of the Dent.

● **Route:**

From the col to the foot of the Dent — *Outline:* From the shoulder 3661 the whole pedestal of broken rock can be seen. This is initially an arête and then becomes steps grooved with couloirs, sometimes snow-filled. From the col the route is direct and then goes up diagonally right to return obliquely left.

Description: From the Col du Géant pass the foot of the Aiguilles Marbrées and go up the glacier to below the Shoulder which has a remarkable gendarme. Climb the snow-couloir — if it is in condition — which leads to

a little col, or take to the broken rocks on the right bank. From the little col follow the ridge which very soon merges into the face in between steps, then climb couloirs to the left and higher on the right to reach the right bank. At the top go back left to turn the base of a large gendarme on the right and follow the snowy crest of the ridge to reach the shoulder facing the S Wall of the Dent (2 hrs).

Rochefort Ridge — *Outline:* This is determined by the ridges which can be well seen from the little shoulder at the beginning of the ridge. There is a remarkable alternation of cornices, some to the right and others to the left.

Description: Follow the ridge (keep away from the edge of the cornices) to the fore-summit (3933m) which is turned below and on the left with the help of an abseil which should be left in place for use on the return. The ridge, now narrower, leads to the piled unstable rocks of the Aiguille de Rochefort. Make an ascending traverse right to climb an ill-defined very open couloir which leads to the ridge a few metres from the summit (1—2 hrs). (Because of the nearness of the téléphérique the Rochefort Ridge is very popular, so the climber will not have the pleasure of making his own path; to make up for it he will generally have the convenience of following a well-planned track made by the Courmayeur guides.)

The Aiguille de Rochefort and the Rochefort Ridges (p. 92 right).
The Dent du Géant (p. 92 left).
The Dent du Géant on the right, Mont Mallet and the Aiguilles de Rochefort on the left (p. 93).
The Dent du Géant from the Col du Géant (above).
The first pitch of the Dent du Géant (right).
The Rochefort Ridge in icy conditions (opposite page above).
The Rochefort Ridge in warmer weather (opposite page, below).

Dent du Géant — *Outline:* Except from a distance, this cannot be seen. The route takes a sort of turning ascending line, S then W round the Dent.

Description: Cross the snow couloir. Skirt the base of the Dent, descending slightly to a detached flake, climb this and the slab above for 5–6m to a belay (large pitons in place). Traverse horizontally left for 10m to a couloir which is climbed for 30m. Exit left onto a platform with a magnificent view of the soaring Burgener Slabs narrowing at the top into an aiguille: the colour, the shape and curves combine to give them an exceptional beauty and lightness. Unhappily they are hung with thick fixed ropes marking the route. You should remember the Maquignaz brothers climbing these virgin slabs in 1882 and imagine what pleasure they must have derived from the route. What skill they had, those early masters, those first venturers into space! Descend a short chimney and a little wall to reach the brèche and from there arrive easily at the NE Summit ($1\frac{1}{4}$ hrs).

It is interesting to make the ascent without using the fixed ropes too much; on the one hand this will give you a certain sense of satisfaction; on the other, and more important, at 4000m it is much more tiring to pull up with the arms than to climb up on the legs. However it is made, the climb is marvellously exposed, and the view admirable on every side.

34. AIGUILLE DE BLAITIERE 3522m
LES CISEAUX — AIGUILLE DU FOU
Traverse
3479–3502m

This route, once very fashionable, is now neglected — a mistake since, whether done in part or as a whole, it is a traverse of great technical interest giving very fine and varied views from the different ridges. The ascent of the Aiguille de Blaitière can be done by different routes: the Rocher de la Corde Ridge up to the central summit, the Brégeault Ridge to the N Summit or else the NW Ridge (Ryan-Lochmatter, a fine route) but I strongly advise you to take the Spencer Couloir. Once you have done the Courtes by the NE Face, the Spencer Couloir on the Blaitière is neither too long nor too difficult, but offers an interestingly angled slope, 51° on average. This being a snow-route facing NE, it must be climbed in the very early morning, which will enable you — since the

couloir itself should take only an hour — to reach the brèche 3449 between the summits of the Blaitière very early. Here you can leave rucksacks and go on after a short rest: N Summit of the Blaitière, then Central and S Summits, the latter by the Ryan-Lochmatter Route, then S Summit of the Ciseaux, then the Aiguille du Fou and its summit block.

● **1st ascent:** Aiguille de Blaitière by the Spencer Couloir, S. Spencer with C. Jossi and H. Almer, 7 August 1898.

Ciseaux, S Summit, Mme Berthelot with J. and E. Ravanel, 22 August 1906.

Aiguille du Fou, E. Fontaine with J. and J. Ravanel, 16 July 1901; first ascent done without lassoing the summit block, Misses E. and Y. Carmichael with A. and G. Charlet, 18 July 1925.

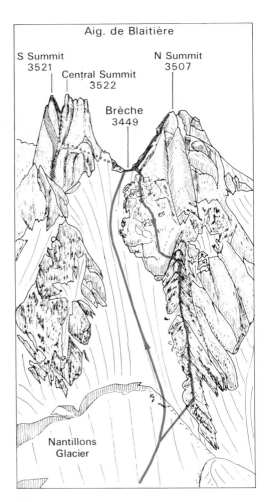

Aig. de Blaitière

S Summit 3521
Central Summit 3522
N Summit 3507
Brèche 3449
Nantillons Glacier

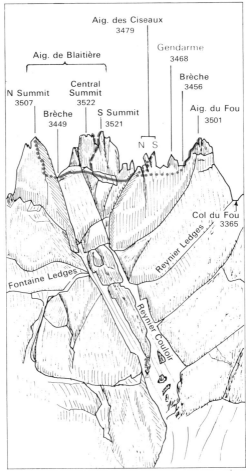

Aig. des Ciseaux 3479
Aig. de Blaitière
Gendarme 3468
N Summit 3507
Central Summit 3522
Brèche 3449
S Summit 3521
Brèche 3456
Aig. du Fou 3501
N S
Reynier Ledges
Fontaine Ledges
Reynier Couloir
Col du Fou 3365

● **Vertical height:** 1300m from the Plan de l'Aiguille Hut to the summit of the Blaitière (from 2202 to 3522m), of which the Spencer Couloir accounts for 150m.

● **Grade:** D with two pitches of V; a steep snow couloir, 51° on average.

● **Time:** 2½ hrs from the hut to the bergschrund. 1 hr for the Spencer Couloir. 2½ hrs for the three summits of the Blaitière. 2 hrs for the Ciseaux-Fou. If you are late you can climb only the N Summit of the Blaitière, which takes 15 mins.

● **Equipment:** Crampons, abseil rope.

● **Starting point:** Plan de l'Aiguille Hut (2202m). Start very early to reach the bergschrund at daybreak.

● **Route** — *Outline:* From the top of the Nantillons Glacier look not only at the Spencer Couloir but also at the Brégeault Ridge by which you will come back. Carefully study the different tints of the snow, which can give some indication of the quality of the snow in the couloir. Above the brèche 3449 (between the Blaitière summits) you take to a different face, and the line is no longer one of ascent but a traverse with ascents and descents. The tricky part is undoubtedly to work out the section below the Ciseaux for the return from the Aiguille du Fou to the brèche 3449. From the training point of view this is a very interesting route-study.

Description: From the top of the Nantillons Glacier, already visited during the Charmoz-Grépon traverse, cross the bergschrund and climb the centre of the Spencer Couloir. The centre, for several reasons: firstly to be more involved — it is better to be in the couloir and immersed in its atmosphere rather than to skirt its edges; secondly if you do this the snow will certainly be better, since in general it is close to the rocks that ice appears either on the surface or just under the snow. Go straight up — this is much more feasible on snow than on rock and much more enjoyable — to reach the brèche 3449.

First climb the N (Chamonix) top, up large blocks and then slabs and short chimneys overlooking the Spencer Couloir. Return to the brèche. Next cross onto the W side (it is one of the interesting aspects of this route that it proceeds on different faces) and skirt the base of the Central and S tops of the Blaitière along an easy ledge. Below the brèche 3506 between these tops climb easy rock then a crack (III) followed by a platform. Go up left to cross a chimney between two flakes; climb the left flake, make a stride into a crack and climb it for 5—6m (IV sup.), exit on the slab to the left and go back right to reach the brèche 3506m. From there climb each of the two summits. Return by the same route, possibly by abseil.

Continue to the Blaitière-Ciseaux col along a ridge like a flake, then descend about 20m down the Envers side by chimneys and slabs and climb diagonally back below the N top of the Ciseaux to reach the brèche between the two tops. Climb the 10m chimney between the two summits and exit on a ledge on the N top. Now make a stride onto the Chamonix side of the S summit and climb the narrow ridge to the summit of the S top (the N top of the Ciseaux has to this day been climbed only by making a difficult lasso, which remains nevertheless a fine manoeuvre, more difficult and elegant than using expansion bolts).

To reach the Aiguille du Fou, first go back towards the Blaitière to the point where by a system of steps and easy ledges you can turn the Ciseaux slabs on the Envers side some 60m below the summit. Now climb up obliquely below the gendarme 3468m to climb a chimney (III) to the brèche 3456 and then, still on the Envers side, arrive at the summit block of the Fou. Gain the N shoulder and climb the fairly rounded NE ridge of the pinnacle (V).

Descent: First return to the Blaitière brèche 3449. If the Spencer Couloir is in good condition, it will be an excellent exercise and the most rapid way of descent. Otherwise descend the Brégeault Ridge, first climbing down and then possibly making some abseils.

The Spencer Couloir (opposite page).
The Aiguille du Fou (below).

35. TOUR RONDE 3792m
North Face

This is an interesting route from several points of view. In the first place, the setting is magnificent: the Tour Ronde has the reputation of being a first-class viewpoint over the Vallée Blanche and the Géant Glacier. The superb background is made up of the Chamonix Aiguilles, of the Drus and of the Verte. But in the foreground, not far away, are the Grand Capucin, that extraordinary granite tower, and the lesser peaks — Chandelle, Trident, Petit Capucin, Pic Adolphe Rey — which are themselves overshadowed by the Aiguilles du Diable rising to Mont Blanc du Tacul.

Lastly, behind the frontier ridge lies the Brenva Face, framed to the left by the Peuterey Ridge, a superb ice ridge coming down from the very summit of Mont Blanc in a series of seracs, and revealing fine sections of red granite.

This is the view which opens out progressively in front of you as you move up the N Face of the Tour Ronde. And already you will be making plans. But as long as you are on the route itself, concentration is essential; this is a steep climb and you should not let your mind wander.

The Tour Ronde has a fairly broad N Face, which has in its centre a depression filled with two snow slopes, one slightly higher than the other and the two linked by a couloir; this is the N Face route, very steep but not too long, only about 350m and framed on the left by a vertical face and on the right by a rock ridge reassuring because it can be joined at several different points and can be used if need be for rest and for belays. There are also several rock outcrops emerging from the snow which can be used as stances.

At the start, the bergschrund can be a problem and an interesting technical exercise; the slope directly above it can sometimes be iced, and if the ice is extensive you may have to cut steps. There are however often steps already cut, since the N Face of the Tour Ronde is a fairly popular route, being interesting and easy of access.

● **1st ascent:** F. Gonella with A. Berthod, 23 August 1886.
● **Vertical height:** About 350m from the slope below the bergschrund to the summit (from 3450 to 3792m).
● **Grade:** A very steep snow slope which can be climbed even if partly ice. It is possible to climb the rocks on the left bank, but the object is to stay on the slope so as not to change the character of the route.
● **Time:** 1½ hrs from the bergschrund to the summit.
● **Equipment:** Crampons, ice-pitons.
● **Starting point:** The Torino Hut (3375m).
● **Route — *Outline:*** This is elegant, fairly straight and slightly oblique from the crossing of the bergschrund to the small horizontal ridge situated before and below the summit.

Description: From the Torino Hut (3375m) reach the foot of the N Face over the Col des

Tour Ronde
3792

Géant Glacier

Flambeaux. Climb the bergschrund on the right and for your own enjoyment try and stay on the face without getting near the ridge on the left bank (halfway up the couloir section, where the face narrows, rock can appear). At the top, gain the horizontal ridge on the left, which leads to the foot of the 30m summit block. This is climbed either by staying on the N side (walls split by cracks, IV), by using the NE Ridge, or most easily by going round onto the E side.

North Face of the Tour Ronde, from in front (opposite page) and from the side (right).

36. AIGUILLES DE TRELATETE 3920m
Traverse

The ridge of the Aiguilles de Trélatête forms the SE shoulder of the Mont Blanc range. It runs from the Col Infranchissable (3349m), which links it with the Dômes de Miage, and over the Tête Carrée (3732m), the N Summit (3892m) and the Central Summit (3917m), then divides into two parts, one going SE to the highest summit of the group, the S Summit (3920m) and the E Summit (3892m), and thence to Petit Mont Blanc (3434m) and the Aiguille de Combal (2837m). The other part goes SW, first to the Col de Trélatête (3515m) then up to the Aiguille de la Lex Blanche (3697m), the Col de la Scie (3609m) and the Aiguille des Glaciers (3815m) which is the southernmost major peak of the group. From this peak three spurs go out to the SE the Aiguille d'Estelette, the second S to the Col de la Seigne and the third to the SW to Mont Tondu.

There are several ways of doing the traverse of the Aiguilles de Trélatête; the most complete goes from the Col Infranchissable to the E Summit, thus crossing all four summits and going from side to side of the ridge. One of the attractions of these relatively easy but long high routes is the discoveries they bring. You can also go from the Central or S Summits towards the Aiguille des Glaciers after having made a

quite short detour to do the E Summit. Finally, there is also the possibility, in case of a change in the weather, of doing only part of the traverse. In any case, alpinism may imply primarily climbing, but it also implies spending whole days on fine snow ridges, between earth and sky, in a wild, remote countryside — and this is becoming rarer and rarer in the Mont Blanc range. Nowhere could be more peaceful than here. In a range so popular, on routes as crowded as the Arête des Cosmiques or the S Face of the Aiguille du Midi, the Bonatti Pillar or the Walker Spur, we have often longed for solitude, silence and the 'wilderness' — I use the English word here, the only one we can use, with all its associations, its idea of melancholy derived from the very air, the colouring of the snow, the rocks and the moraine, and derived also from the lines of the mountains which, even far down, have a sort of luminosity. On this route, as on the Dolent traverse, we can find such a wilderness.

From the technical point of view, this is a very interesting route for any novice or rather for any climber who wants to achieve harmony with the snow and the high mountains, and to develop a sense of route-finding. For this is a long, sustained route, where the times must be kept to.

● **1st ascent**: A. Reilly and E. Whymper, with M. Croz, M. Payot and H. Charlet, 12 July 1864.

● **Vertical height**: 1950m from the Trélatête Hotel to the summit (from 1970 to 3920m).

● **Grade**: A long snow route (narrow corniced crests).

● **Time**: As speed depends on the snow conditions it is important to start out very early and keep to time. 6–7 hrs from the Trélatête Hotel to the Central Summit. 45 mins–1 hr from the Central Summit to the E Summit. $2\frac{1}{2}$–3 hrs from the Central Summit to the Dôme de Neige. 1 hr from the Dôme de Neige to the Aiguille des Glaciers. 3–4 hrs from the Dôme de Neige to the Trélatête Hotel, making 10–15 hrs in total.

For the descent on the Italian side, $2\frac{1}{2}$ hrs from the E Summit to the Petit Mont Blanc Hut (2850m) and Lac Combal, 3 hrs from the S Summit to the Estelette bivouac hut (2858m) and the Elisabetta Hut. 10–12 hrs in all.

● **Equipment**: Crampons.

● **Starting point**: Trélatête Hotel (1970m).

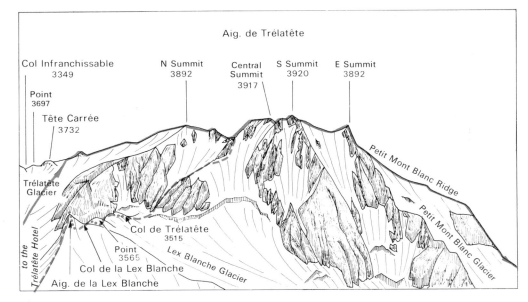

Aig. de Trélatête

Col Infranchissable 3349

Point 3697

Tête Carrée 3732

N Summit 3892

Central Summit 3917

S Summit 3920

E Summit 3892

Petit Mont Blanc Ridge

Petit Mont Blanc Glacier

Trélatête Glacier

to the Trélatête Hotel

Col de Trélatête 3515

Point 3565

Col de la Lex Blanche

Aig. de la Lex Blanche

Lex Blanche Glacier

● **Route** – *Outline:* The ridge is reached up the Trélatête Glacier and a ridge of broken rock right of the Tête Carrée. Then the line of ascent is determined by the ridge linking the Aiguilles.

Description:

N Aiguille or Tête Blanche (3892m). From the Trélatête Hotel follow the route to the Col Infranchissable. At the lower part of the saddle of the col, go up right along a ridge of broken rocks leading to the frontier ridge. Leave the Tête Carrée on the left to follow the mixed corniced ridge with a steep slope up to the top of the N Aiguille.

Central Aiguille (3917m). Continue along the snow ridge, with a short easy descent, then climb the first gendarme on bad rock. Then there are cornices to be avoided, mainly on the right, the second gendarme turned partly on the right and then climbed, and rock flakes passed on the left. The summit slope of the Central Aiguille can either be climbed directly or by a couloir on the right leading to the summit.

S (3920m) and E (3892m) Aiguilles. Follow the narrow corniced ridge. The descent to the Petit Mont Blanc bivouac hut

by the SE Ridge is easy. To reach the Petit Mont Blanc first take the narrow ridge, then a couloir descending to the Petit Mont Blanc Glacier. Climb the Petit Mont Blanc up a rock couloir or turn it on the S side and follow a snow ridge to the hut, from where the descent is made to Lac Combal.

You can also descend the easy S Ridge to the Estelette bivouac hut following the ordinary route.

Aiguille des Glaciers (3816m). From the Central Trélatête Aiguille (or from the S Aiguille after a traverse) descend the SW Ridge to the Col de Trélatête (3515m). This ridge is fairly sharp and although it is probably corniced and sometimes rocky, it is not difficult. From the Col de Trélatête reach without difficulty the Col de la Lex Blanche (3557m), then follow the N Ridge, first rock and then a very narrow snow ridge, to the Aiguille de la Lex Blanche (3697m). From here descend a sharp, corniced snow ridge to the Col de la Scie (3615m). Leave the ridge, go onto the W side and climb the Dôme de Neige; do not take the Arête de la Scie which has many teeth made up of rotten rock, but follow the snow couloir to

the S which leads back to the ridge and continue along it to the summit.

The descent from the Aiguille des Glaciers can easily be made by several routes: to the Elisabetta Hut down rocks and easy snow slopes; to the Col de la Seigne following the long S Ridge which leads slowly down to the pastures; to the Trélatête Hotel by the W Ridge of the Dôme de Neige (the ordinary route); or by the Col des Glaciers, from which there is also a descent to the Mottets valley.

The Aiguilles de Trélatête from the north (opposite page). The Aiguilles de Trélatête from Mont Blanc, with the Oisans range in the background left (above).

37. TRIDENT DU TACUL 3639m
Lépiney Route

This is not a major route, but it can bring all the satisfaction due to its magnificent setting and situation to the quality of the rock and to the superb view both of the climb itself from the middle and far distance. But many alpinists will be inspired principally by the memory of Jacques de Lépiney who, in 1919, did this climb free. Climbers' pride in him should lead them to be worthy of their inheritance and themselves climb free, at least as well as Lépiney himself did, the more so because equipment and technique have both improved since his time. If this contention is true, we must ask ourselves: have climbers themselves made any real progress? It may well be not, since so often they first put in belay pitons, then pitons to hold or pull up on, and this is in itself a form of artificial climbing.

Once you have done the crux pitch and moved onto the E Face, the view of the Grand Capucin is striking. It may also remind you of another extraordinary climber, W. Bonatti, whose first great exploit was undoubtedly the making of a route up that magnificent red granite face. The last few moves onto the summit of the Trident are very fine, and the summit itself is very exposed. So there are a number of reasons for enjoying this climb.

● **1st ascent:** Mme A. Damesme, M. Damesme and J. de Lépiney, 13 September 1919.
● **Vertical height:** About 200m from the start to the summit (from 3450 to 3639m).
● **Grade:** D with a pitch of V.
● **Time:** 3 hrs from the start to the summit.
● **Equipment:** Crampons, abseil rope.
● **Starting point:** The Torino Hut; the route can also be done in the day by taking the first cable car.
● **Route** – *Outline:* This is not a direct route; on the contrary, it takes an oblique line from left to right. It starts on the SW Face then slants across the S Ridge and climbs the summit up the E Face.

Description: From the Col du Géant (or the Col du Midi) go up the Géant Glacier, passing beyond the Trident (but take a good look at the S side and the S Ridge) to ascend for about 100m the snow couloir W of the Trident. Then climb on the Trident up ledges and stepped dièdres (III) to reach on the right a large platform forming a balcony on the right. Traversing right you can see a big couloir-chimney bounded on the right by a ridge; this is the crux pitch. Higher up the granite whitens and becomes overhanging. Climb obliquely towards the couloir-chimney which becomes a dièdre (V), then traverse right (V) to pull up onto the ridge and reach a good belay. Move right onto the E Face and slant across to a zone of terraces at the foot of the final 80m wall. Here the rucksacks can be left and collected on the return. Climb a chimney (IV) and then a series of cracks below the brèche between the Central and S Summits to a large platform. Continue straight up for 10m or so, and traverse right to reach a crack which leads to the Central Summit (IV). Descend to the brèche and gain the S Summit by an exposed traverse on the E Face.

Descent: Abseil down to the terraces. From there climb mixed ground to reach the top of a couloir-chimney; an abseil leads to the snow couloir separating the Trident from the Grand Capucin.

The Trident from the East (opposite page).
The crux of the Lépiney Route (right).

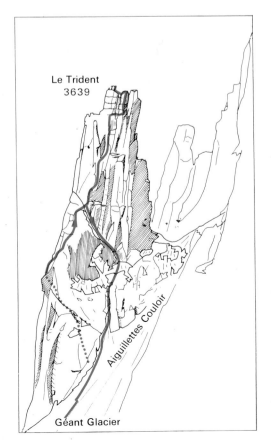

38. LES COURTES 3856m
AIGUILLES RAVANEL — MUMMERY
Traverse
3696–3700m

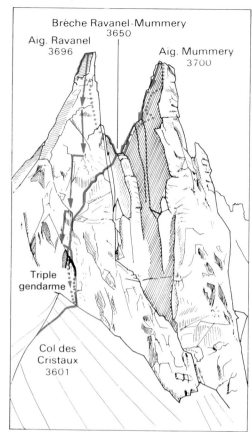

The ascent and traverse of the Courtes early in the morning when the snow is good and firm, and then the ascent of the Ravanel and Mummery Aiguilles (already seen and admired from the Courtes) when the rock is warmer is a delightful way of spending a whole day high in the mountains.

You should calculate the time of departure from the Couvercle Hut so that you will reach the Col des Cristaux between 8 and 9 am; any earlier and the rock will still be cold, any later and the route will be longer, the descent unpleasant and tiring. You can leave rucksacks at the Col des Cristaux to go and do the ascent of the Ravanel and Mummery Aiguilles. The climbing is varied and the route-finding intricate. Use your own head; do not gain too much height on the Ravanel, then take care to protect the traverse moves into the Ravanel-Mummery Brèche. Then do the Aiguille Mummery first, a fine balance climb on excellent granite. Then abseil down, climb easily up the Ravanel and abseil down again to the Col des Cristaux.

This may be a mixed route, which spreads out the effort, but it is long and demands proper concentration; remember you may be tired coming down the abseils off the Ravanel. Do not tense your muscles when abseiling; you should be physically relaxed. On the other hand you should pay the greatest attention to the placing of the ropes, the checking of the abseil loops in place — always change them if they are at all doubtful. You should also avoid knocking down stones.

● **1st ascent:**

Les Courtes (by the WNW Ridge): O. Schuster and A. Swaim, 17 August 1897. 1st descent by the SE Ridge: E. Fontaine,

J. Ravanel and L. Tournier, 11 July 1904.
Aiguille Ravanel: E. Fontaine with J. Ravanel and L. Tournier, 22 August 1902.
Aiguille Mummery: E. Fontaine with J. Ravanel and L. Tournier, 16 July 1903.

● **Vertical height:** 1169m from the Couvercle to the summit (from 2687 to 3856m).

● **Grade:** Sustained D; some sections are delicate and exposed.

● **Time:** 4 hrs from the Couvercle Hut to the summit of the Courtes. 1–1½ hrs from the summit to the Col des Cristaux. 3–4 hrs for the traverse of the Mummery and Ravanel. 1½ hrs from the Col des Cristaux to the Couvercle Hut.

● **Equipment:** Crampons, abseil rope.

● **Starting point:** Couvercle Hut (2687m).

● **Route** — *Outline:* The snow couloir S of the Col de la Tour des Courtes, then the ridge to the Col des Cristaux turning the Aiguille Croulante on the S and the Aiguille qui Remue on the N.

From the Col des Cristaux ascend skirting the Aiguille Ravanel to reach the Ravanel-Mummery Brèche. Climb the E Face of the Aiguille Mummery, abseiling in descent, and then climb the E Face of the Aiguille Ravanel and abseil down to the Col des Cristaux.

Description: From the Couvercle Hut (2687m) take the path (to be reconnoitred

the evening before) to the Jardin de Talèfre, then go beyond it before aiming for the slope descending from the Col de la Tour des Courtes. Ascend this slope to reach the col. There follow the snow ridge to the summit (if it is too sharp or too corniced, you can use the rocks below on the Talèfre side). From the summit continue along the ridge, climb the Aiguille Chenavier, turn the Aiguille Croulante on the Talèfre side and then the Aiguille qui Remue on the Argentière side to reach the Col des Cristaux.

From the Col des Cristaux follow the ridge to the foot of the triple gendarme at the base of the Aiguille Ravanel. Descend a chimney, then a couloir, on the Talèfre side to gain an ill-defined hollow on the Ravanel wall. Climb cracked slabs for 30m to a big overhanging block. Above this are the Ravanel Slabs. Climb these (IV) and continue on the right directly up a system of crack-chimneys (IV to IV sup.) leading to a good terrace. Slant up to the ridge on the right to reach an enormous block on a level base (slightly overhanging IV). Climb 3m above the block, then traverse almost horizontally (IV) to the Ravanel-Mummery Brèche. You change faces to start the Aiguille Mummery. Reach the terrace below the NE Ridge either by a crack in the E Face (IV) or by the N side of the ridge. Go left and ascend to the NE Ridge up a short chimney-dièdre (IV), cross the NE Ridge and go onto the E Face. Follow a ledge left to a detached flake. Go back right, climb a vertical 6m crack (IV) and exit left to gain the upper terrace. Go right. Climb an overhang by a twisting crack and go up a slab set on its side to the start of the final, very open, 8m chimney (IV) which leads to the summit. Three abseils down the E Face and the NE Ridge, and an easy traverse lead to the brèche at the foot of the small ESE Face of the Aiguille Ravanel. Climb easy steps, turn a large block on the right and gain the summit on the Argentière side.

Descent: From the summit make four abseils down the Talèfre side to 10m above the brèche between the Aiguille Ravanel and the triple gendarme. From here abseil to the southern base of the triple gendarme and then traverse onto the ridge and gain the Col des Cristaux.

From the Col des Cristaux, descend diagonally across the snow slopes and rock outcrops to gain a zone of broken steps at the foot of a wall flanking a rock pinnacle. Reach the rocks on the left bank of the couloir between the Aiguilles Chenavier and Croulante, and gain the Talèfre Glacier.

The Aiguille Ravanel on the left, the Mummery on the right (opposite page).
The Courtes and the Aiguilles Ravanel and Mummery from the casque d'Argentière (below).

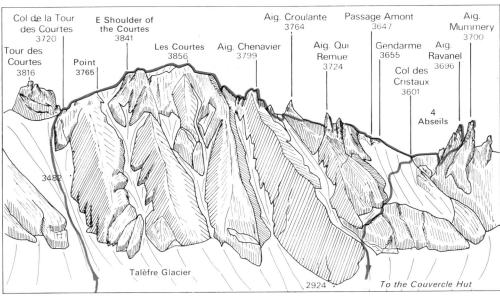

Col de la Tour des Courtes 3720

Tour des Courtes 3816

Point 3765

E Shoulder of the Courtes 3841

Les Courtes 3856

Aig. Chenavier 3799

Aig. Croulante 3764

Aig. Qui Remue 3724

Passage Amont 3647

Gendarme 3655

Col des Cristaux 3601

Aig. Mummery 3700

Aig. Ravanel 3696

4 Abseils

3482

Talèfre Glacier

2924

To the Couvercle Hut

39. PETITES JORASSES 3649m
South Ridge

Can these really be called individual peaks, or are they only a part of the ridge going from the Aiguille de Leschaux to the Grandes Jorasses? They have their own names, true, their own shape and appearance, and even if they were called 'petites', they could still be pointed, light and airy. No such thing. The Petites Jorasses are mixed in structure and are no more than a massive shoulder on the ridge. They might do better if they had a name which was not so reminiscent of their sister mountain to the W, inspiring, soaring up to more than 4000m. But after all, if the Petites Jorasses were more outstanding, more individual, if they stood out better against the sky, we would be less awed by the Grandes Jorasses.

In any case, to make up for these handicaps, the Petites Jorasses have a ridge and a face more than worthy to put them among any list of one hundred finest routes in the Mont Blanc range. Here the attraction is less the summit itself than two particular features: the S Ridge, 400m high, and the W Face, 700m high, which each in its own way seems to have been created for the pleasure and the happiness of the climber.

Both are very fine climbs in themselves, and, from the training point of view, demand the use of all the climber's technical resources; he will realise that these allow him to get up and to do so safely and without becoming too tired. These are essential stages in the training of an alpinist.

Whereas the W Face goes directly to the summit of the Petites Jorasses, the S Ridge is completely apart from it; it rises, boldly and unerringly, without deviation, overlooking an unbroken stretch of slabs, from the Frébouzie Glacier, and narrows as it goes upwards to the sky. At 3550m it becomes a snow ridge, very gradual, and continues straight on up to the summit.

The S Ridge of the Petites Jorasses is not a major route; the vertical height is not great and nor is the altitude, but the setting is remote and the climb itself is sustained and very attractive on good granite; it is a route which, mistakenly, is not very popular. Being steep and facing south, it quickly comes into condition.

This route is not only suitable for high summer, but can also be done early in the season when the climber is longing to get to grips with good granite, and in the autumn when it is no longer too hot and the sun gives colour to the rock rather than draining it away; but at the end of the season there can be some difficulties on the descent because of open crevasses on the glacier.

- **1st ascent:** A. Castelli and M. Rivero, 18 August 1935.
- **Vertical height:** 400m from the hut to the start proper; 400m roughly from the start

to the summit. In all 816m (from 2833 to 3649m).

● **Grade:** D with a pitch of V.
● **Time:** 5 hrs from the hut to the summit.
● **Equipment:** Crampons as far as the start proper.
● **Starting point:** The Gervasutti Hut (2833m).
● **Route** – *Outline:* This can be divided into three sections. First the approach to the ridge itself follows a diagonal line across the W flank from the Frébouzie Glacier to the foot of the ridge proper. Then the ridge, which is simple to follow and direct. Last, the upper part, formed by a snow ridge which leads to the summit.

Description: From the Gervasutti Hut (2833m) turn the foot of the S Ridge on the left. Go up the snow slope on the W side and traverse right up a snow tongue towards the ridge. At the end of the snow tongue slant up right to gain the ridge where it stops bulging and becomes narrow, and so reach a terrace on the E side (about 3430m).

Climb the crest of the ridge for 10m (IV) to a small platform on the right from which you can climb straight up to a pointed block on the ridge (IV). Go onto the W flank, descending slightly to gain a red dièdre 20m high (IV) closed by a roof. Below the roof

move right to exit onto the ridge (V; this is the hardest section of the route) where there are good holds above the overhang. Climb up to a platform 2m above (IV). The rest of the climbing stays fine, exposed and interesting, but becomes easier (III and III sup.), often taking the left flank (W). Reach the top of a rock ridge from which begins the snow ridge leading to the summit.

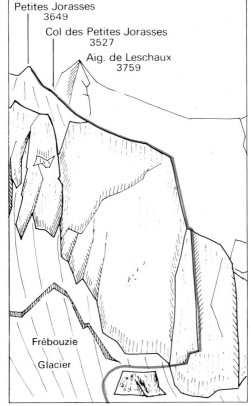

The South-West Face of the Petites Jorasses from the side, with the South Ridge on the right (opposite page). South Ridge of the Petites Jorasses (above).

40. PETIT DRU – GRAND DRU
Traverse
3733m–3754m

If any mountain can be said to have a legend, surely it must be the Drus. And for many excellent reasons: name, shape, appearance, history, all contribute to their legendary quality. The name is short and sharp; the shape is simple, unadorned, without frills; historically, each first ascent on the Drus marks a new step in mountaineering progress.

The Drus can be seen from the valley, especially from Les Praz, but their true, symbolic beauty can best be seen from the Montenvers. And even if you climb nothing but the ordinary route, it is this impression of purity of line, of austerity, that you will remember, and rightly; besides, even by the ordinary route which follows the line of the first ascent on the Charpoua side, the traverse of the Drus is a major route, in a wild remote setting.

Other climbs have changed; not so the traverse of the Drus, and this is its attraction. The little hut – a real *refuge* as the French say – is unchanged and the traverse is still a long route (10–12 hrs at a good pace), strenuous and committing.

The route is intricate, a little difficult to find on the way up and even more so on the descent.

You should arrive at the hut early enough to reconnoitre the Charpoua Glacier and find the snow tongue leading to the rock. From the Petit Dru the sight of the Z pitch is a bit awe-inspiring, but the pitch is not difficult except in poor conditions. On the descent of the Grand Dru, anticipation is essential; you should be aware of the sequence of pitches which go below the Col des Drus to the Pendulum Pitch, and should not set off blindly abseiling even if old abseil loops seem to suggest it. To sum up: this is an excellent route not only for its appeal, but also as training for the future alpinist; safe but quite strenuous climbing; several short Chamonix-type cracks on the ascent of the Petit Dru; good stances; possible stonefall in the afternoon when the sun has melted the snow patches.

● **1st ascent:**
Grand Dru: C. T. Dent and J. Walker Hartley with A. Burgener and K. Maurer, 12 September 1878.
Petit Dru: J. Charlet-Straton, P. Payot and F. Folliguet, 29 August 1879.
Traverse from the Petit to the Grand Dru: E. Giraud with J. Ravanel and A. Comte, 6 September 1903.
● **Vertical height:** 913m from the hut to the Grand Dru (from 2841 to 3754m).
● **Grade:** D – fairly strenuous, sustained from the Shoulder to the summit.
● **Time:** 2½–3 hrs from the hut to the Shoulder. 3–3½ hrs from the Shoulder to the Petit Dru. 1 hr from the Petit Dru to the Grand Dru. 3–5 hrs from the Grand Dru to the hut. 9½–12½ hrs from hut to hut.
● **Equipment:** Abseil rope. Light crampons and one axe per party.
● **Starting point:** The Charpoua Hut (2841m).
● **Route** – *Outline:* The Charpoua Glacier; the ledge on the left and the couloir leading to the Shoulder; from there the ridge above which merges into the face; the traverse to the Grand Dru by the Z pitch; the descent of

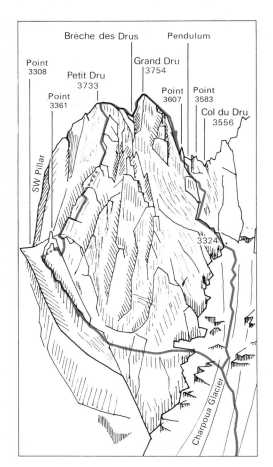

the Grand Dru by the E Ridge in the upper part and by the SE Face lower down, bearing right (E) to the Pendulum Pitch and from there straight onto the glacier.

Description: From the hut ascend the rock rognon then the Charpoua Glacier to a slanting snow line which is followed. This well-marked line slants left up the spur descending from the Grand Dru. Continue the traverse along a ledge leading to the foot of a system of couloirs coming down from the Shoulder. Follow rising ledges to ascend the first couloir and gain the second which is climbed to the Flammes de Pierre Ridge (3308m). On the right a chimney (III, which can be reached directly from the couloir) leads to a brèche on the ridge SE of the gendarme 3361m. Climb the ridge to the Shoulder; there is an impressive view of the Bonatti Pillar. Traverse right and climb the ridge for about 100m up cracks, chimneys, slabs and rock steps until it merges with the face proper. Climb first one crack then a second (a move of IV at the beginning of the second) and go back left along a ledge to reach a chimney system over towards the great couloir on the left descending to the foot of the Bonatti Pillar. Climb four 15 to 20m pitches to a horizontal shoulder (the 'dining room'). Climb a crack (IV), exit left on a big terrace, return up a deep couloir and climb either the ice chimney or the step on the right (IV). Ascend steps to a sloping slab split by a crack. Climb either the slab itself, on the right, or the crack in the centre. Go left, climb two short chimneys, pass a small overhang and exit left (IV). Climb a short easy-angled dièdre (III) which leads back right to a horizontal ledge and there either go through a 'letter-box' or climb up the outside. Continue up a grooved arête for 4–5m

(IV) which leads to the summit couloir and up a last short step to the summit of the Petit Dru (5½–6½ hrs from the hut).

From the Petit Dru descend the easy ridge on mixed ground to the Brèche des Drus (3697m). Above is the 'Passage en Z' leading to the summit of the Grand Dru. The whole route is visible, except for the exit chimney which is on the N Face. The most impressive section is the ledge between the top of the Z and this exit chimney. Climb 7–8m up a crack (IV) then traverse right for 10m along a horizontal ledge. Slant back up left almost to the arête. Climb up 5m to a belay platform. Climb 7–8m further up below the big overhang and exit left, using a crack-ledge for the hands (IV). Climb the crest of the ridge to go onto the N side and ascend an open chimney for 5m (belay). Above get into a deep chimney leaning to the left and exit on a shoulder from which a short pitch leads to the Grand Dru (3754m, 1 hr).

Descent: From the summit follow the E Ridge slightly below the crest for about 100m to where there is a large horizontal area, in the middle of which is a large block (sometimes buried by snow). Go some way onto the Charpoua side by abseiling down two chimneys. Traverse left (N) and abseil down a third chimney. Descend terraces to reach a slanting chimney and make a fourth abseil obliquely left (IV) to descend 10m or so down a couloir-chimney abutting on a short 4–5m spur. Climb up 1m and traverse over to the large Pendulum Terrace from which a diagonal abseil is made down the left (N) couloir. Cross the couloir to reach a second couloir (either climb or abseil) and gain on the left (N) a system of terraces and sloping ledges still on the left bank of the couloir. After descending about 200m, cross the couloir and descend the spur right of the couloir for 100m. Go back left and then, on the edge of the couloir, make a long abseil (30m) across the bergschrund and reach the glacier (2½–3 hrs).

Right to left: Petit Dru, Brèche des Drus, Grand Dru, Z Pitch (opposite page).
The Charpoua cirque with, on the left, the Petit Dru and the Grand Dru, and on the right, the Aiguille Sans Nom and the Aiguille Verte (above).

41. AIGUILLE VERTE 4121m
Whymper Couloir

Verte and Whymper, these are two august names. The Verte is a fine peak, for its height, its setting and its appearance. There is no easy route to the summit; the ordinary route, whether the Whymper Couloir or the Moine Ridge, is itself a major route. It is on the Verte that you become a mountaineer.

The Whymper Couloir is a fine snow route, direct and elegant. Amusingly enough,

Whymper and his guides Almer and Biener followed only the lower third of the Whymper Couloir and then took to the mixed terrain of its right flank, joined the Moine Ridge and so reached the summit. The central part of the couloir is in fact steep and formidable, the upper part being perhaps wider but its average angle (47° between 3700 and 3950m) is 55° from 3950 to 4051m at the

Col de la Rocheuse. This route must not be undertaken except in good conditions, that is when the couloir is snow and not ice, and after a freezing night; when you yourself are fit, that is able to crampon up well, and keep to a timetable which will get you away from the Couloir at 9 am at the latest — and for this, you must leave the Couvercle Hut very early, at around midnight. The Whymper Couloir is in fact a prime example of the sort of difficult route that can become dangerous: the steepness of the slope does not change, but if you are late the couloir becomes a trap, since the snow, melted by the sun, is not so good for cramponning, may avalanche and can even allow stonefalls from stones frozen in and now melted out. In good conditions, it is on the contrary a very safe route.

I myself have done it solo. It was mid-June, and there was also a guides' course on the route, and what with the different instructors and the trainee-guides who wanted to prove their competence, it developed into something of a race; it was also a moment for taking stock. All of us were very fit; there was no question of tiredness, and the route demanded technique and clear thinking: proper cramponning. This of course is automatic, but in spite of the temptations of the setting, the attention must not wander even for a second, a millionth of a second. No time for dreams here; dreams are for the summit. I was to precede the main party, because I wanted to film it arriving on the Col de la Rocheuse and following the summit ridge, and for this purpose the best place is the Grande Rocheuse Ridge. I was already aware it would be beautiful, but that morning, very early — it must have been about 6 am — it was extraordinary, with the sun and the men bringing animation to those cold, impassive slopes, which trembled into life under the dancing rays of the dawn.

● **1st ascent:** E. Whymper with C. Almer and F. Biener, 29 June 1865.

● **Vertical height:** About 800m from the Couvercle Hut to the bergschrund (about 3500m); about 600m from the bergschrund to the summit; in all 1425m (from 2696 to 4121m).

● **Grade:** A steep snow slope, but the difficulties are essentially of a different type: to be able to crampon well, keep to time and be able to return to the bottom before the snow becomes dangerous.

● **Time:** 2 hrs from the hut to the bergschrund. 3–5 hrs from the bergschrund to the summit.

● **Equipment:** Crampons.

● **Starting point:** Couvercle Hut (2696m).

● **Route** — *Outline:* This is very fine and direct: up the couloir (note any runnels there are to cross) and then the ridge.

Description: From the Couvercle Hut go up the Talèfre Glacier skirting the foot of the Moine chain to the bottom of the Whymper Couloir which comes down from the Col de la Grande Rocheuse (2 hrs). Cross the bergschrund (at about 3500m; can sometimes pose problems) on the right of the slope near the rocks of the S buttress of the Grande Rocheuse. Climb the slope, then a short couloir parallel to and on the right (E) of the Whymper Couloir. Move left onto the rock crest separating this from the main couloir and go up it. Cross a tributary couloir of the main one descending from the Grande Rocheuse. Go up a ridge dotted with rocks on the left bank of the main couloir, then slant up left and go up either directly to the Col de la Rocheuse, or cross the Whymper Couloir and ascend the right bank to reach the summit ridge above the Col de la Grande Rocheuse. Follow the ridge to the summit. The exact route depends upon the conditions.

Descent: By the same route. You must, however, time the ascent to allow for the descent; in other words, you should descend the couloir before the snow is too soft, that is before 9 am.

If you are late you must take the Rocheuse Spur. This is a fairly difficult, but at the same time safe, route except in the lower part

which it shares with the route up the Whymper Couloir. From the Col de la Grande Rocheuse climb the W Ridge of the Grande Rocheuse then abseil down the well-marked S spur. Pass the foot of a first, well-defined gendarme 3996m, then a second at 3835m which is turned on the Whymper Couloir side. Then rejoin the lower third of the Whymper Couloir.

The Aiguille Verte and the Col de la Grande Rocheuse, and the Grande Rocheuse from the Talèfre side; the Whymper Couloir coming down diagonally from the Col de la Grande Rocheuse (opposite page). The Grande Rocheuse and the summit ridge of the Aiguille Verte, with the Moine Ridge on the left and on the right the upper slope of the Verte (above).

42. AIGUILLE CROUX 3251m
South-East Face

Because of its marvellous setting, going back to the Aiguille Croux is always a pleasure, the more so as the route I am now proposing takes the Frêney Glacier side with its fine atmosphere and its striking views of the Aiguille Noire de Peuterey. On this fairly short steep wall, rounded like a shield, there are three routes: the Ottoz-Hurzeler Route on the SE Face, the first route done on this side (TD) and now a classic; the Ottoz-Nava Route up the ENE Spur which is more difficult; and between the two, the Bertone-Zappelli Route following the SE Spur, which is very difficult (ED). Anyway, all three of these routes soon come into condition, even after heavy low-level snowfalls, since the Aiguille Croux is fairly low and its Frêney Face is steep enough not to hold the snow; finally the Ottoz-Hurzeler Route, facing SE, has all the advantages of facing the sun, so that there are even grass and flowers on some of the cracks and ledges; this gives a less overpowering atmosphere, as opposed to

East Face of the Aiguille Croux (left).
In the left foreground the Col de l'Innominata and the Aiguille Croux; in the background the Dames Anglaises and the Aiguille Noire de Peuterey (opposite page).

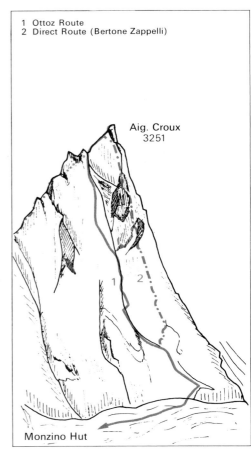

1 Ottoz Route
2 Direct Route (Bertone Zappelli)

Aig. Croux
3251

Monzino Hut

the impression given by the stark Aiguille Noire de Peuterey on the other side.

The climbing is difficult, sometimes very exposed, and delicate rather than strenuous in spite of being on granite.

● **1st ascent:** E. Hurzeler and the guide A. Ottoz, 5 July 1935.

● **Vertical height:** About 360m from the hut to the start proper; about 300m from here to the summit; in all 661m (2590 to 3251m).

● **Grade:** TD.

● **Time:** 5–6 hrs from the Monzino Hut to the summit.

● **Starting point:** The Monzino Hut (about 2590m).

● **Route** – *Outline:* This is indicated by a slight open hollow marked by big black streaks coming down from the brèche (on the S Ridge at the foot of the slab) above the small névé at the foot of the SE side of the Aiguille. Within this hollow the route makes several slight zig-zags dictated by the terrain which, unlike the Aiguilles, although granite

does not have those pure geometrical lines on it; this could at first disconcert the true Chamonix climber, but he will come to find it interesting because the line of the route depends on understanding the rock.

Description: From the Monzino Hut (2590m) follow the path passing below the foot of the S Ridge which leads to the base of the wall on a sort of balcony more or less filled with névé depending on the season, and ending on the right in a rounded buttress, the NNE Spur overlooking the Frêney Glacier. Go up the névé on the right to set foot on the gently-angled buttress and climb up slabs (III). After two pitches when the buttress steepens (above on the right is the Bertone-Zappelli Route), traverse left to the hollow, below the brèche of the S Ridge, which marks the general line of ascent. The hollow is mainly open with some bulges. Climb first up rocks on the right bank then traverse right to return to the centre (V), where a chimney is climbed for 50m (IV with

a move of V). This opens out into a Y; take the left fork to the foot of a step. Either climb the crack running up this step (the route used on the first ascent) or, better, the wall right of the crack which overhangs slightly in the upper part (V). Now slant left and climb a second wall (V) to go left into the slanting couloir above the crack used on the first ascent. Climb a deep chimney (IV) exiting on the left (V), then another chimney which leads to the last difficult section on loose rock. Slant right up a slab and above return left (V) to gain the easy couloir leading to the brèche on the S Ridge at the foot of the 'grande plaque' (great slab) of 40m (IV) and climb the slab to the summit.

43. AIGUILLE DU CHARDONNET
North Spur   3824m

From the Albert Premier Hut you can see the N and W faces of the Aiguille du Chardonnet rearing up, broad and well-formed. If you go up to the Col or the Aiguille du Tour, the whole face seems to grow higher and more magnificent, especially the N Spur between the two faces, which rises directly from the glacier to the summit. The elegant line and even more so the way it stands out makes it very alluring. There it is, two snow ridges straight as a die over two bands of granite. It is an elegant mixed route, with a fine setting, of no very great difficulty and with few objective dangers — as opposed to the N Face to its left, badly exposed to falling seracs. The route is not very high, only about 500m in vertical height, about half as high as the major routes I shall propose later.

The first time I climbed it I was guiding a young Belgian climber and I realised with pleasure that, both as technical training and as an enjoyable experience for my young friend, this was an excellent step on the way to the great routes, and one which could be done without danger or risk.

After a snow ridge between two rock buttresses, the final section is a snow slope which goes up from a ridge and gets steeper towards the summit.

An early start is essential and all the approach should be done with head-torches so as to be on the spur itself at daybreak.

There are very fine views during the whole route, but especially at two points, and this for different reasons: just above the rocks, because you are moving close to an extraordinary line of seracs, and at the top, on the last slope, which is pure, detached and exposed.

● **1st ascent:** A. Migot with C. Devouassoux, 25 July 1929.
● **Vertical height:** About 600m from the Albert Premier Hut to the start of the difficulties; about 500m from there to the summit; 1122m in all (from 2702 to 3824m).
● **Grade:** Some rock, but almost entirely ice.
● **Time:** 2 hrs from the Albert Premier Hut to the start of the difficulties (by starting from the Trient Hut you gain 30 mins). 5–6 hrs from here to the summit.
● **Equipment:** Crampons.
● **Starting point:** Albert Premier Hut (2702m) or the Trient Hut (3170m), crossing the Col du Tour (3282m).
● **Route – *Outline:*** The N Spur is well-marked and the crest is taken except in the lower section, where the first snow ridge is approached on the W Flank of the rock buttress.

Description: From the Albert Premier Hut do not descend to the glacier to cross directly to the Spur, but follow the route to

the Col du Tour to below the col and then traverse almost horizontally towards the foot of the N Face, with a slight descent to reach the vast glacier bay right of the Spur.

Turn the large crevasses on the right and go up the gentle slopes of the bay, then steep slopes on the left to exit at the snow saddle at the top of the first rock buttress.

Climb the snow ridge, then the steep rocks of the second buttress, keeping on the crest as much as possible and never on the left, to keep away from directly below the threatening seracs.

Go up to and climb the second snow ridge which merges into the final slope. This steepens considerably and leads to the summit. If this last slope is ice rather than snow, it is often better to bear left where there are good rock spikes for protection.

North Face of the Chardonnet (opposite page).
On the North Spur route near the seracs (right).

Aig. du Chardonnet
3824

3424

Tour Glacier

44. DENT DU REQUIN 3422m
East Face

Above the Mer de Glace is the broad face of the Dent du Requin, the E Face, between the Chapeau à Cornes Ridge to the left and the Mayer-Dibona Ridge to the right. Both ridges are very fine, and you will already have done the first, the Chapeau à Cornes; I advise you also to do the Mayer-Dibona, a climb which is unfortunately broken and not sustained but which is nevertheless worth climbing. It has two particular features: firstly, the climb up the dark, enclosed, mixed couloir which has a lot of character and leads to the brèche where you meet sun and light, all the more pleasurably because the whole landscape, the Envers des Aiguilles with its spurs and couloirs, seems to be unfolding under the morning sun; and secondly, higher up, after a rather uninteresting section, the final ridge grows narrower and reveals yet further fine views.

But the most interesting route on the face, especially for the climbing, is the one on the central spur. It is an elegant, direct route of sustained difficulty. The rock is excellent, and after each pitch there is a good stance. On the other hand, there is one disadvantage: you can escape from the climb before getting to the red slabs.

● **1st ascent**: Mme J. Renaudie and J. Renaudie, 4 August 1946. There have however always been difficulties in establishing the details of the first ascent, especially as far as the red slabs are concerned. The route is sometimes called the Contamine Route. The first rope to have done the whole route described below was that of L. Lachenal and G. Robino, with a party of students from the École Nationale de Ski et d'Alpinisme, in August 1948.
● **Vertical height**: About 500m from the Requin Hut to the start of the difficulties; about 400m from there to the summit; 906m in total (from 2516 to 3422m).
● **Grade**: D with two pitches of V.
● **Time**: 1 hr from the hut to the start. 5 hrs from there to the summit.
● **Equipment**: Carabiners, wooden wedges, large pitons.
● **Starting point**: Requin Hut (2516m).
● **Route** – *Outline*: The red pillar right of the big crack down the face below the summit. Right of this pillar there is a depression, a big, light-grey couloir ending below in an amphitheatre, also light-grey, on the Morin-Langlois Route (undoubtedly the shortest route on the E Face, quicker than the Voie des Plaques). Left of the big crack is a second large red pillar. Finally left again are the Voie des Plaques and the Chapeau à Cornes Ridge.

Description: Start as for the Voie des Plaques at a small terrace on the right about 30m before the gully at the top of the glacier. A system of ledges cut by short

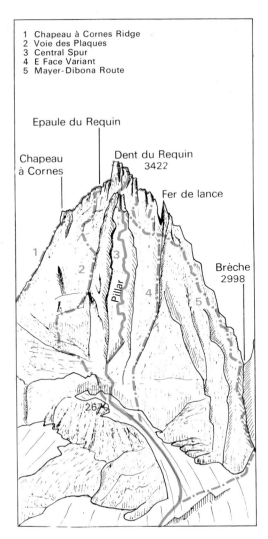

1 Chapeau à Cornes Ridge
2 Voie des Plaques
3 Central Spur
4 E Face Variant
5 Mayer-Dibona Route

Epaule du Requin

Dent du Requin
3422

Chapeau
à Cornes

Fer de lance

Pillar

Brèche
2998

2679

steps leads diagonally right towards the bottom of the NE Ridge. Take this line for about 100m. Go up initially in the direction of the light-grey amphitheatre, then slant left towards the base of the red pillar. This base looks like an enormous vertical pile made of darkish blocks. A little before this wall there is a small cave on the left with another even smaller cave above. Go up right of these caves and take an ascending gangway which narrows and steepens (IV) to reach the ridge. Follow this for about 40m climbing short steps (III) initially, going slightly right then returning sharply left to a point about 30m from the big crack separating the two red pillars. You reach a large terrace at the foot of fine red slabs. Do not take the ledges leading back right to the big light-grey couloir. Take a fine rib up the red slabs on the left. Go slightly right without getting too far from the centre of the slabs, up a slanting crack filled with flakes (IV). Arrive below a block and exit left up a series of flakes on excellent rock (IV). Climb a

vertical crack beside a rib, on the outside for the last few metres (V at the start, 1 wedge, then IV sup., 1 piton). Rejoin the crest of the ridge and follow it for about two rope-lengths, then traverse left to the foot of two parallel dièdres slanting to the right. It is better to climb the left-hand dièdre (IV). This leads to a horizontal ledge which is followed to its right-hand end. Continue slightly right up the crest of the spur for about 100m (III and IV). You arrive below a vertical, concave wall. Climb this wall in two rope-lengths by the right-hand vertical crack which is blocked halfway by a chockstone which must be climbed (V); the exit is overhanging (V). This now leads to the shoulder at the top of the two red pillars of the E Face. Follow the ridge of the shoulder towards a blackish, overhanging dièdre which forms the NE boundary of the summit block of the Requin.

After gaining the foot of this dièdre, climb up a dièdre-chimney slanting up right and leading (IV sup., 2 pitons) to a V brèche on

the NE Ridge. A short thin arête, then a short very exposed vertical wall lead to a terrace from which the summit block is climbed on the N side.

The East Face of the Dent du Requin (opposite page). The Requin Hut with the Drus and the Aiguille Verte behind (above).

45. MONT DOLENT 3823m
North Ridge

Situated in the E section of the range, at the junction of the long ridges coming from the Jorasses to the W and the Aiguille d'Argentière to the N, Mont Dolent is an important peak. Climbing it will help your understanding of the geography of the range, and of the appearance and structure of certain faces which are seldom visited. There is a superb view, very extensive, over a whole series of different landscapes, from the wild to the pastoral.

The ordinary route is nothing more than a long walk, needing little technical expertise. The N (or to be more exact the NNW) Ridge is however interesting as a mixed route at high altitude, and it is joined at the Brèche de l'Amône, which is in itself a worthwhile route. Climbers coming from Switzerland go up the Neuve side, by far the more attractive, but this involves a very long approach-march, 7—8 hrs, over a crevassed glacier and then up a rocky spur angling gently up above the brèche. From France, alpinists must go up to the top of the extraordinary enclave of the Argentière Glacier, then cross a band of slabs cut by a couloir leading to the brèche. This route is undoubtedly preferable because it offers more variety: a fine walk up, not too difficult, from the glacier, an interesting rock-

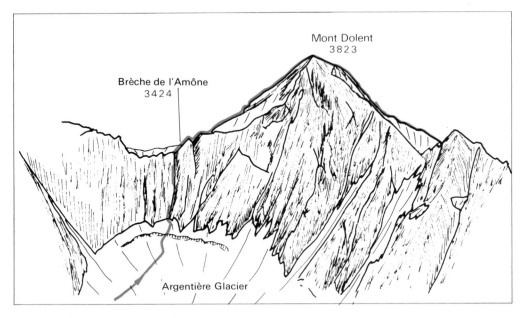

Mont Dolent
3823

Brèche de l'Amône
3424

Argentière Glacier

climb, particularly the last pitch leading to the brèche, and the whole giving an interesting contrast with, and completing, the mixed climbing on the N Ridge itself. You will also derive different, and complementary, impressions from the different sides of the mountain: the wild, starker Argentière side, and the sunny, pleasant Neuve side.

Higher up, this impression of traversing, or journeying across a changing countryside, will be accentuated when you see, after crossing the frontier point on the N Ridge just before the summit, the mountains and valleys of the Italian side. The descent is in fact on the Italian side by the Pré de Bar Glacier, and you can choose at the foot whether to come back by the Italian Val Ferret or the Swiss Val Ferret; I would suggest the latter, here also to make the traverse a more rewarding experience from all points of view, and also because it will allow for a view of a different aspect of the Dolent, from La Fouly.

● **1st ascent:** G. Bolaffio and J. Kugy with J. Croux and D. Proment, 29 July 1906.
● **Vertical height:** 653m from the Argentière Hut (2771m) to the Brèche de l'Amône (3424m); 399m from the brèche to the summit; 1052m in all (from 2771 to 3823m).
● **Grade:** D for the ascent to the brèche. From there mixed terrain and snow.
● **Time:** 4–5 hrs from the Argentière Hut (2771m) to the brèche. 7–8 hrs from the Neuve Hut (2729m) to the brèche, or more accurately to a point slightly higher than the brèche at 3534m. 3 hrs from the brèche to the summit.
● **Equipment:** Crampons, carabiners.
● **Starting point:** the Argentière Hut (2771m) or the Neuve Hut (2729m).
● **Route** – *Outline:* Initially up the couloir cutting through the barrier of slabs and leading to the brèche, then the ridge proper.

Description: From the Argentière Hut go up long easy slopes at the head of the glacier to gain the foot of the couloir. Cross the bergschrund. Go up the couloir or its right bank. When it steepens and forms a huge dièdre, exit right along a ledge and climb the fairly smooth rock slabs (IV). Return into the couloir and climb the steep 25m exit wall slightly on the right (IV). From the Brèche de l'Amône follow the N Ridge, initially rocky then mixed, and finally mainly snow with broken rock from time to time, particularly at the frontier point where it steepens to the summit.

Descent: By the S Flank and the SE Ridge. From the summit follow the ridge – big easy blocks and snow – which descends to the Shoulder at 3774m. Then by a couloir of easy but loose rock reach the snowy SE Ridge and follow it to a large snow saddle NW of Point 3580m. From here after crossing the bergschrund, descend the Pré de Bar Glacier passing round the foot of the buttress at 3083m. At 2900m return to the left bank of the glacier below the slopes of Mont Allobrogia to reach the Fioria bivouac hut (about 2800m). From there traverse left across the wide slopes and make a slight reascent to reach the Petit Col Ferret (2490m) and La Fouly.

Going up to the Argentière Hut, with Mont Dolent in the left background, and the Triolet on the right (opposite page).
Mont Dolent from the Neuve side, with the North Ridge in the centre (below).

46. AIGUILLE DE L'M 2844m
Ménégaux and Couzy Routes

1 Ménégaux Route
2 Couzy Route

Aig. de l'M
2844

NNE Ridge

On its NW side looking towards Chamonix, the Aiguille de l'M rises vertically out of a scree-slope and a few névés. The face is small, but being steep and at low altitude it is always in condition. It is therefore very popular, like the NNE Ridge close at hand, and especially when, because of new snow or doubtful weather, routes over 3000m are impossible. There are three routes on the face: the Leininger Route on the right leading to the Pic Albert or SW Summit, and the Ménégaux and Couzy Routes which come out on the NE summit-ridge of the M. The last two are very popular; the rock is better and the climbing more sustained than on the Leininger. The Ménégaux and Couzy Routes are of a fairly similar standard of difficulty, the Ménégaux being more difficult and requiring more artificial climbing. But you can set off leaving the choice until the last moment and then do one or the other according to mood, or according to which is the less crowded. In any case, in any summer there will be a number of days when the high routes are impossible, and so you will undoubtedly come back later to do the remaining route; it is one of the major attractions of this extraordinary range that one can do a number of interesting routes, without long approach-marches, on clear days or half-days during a period of poor weather.

Ménégaux Route:

● **1st ascent:** J. C. and S. Ménégaux and J. Poullain, August 1948.

● **Vertical height:** About 200m (from 2650 to 2844m).

● **Grade:** Sustained TD, with a pitch of V. The rock at the base of the wall is often wet.

● **Time:** 1¼ hrs from the Plan de l'Aiguille to the start. 3—4 hrs from here to the summit.

● **Equipment:** Carabiners, étriers.

● **Starting point:** Plan de l'Aiguille (2310m).

● **Route** — *Outline:* This follows a big couloir-dièdre about 150m high slanting slightly right, which merges into the final wall. For the first third of its height it is beside a well-defined pillar ending at a large platform.

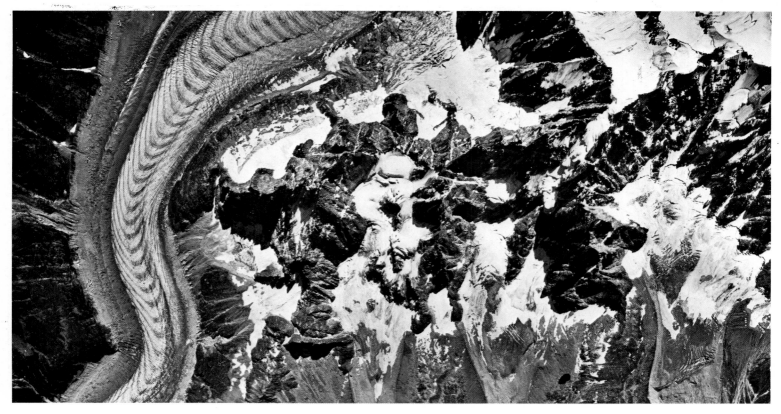

Description: Three rope-lengths (III, V and IV) lead initially to the platform at the top of the pillar. Above there is a large detached flake; climb this on the left (V, a strenuous jamming crack). The top of the flake makes a good belay. To the left gain the edge of the dièdre and get into it, then climb a vertical crack, exiting on the right, to reach a good stance on the left. Climb a short wall (IV) then the dièdre (V) for two rope-lengths, leading to an overhang (V sup.) and then to a platform on the right. Now climb a chimney (IV sup.), then a wall with a detached flake, a short difficult section (V) and another wall on the left (V), which leads to a slightly descending traverse on the left climbed with the help of a detached flake. Then a crack-chimney (IV) and easy rock (III) lead to the summit.

Couzy Route:
● **1st ascent:** J. Couzy and M. Prost, 25 July 1952.
● **Vertical height:** About 180m (from 2670 to 2844m).
● **Grade:** Sustained TD.
● **Time:** 2–3 hrs from the start to the summit.
● **Equipment:** Carabiners.
● **Route** – *Outline:* A dièdre slanting right directly below the summit right of the pillar finishing on the ridge right of the summit.

Description: Where the Ménégaux starts left of the well-defined 50m pillar, the Couzy Route starts to the right. 15m of easy climbing lead to a big slanting dièdre which is climbed on the right wall (IV) then at the back using a crack running up it (V and IV, sustained). This is pleasant climbing often with wide bridging, to the point where the dièdre is blocked by an overhanging wall. Turn this by a crack on the left which itself has two overhangs (V exposed).

A less steep and less difficult couloir-dièdre (IV) leads to the crest of the ridge right of the summit.

Aerial view of the Aiguille de l'M (opposite page). The Ménégaux Route seen from the start (right).

47. AIGUILLE DU PLAN 3673m
Ryan-Lochmatter Ridge

The E Ridge, or Ryan-Lochmatter Ridge, on the Aiguille du Plan is one of those superb routes done as far back as 1906 by that remarkable rope V. J. E. Ryan and the Lochmatter brothers.

The E Ridge is at the very top of the glacier cirque of the Envers de Blaitière. As you go up you feel you are walking deeper and deeper into an enclosure; the glacier narrows, and you are surrounded by great faces and pillars of granite; then, the higher you climb on the ridge, the more the horizon broadens before you, away from those sheer, enclosing faces.

The main problem of this route is the bergschrund, which can at times be very difficult. The ridge itself is not particularly steep; it is made up of a series of big steps cut by cracks and brèches, usually with excellent belays. The granite is invariably good and rough; the difficulty is sustained and consistent; each pitch gives you some interesting moves, with safe, fairly strenuous climbing; there are some delicate moves, but little sense of exposure.

From the summit of the Aiguille du Plan, the descent is usually down to the Requin Hut and the Montenvers by the Envers du Plan Glacier and the Mer de Glace. Another possibility is to go up from the Col Supérieur du Plan to the Aiguille du Midi and take the téléphérique down to the valley. This may be less obvious as a descent, but it is a very fine one; after a very fine rock route, you follow a snow ridge which you know already — this is not in fact a disadvantage, since you will be seeing the ridge at a different time of day and in a quite different light. It will also allow you to spend a few more hours in an extraordinary world between the airy N slopes overlooking the valley on the right, and the great glacier mass at the centre of the range going up to Mont Blanc on the left and in front. Finally, from the technical point of view, you cannot fail to derive a great knowledge and understanding of snow techniques, of snow ridges and of cornices.

● **1st ascent:** V. J. E. Ryan with F. and J. Lochmatter, 20 June 1906.
● **Vertical height:** 600m from the Envers des Aiguilles Hut to the bergschrund; 550m from the bergschrund to the summit; 1153m from the hut to the summit (from 2520 to 3673m).
● **Grade:** D sup. (several pitches of IV and IV sup.), mainly crack climbing. A fairly strenuous climb.
● **Time:** 1½ hrs from the hut to the bergschrund. 6–7 hrs from the bergschrund to the summit. 2½–3½ hrs from the summit to the Aiguille du Midi.
● **Equipment:** Crampons, carabiners.
● **Starting point:** Envers des Aiguilles Hut (2520m).
● **Route – Outline:** The ridge is well-defined. At the bottom the exact line depends on the state of the bergschrund.

Description: From the hut cross névés and scree below the N end of the Envers de

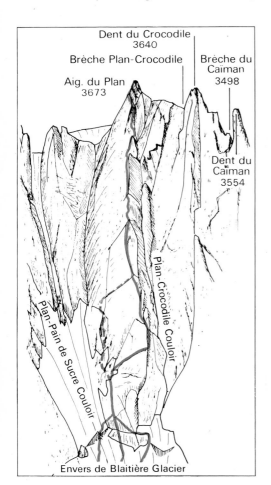

Dent du Crocodile 3640
Brèche Plan-Crocodile
Brèche du Caiman 3498
Aig. du Plan 3673
Dent du Caiman 3554
Plan-Crocodile Couloir
Plan-Pain de Sucre Couloir
Envers de Blaitière Glacier

Blaitière Glacier and then go up the glacier (S end) towards the foot of the buttress coming down from the Aiguille de Blaitière and also from the Ryan-Lochmatter Ridge. The slope steepens as the bergschrund is reached. Cross this left of the Ryan-Lochmatter Ridge (on the Pain de Sucre slope) and go back right onto the ridge 80m above its lowest point. If the bergschrund is impassable, it is possible either to climb the bottom of the ridge by two fairly steep cracks of 20m (IV), provided that the glacier touches the rock here, or to cross the bergschrund on the right, that is towards the Plan-Crocodile Couloir (beware of stonefall) and go back left up a diagonal line, a ledge and rock steps leading to the ridge.

Climb directly up blocks and then cracked slabs, leaving a large horizontal ledge on the right (on the left are bivouac sites between a flake and the wall) to a second ledge which slants up right and narrows into a dièdre (III) leading to the Plan-Crocodile Couloir. On the right take a look at the route up the E Face of the Dent du Crocodile which I shall describe later on. Climb the right bank of the couloir quickly, watching out for possible stonefall, and go up rocks, often snowed up

and tricky, to reach the Shoulder at about 3300m. It is also possible to reach this point on the left of the ridge if the rocks in the couloir are too snowed up. To do this go up a secondary snow couloir between the Plan-Pain de Sucre Couloir and the Ryan-Lochmatter Ridge, then up rocks (IV) between a gendarme on the left and the flank of the Ryan-Lochmatter Ridge. Above climb a slab (IV sup.) and a narrow chimney (IV sup.), then bear right to gain the rock steps of the Shoulder.

Above the Shoulder climb the crest of the ridge to reach the first step. Two cracks (IV) lead to the foot of an ice-choked chimney. Gain the chimney (IV, delicate) and climb it to the top of the first step. Follow the crest of the ridge made of broken steps climbing a series of cracks and chimneys (IV) one of which, the 'Grand-Mère' Crack (IV sup.), is slightly slanting and grows steeper. Above do not take the vertical Y-shaped crack but follow the overhanging crest of the ridge (IV) leading to the foot of the final step which is climbed entirely on its left side. Climb a delicate crack (IV sup.). Go along a ledge (slight descent) to climb a chimney going up to the ridge which is left in its upper

section in order to gain easier ground with a stride (IV sup.). For three rope-lengths climb walls cut by platforms. Above, the upper part of the step is split by a Y-shaped crack. To reach the bottom of this make a detour left climbing a crack-chimney with two jammed blocks (IV) and immediately above, a deep chimney concealed by a jammed flake (IV sup.). Then climb the Y-shaped chimney avoiding the left branch (IV sup.). An easy ledge leads left up the last easy steps to the summit.

The upper part, and the bergschrund, of the Ryan-Lochmatter Ridge (opposite page).
The Envers des Aiguilles, and the Ryan-Lochmatter Ridge above the Envers de Blaitière Glacier (above).

48. PAIN DE SUCRE D'ENVERS DU PLAN 3607m
North Face

There are not many snow and ice routes on the Aiguilles of Chamonix: the N Face of the Pain de Sucre, the Frendo Spur, the N Face of the Plan. But they all share a certain particular character arising from their being enclosed by those magnificent granite pillars. During previous routes you will have seen and often admired them, looking a little strange and slightly out of place. In choosing such routes, you will feel that you are escaping from something that is almost a routine, no longer a surprise: rock-climbing, often very difficult, true, but beautiful, safe and with good belays.

Moreover, taking a longer-term view of a climbing career, these Aiguilles snow routes are excellent training for the major, high altitude snow routes, both technically and because of their atmosphere. On the hanging glacier of the Plan, on the Pan de Rideau, you will learn a lot; you will start the process of becoming an alpinist, and you are making preparations for the day when you will become a true mountaineer and will do the Innominata, or the Sans Nom on the Verte, or the Peuterey. The altitude of the Aiguilles is less, the setting less beautiful but also less dangerous than at 4000m; to be near well-known names and popular routes is reassuring, but the bergschrund can be as difficult and the slopes as steep — and it is this which is so profitable technically.

At the foot of the Pan de Rideau, the original route goes right to come out to the right of the Pain de Sucre. I consider it better, and much more enjoyable, to go left and spend longer on the fine snow-slopes of the Pan de Rideau, and then reach the summit by the E Ridge. There is a further very interesting route on the Pain de Sucre, up the E Spur; this is a fairly long route, rock lower down rock and mixed higher up, with superb views.

Finally, there is a direct route leading up from the lower snow slope to the Col du Pain de Sucre, but it is very difficult and must be exposed to stonefall.

● **1st ascent:** The left-hand route, by R. Gréloz and A. Roch, 4 July 1937.
● **Vertical height:** About 500m from the bergschrund to the summit (from 3100 to 3607m).

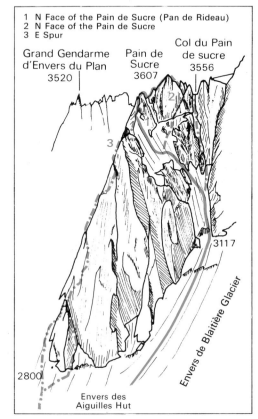

1 N Face of the Pain de Sucre (Pan de Rideau)
2 N Face of the Pain de Sucre
3 E Spur

Grand Gendarme d'Envers du Plan 3520

Pain de Sucre 3607

Col du Pain de sucre 3556

3117

2800

Envers de Blaitière Glacier

Envers des Aiguilles Hut

- **Grade:** A very steep snow route exposed to the sun from early in the morning.
- **Time:** 6–7 hrs.
- **Equipment:** Crampons.
- **Starting point:** The Envers des Aiguilles Hut (2520m).
- **Route** – *Outline:* The N Face of the Pain de Sucre is composed of two snow slopes staggered one above the other and joined by a middle zone of snow, or rock if the snow has melted off. The line follows the first slope, goes up the middle zone and above splits into a Y, going left or right of the summit according to the route chosen.

Description: From the Envers des Aiguilles Hut (2520m) climb the three bergschrunds above the Envers Glacier and gain the long slope. Go up this bearing left to climb the middle zone by more or less snow-covered slabs and blocks which lead to the Pan de Rideau and the upper slope. The right-hand route skirts the rock and, when the snow slope ends, follows a deep ice couloir which becomes very steep at the exit to the brèche. The left-hand route is undoubtedly less difficult but more beautiful; it does a complete ascent of the Pan de Rideau to exit on the E Ridge which is followed to point 3548. From there the SE Ridge leads, with pitches of III and one of IV, to the summit.

Descent: Easily by the S Face to the Envers du Plan Glacier.

The Pan de Rideau with the Grandes Jorasses behind (opposite page).
The North Face of the Pain de Sucre (above).

49. AIGUILLE DE BIONNASSAY 4052m
North-West Face
MONT BLANC 4807m
Traverse

The Aiguille de Bionnassay is that sturdy yet delicate shoulder of Mont Blanc which faces west, and its NW Face is made up of a glacier cascading elegantly from the summit. It is a very fine snow route, more than 1000m long, and individual in that it is oblique, along the contour of the slope, so that you feel as if you were moving along a balcony; it is always exposed and often vertiginous.

From the summit of the Aiguille de Bionnassay (4052m) the summit ridge, sometimes narrow, sometimes corniced, goes slightly downwards to the Col de Bionnassay (3892m) and then up to the Dôme du Goûter; from here you can go down to the Aiguille du Goûter and thence to the valley. But except in poor weather, I strongly advise you to go on to do the 'traverse' of Mont Blanc. For this there are

several reasons: in the first place, if you end the climb on the Dôme du Goûter you may feel it incomplete. Again, if you are thinking in terms of effort, the only really laborious part of the traverse of Mont Blanc is the ascent of the Dôme du Goûter — and this, necessarily, you will already have done. Moreover, you will now be coming to the Bosses Ridge, which I consider to be one of the finest of all high ridges, and the ascent of which, from the Bosses to the last slender ridge, soaring up into the sky, is varied and not monotonous. Finally, there is Mont Blanc itself and reaching that summit is always a worthwhile moment. From the summit you will see a new panorama: the Mur de Côte, the Col de la Brenva where the wind sculpts great cornices, the architecturally pure lines of Mont Maudit, Col Maudit

and the view over the Aiguilles du Diable, and finally the descent from Mont Blanc du Tacul to the Col du Midi. Here you can either go up to the Aiguille du Midi to take the téléphérique, or, to extend this high-altitude route still further, you can spend the night at the Cosmiques Hut which is always pleasant and then go down the next day to Montenvers by the Vallée Blanche and the Mer de Glace. If you make the latter choice, the whole route, as well as its different parts (even the rather crowded Vallée Blanche) will take on a new dimension.

● **1st ascent:** Of the NW Face of the Aiguille de Bionnassay, E. N. Buxton, F. C. Grove and R. J. S. MacDonald with J.-P. Cachat and M.-C. Payot, 28 July 1865 (the same year as the first ascent of the Matterhorn).

● **Vertical height:** About 1050m from the foot of the NW Face to the summit (from 3000 to 4052m); 750m from the Aiguille de Bionnassay to Mont Blanc; 1750m in all (from about 3050 to 4807m).

● **Grade:** A snow route having a certain seriousness. The ascent up the face is followed by the traverse of the ridge. Above the Dôme du Goûter the traverse of Mont Blanc, while a major route at high altitude, presents no serious technical difficulties.

The descent from the Col du Mont Maudit can however require an abseil if the bergschrund is high and open.

However, for the whole route considerable experience of snow is required. It is also useful to spend a whole day on snow and to realise how far it varies in quality according to the slopes, the ridges, their orientation and, especially, the sun.

● **Time:** 4–5 hrs from the Tête Rousse Hut (3167m) to the summit of the Aiguille de Bionnassay. 1½–2 hrs from the Aiguille to the Dôme du Goûter. 2 hrs from the Dôme du Goûter to Mont Blanc. 4 hrs from Mont Blanc to the Col du Midi. 11½–13 hrs in all.

● **Equipment:** Crampons (a wooden stake or an ice-screw for the possible abseil at the Col du Mont Maudit).

● **Starting point:** Tête Rousse Hut (3167m).

● **Route** – *Outline:* This can be seen from the Tête Rousse Hut and you can have the pleasure the evening before of studying the ascent route. This is formed by a fine diagonal line ascending from the right to left to lead either to the summit or slightly right of the summit to the Arête du Tricot. If the traverse of Mont Blanc is made from the Dôme du Goûter, the route generally follows the ridge on the N side.

Description: There is a couloir slightly above the Tête Rousse Hut. Go up to this and descend it to reach the plateau of the Bionnassay Glacier. Cross this towards the slopes of the NW Face which slant down from the summit to join the glacier on the right. Ascend the entire length of these steep slopes cut by crevasses and seracs; I suggest this because on the one hand the ascent in crampons is not as monotonous as it could be up a couloir and, on the other, you can so arrange it that very steep sections can be followed by level or at least less steep sections. On the upper part of the slope you can gain the Arête du Tricot on the right or alternatively traverse left and stay on the N Face, going up it directly to the summit.

At the summit (4052m) follow the sharp corniced crest descending to the Col de Bionnassay (3892m) and then ascend to the Dôme du Goûter, passing a first shoulder (4003m), from which the Aiguilles Grises Ridge goes down to the S, then a second shoulder (4153m) where the great SW Buttress of the Dôme du Goûter starts. Traverse the slopes of the Dôme, leaving the summit on the left, to reach the Col du Dôme and the Vallot Hut (4362m). From here follow the Bosses Ridge to reach the summit of Mont Blanc.

Descend the E slope and the Mur de la Côte to reach the Col de la Brenva (4303m).

Climb Mont Maudit (4465m) up a long snow slope, descend directly and then slant across to Col Maudit (4035m). You can avoid the summit by gaining on the left the Col du Mont Maudit (4354m) from which the descent, at the start, sometimes requires an abseil over the bergschrund.

From Col Maudit, make an ascending traverse and pass the Shoulder of Mont Blanc du Tacul, from which a descent is made to the Col du Midi.

The corniced ridge between the Col de Bionnassay and the Dôme du Goûter (left).
On the North-West Face of the Aiguille de Bionnassay (below).

Overall view from the North-West Face of the Aiguille de Bionnassay (right background) to the Aiguille du Midi (left), over the Dôme du Goûter, Mont Blanc, Mont Maudit, Mont Blanc du Tacul;

the Bossons Glacier is directly below the summit of
Mont Blanc (above).
A party on Mont Maudit (above right).

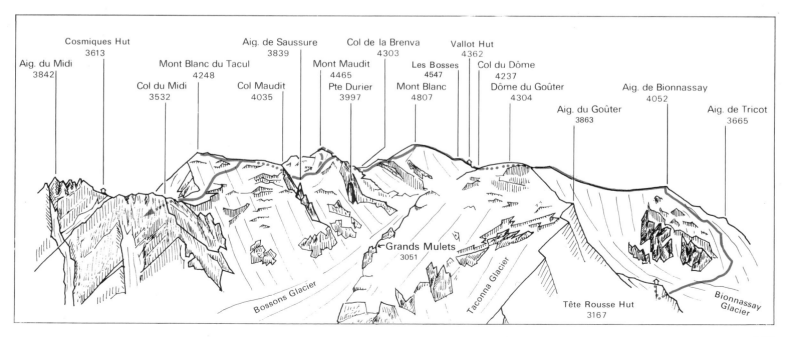

Aig. du Midi
3842

Cosmiques Hut
3613

Col du Midi
3532

Mont Blanc du Tacul
4248

Col Maudit
4035

Aig. de Saussure
3839

Mont Maudit
4465

Pte Durier
3997

Col de la Brenva
4303

Les Bosses
4547

Mont Blanc
4807

Vallot Hut
4362

Col du Dôme
4237

Dôme du Goûter
4304

Aig. du Goûter
3863

Aig. de Bionnassay
4052

Aig. de Tricot
3665

Grands Mulets
3051

Bossons Glacier

Taconna Glacier

Tête Rousse Hut
3167

Bionnassay
Glacier

50. MONT MAUDIT 4465m
Tour Ronde Ridge

This is a major ridge route, mixed climbing at high altitude, which could not be more different from routes like the Ménégaux and Couzy Routes, or even the Mer de Glace Face of the Grépon; but this after all is precisely the point of the programme that I suggest, that it offers a huge variety of possibilities for all weathers, at all altitudes, and that it gives a host of pleasures complementary to each other, rather than negating each other. This climb, the Tour Ronde Ridge of Mont Maudit, is in the most magnificent surroundings along a frontier ridge (not that that has anything to do with it), a ridge which separates two wild and widely differing worlds: the Combe Maudite on the right and the Brenva cirque on the left. You will move sometimes on snow, sometimes on rock, and some corniced pitches can be delicate. The route is long, but without major difficulties and likely to inspire you with the wish to go on to do the great high-altitude climbs like the Peuterey dominating the skyline on your left; moreover it will give you some of the experience necessary to fit you for it. Remember that the weather may turn bad, that you may have to turn back — or consider that you may have to emerge onto the Shoulder in mist. If you are to undertake

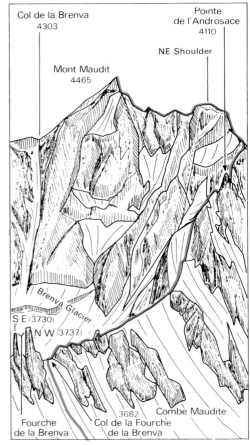

this route, you should be capable of retreating from it in bad weather.

The route has a fine red tower, the Pointe de l'Androsace, flowerlike in that barren world, a reminder of the four men, members of the Androsace Club of Geneva, who made the first ascent of it. The ordinary route avoids it to the left, but you can climb it if the conditions on the Brenva side are poor, or just because you feel like it, even if this particular ascent is scarcely in keeping with the character of the rest of the climb. The ridge comes out not on the summit of Mont Maudit but on the NE Ridge coming down from it; you follow the latter to get to the Shoulder (4336m) and Mont Maudit itself (4465m).

● **1st ascent**: M. von Kuffner with A. Burgener, J. Furrer and a porter, 2–4 July 1887.

● **Vertical height**: About 800m from the Col de la Fourche to the summit (from 3680 to 4465m).

● **Grade**: A long mixed route at high altitude.

● **Time**: 4–7 hrs from the hut to the summit.
● **Equipment**: Crampons.
● **Starting point**: The Col de la Fourche Hut (3682m), reached in 2 hrs from the Torino Hut by the Géant Glacier, the Combe Maudite at the foot of the Tour Ronde and, after the bergschrund, by a fairly steep slope leading to the col.

● **Route** – *Outline*: This is the fine curve sweeping up from the col to the Col Maudit-Mont Maudit Ridge.

Description: From the hut follow the snow and rock ridge which is at first horizontal (passing a small gendarme on the right), and then steepens into a narrow snow ridge going up to the foot of the great lower step. Go up right of the crest of the step by a couloir, then follow the crest to a narrow exposed shoulder from which a short descent leads to the foot of the Point de l'Androsace, which, along with the small teeth above, is usually turned on the Brenva side. If you wish to climb it, go up by a deep chimney on the right (IV) which leads to a narrow platform. Climb a slab and a short

couloir to a ledge (belay piton in place). Slabs and a crack lead to the summit. Abseil (20m) down the Brenva side. You reach a snow saddle at the foot of the upper step, which is fairly steep, ice, snow and rock. Climb this taking a line depending on the terrain, initially to the left on the Brenva side to gain a slanting couloir; go up this latter. Go back right then left to reach the NE Ridge of Mont Maudit. Follow this passing the Shoulder (4336m), then continue first on the Brenva side and later on the French side below the summit tower to reach the summit from the W.

In the foreground above a sea of cloud, the Tour Ronde Ridge and the Fourche; in the background the Grivola and the Gran Paradiso (opposite page). On the ridge just before the gendarme de l'Androsace (above).

51. AIGUILLE DU MOINE 3412m
East Face

Above the Talèfre Glacier is the fine rock wall of the Moine: the E Face, between the SE Ridge to the left and the N Ridge on the right. It is seamed with straight steep couloirs and pillars, which make it very attractive, and indeed it attracted the attention of climbers early. In 1932, Mlle Morin, W. Carmichael and G. Charlet made a rather meandering but fine route. Ten years later, J. Aureille and Y. Feutren reached the SE Ridge 50m from the summit by a route whose line follows the main couloir, a very worthwhile route graded TD with six pitons; finally, in 1954, P. Labrunie and A. Contamine made a more difficult and more sustained direct route, which is described below. This is a very fine route on good granite, of a high standard of difficulty but in pleasant surroundings, in sunlight because the wall faces E. The descent, by the ordinary route, poses no problems.

● **1st ascent**: P. Labrunie with A. Contamine, 25 July 1954.

● **Vertical height**: About 400m (from 3000 to 3412m). The Couvercle Hut is at 2687m.

● **Grade**: TD sup., sustained particularly in the lower and upper thirds.

● **Time**: 40 mins from the Couvercle Hut to

1 Labrunie-Contamine Route
2 Aureille-Feutren Route

Aig. du Moine
3412

Talèfre Glacier

the start of the difficulties. 4–5 hrs from there to the summit.

● **Equipment**: Carabiners and 15 pitons (étriers can make the climbing easier lower down).

● **Starting point**: Couvercle Hut (2687m). Try to combine this route with a second to be done the next day from the same hut, preferably a snow or mixed route. As you return to the hut early from this route there is plenty of time to sleep during the afternoon, and so it is easy to set out again at midnight.

● **Route** – *Outline:* There is a depression right of the central buttress coming down from the summit, where there is a very open dièdre capped by a large and obvious roof right of two high parallel chimneys. This is the start, and the route generally follows the extended line, with a detour right to gain a large couloir and higher a traverse left to regain the central buttress at its final step.

Description: From the Couvercle Hut (2687m) turn the bottom of the SE Ridge of the Moine and go up the Talèfre Glacier to reach the foot of the face. Go past the buttress coming down from the summit which sticks out a little into the glacier; then go past two high parallel chimneys to start up an ill-defined dièdre, which is very open and 50m high. Depending on the state of the glacier it can sometimes be difficult to gain the rock. Climb the dièdre (V then III and IV) and leave it in the upper part to follow a crack on the right leading (V) to the ridge. Follow a narrow balcony formed by a flake attached to the wall (IV, then V). Go round the ridge on the right (IV sup.). Above climb the dièdres (IV and V) to reach the terraces of the big couloir which is climbed. Ascend easy slabs for about 100m to a black step. Take a first rounded and wet dièdre on the left (V sup.) and then a second leading to snowy terraces. Regain the pillar on the left, follow the right side of the arête (IV, V) and reach the final step. Grooves (IV sup.) and then two dièdres (IV, IV sup.) lead to the summit.

East Face of the Moine (opposite page).
The Moine and the Talèfre Glacier from the Whymper Couloir (above right).
The seracs of the Talèfre Glacier from the East Face of the Moine (right).

133

52. AIGUILLE DU PEIGNE 3192m

Papillons Ridge (West Ridge proper), West-North-West Face, North-West Pillar, North-West Face, North Ridge

This is not a major route, not even a particularly consistent one; it is more of a traverse, uniting several different routes in a clever combination, and leading with a certain elegance to the summit of the Peigne. It is a low- rather than high-altitude climb, and its popularity stems in part from this, the fact that it is possible even when the snow is low down or the weather is poor.

The lower part is made up of the Papillons Ridge proper, which is in itself a pleasant route (with one very delicate slanting pitch, IV sup. with 2 moves of V) if the weather and conditions higher up are poor; this lower part poses no problems.

You should not, on the other hand, undertake the upper part, or at least should not climb the summit block, in storm conditions; the summit of the Peigne being a pointed one is particularly liable to attract lightning, and more than one party has been struck, with serious consequences. This is a danger you must never forget; do not allow yourself to be lulled into a false sense of security by the nearness of the valley.

On the upper part of the climb, you have the choice of four different routes: the WNW or Chamonix Face overlooking Les Houches; the NW Pillar separating the WNW Face from the NW Face; the NW Face, more difficult than the two preceding

routes; and finally the very difficult N Ridge, a remarkable climb, of exceptional character because of its style and its consistency. In spite of its name, the N Ridge, of compact granite, is not itself climbed; the route follows rather a groove between the ridge and the beginning of the wall of slabs on the NE Face. This groove forms a huge dièdre 170m high, remarkably straight, parallel to the ridge, overlooked, even partly hidden, by it; it is this which gives it not only elegance, but a certain starkness.

You can do the whole route by doing the same as R. Gabriel and G. Livanos and climbing the lower part of the ridge from the very bottom of the Peigne; this gives a route of some 600m of vertical height, but has the disadvantage that it, like the intégrale of the Grütter Ridge, allows the climber to escape at several different points, or to rejoin the route; this detracts from the character and style of the N Ridge proper.

Normally, you follow the Papillons Couloir to get to the brèche of gendarme 3009m and from that point, when you have traversed left and turned the lower point of the N Ridge itself, the whole atmosphere of the face changes and so does the character of the climbing. I have done the ridge six or seven times myself, but my strongest memories are of attempts at climbing it, before the first ascent, with G. Bellin. It was an overwhelming but exhilarating experience to go into the dièdre. It is dark, the rock is sometimes covered with verglas, or indeed snowed or iced up; whatever the conditions, it is always damp. The lines of the rock are straight and vertiginous, sheer beneath your feet. The rock is excellent but cold; the climbing is especially strenuous in spite of occasional delicate moves. It is of very sustained difficulty.

Papillons Ridge
- **1st ascent:** K. Gurékian, L. Pez and A. Subot, 10 September 1948.
- **Vertical height:** About 200m.
- **Grade:** D with two moves of V.
- **Time:** 1½–2 hrs.

Upper part (WNW)
WNW Face:
- **1st ascent:** R. Ferlet and L. Terray, 2 August 1943.
- **Vertical height:** About 100m.
- **Grade:** D with two pitches of V.
- **Time:** 2 hrs.

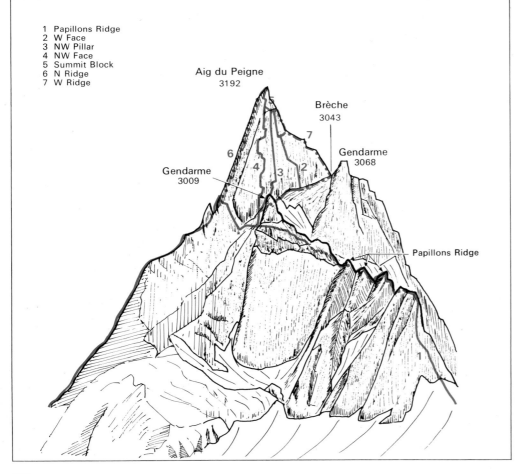

1 Papillons Ridge
2 W Face
3 NW Pillar
4 NW Face
5 Summit Block
6 N Ridge
7 W Ridge

Aig du Peigne
3192

Brèche
3043

Gendarme
3068

Gendarme
3009

Papillons Ridge

The Lépiney Crack (opposite page, left).
In spite of snow the Aiguille du Peigne is still feasible (opposite page, right).

NW Pillar:
- **1st ascent**: R. Mazars with G. Rébuffat, 19 August 1969.
- **Vertical height**: About 130m.
- **Grade**: TD with two pitches of V and a pitch of A1.
- **Time**: 2 hrs.

NW Face:
- **1st ascent**: J. L. Massenet, P. Meyer and B. Perrin, 13 July 1959.
- **Vertical height**: About 150m.
- **Grade**: TD sup.
- **Time**: 3 hrs.

Summit block: J. Lépiney climbed the crack on 6 September 1921; the exit however was first climbed without external aids or lassoing by G. Rébuffat and L. Terray, 6 June 1943.
- **Grade**: V and A1 (pitons in place).
- **Time**: 30 mins.

N Ridge:
- **1st ascent**: F. Aubert, J. C. Martin, J. C. Ménégaux, M. Schatz, 2 August 1947.
- **Vertical height**: N Ridge proper, 170m; 400m from the foot of the wall.
- **Grade**: TD sup., very sustained, strenuous.
- **Time**: 1½ hrs from the Plan de l'Aiguille to the foot of the ridge by the Papillons Couloir. 3–4 hrs from the Plan de l'Aiguille to the foot of the ridge by the lower part of the ridge. 3–4 hrs from the foot of the ridge to the summit.

- **Equipment**: Carabiners, étriers. Pitons are usually in place on the ridge; but you should take a selection of gear, including a few wedges or very large angles.

- **Route** – *Outline*: The ascent splits into three sections: the Papillons Ridge with its four towers; the middle section, a long diagonal ascent; the upper section with four possibilities, the WNW Face on the right, the NW Pillar in the middle, the NW Face on the left and the N Ridge further left still.

Description:

The Papillons Ridge: From the Plan de l'Aiguille ascend grass and then scree slopes to the foot of the ridge. Start level with a small horizontal ledge. Follow a small ledge-crack (4–5m) to the S and return left by a crack-chimney (15m) ending in a double crack climbed by hand- and foot-jams (III). A short horizontal ridge and platform follow. Climb a step by a system of grooves (25m, IV). Go up several metres to a block overlooking a small deep brèche 2m. Get onto the block, swing across to a slab and climb this by a thin crack to a little ledge 3m higher up. Now continue up a cracked slab initially keeping right, then returning left by a slanting crack to gain the summit of the first step (V). Follow the horizontal easy ridge, then climb the second step by cracks (III). From the top of the second step, descend slightly to a first small

brèche, traverse horizontally for several metres to a second brèche (from the first small brèche it is possible to escape in bad weather by descending an earth ledge slanting S and then descending the couloir it leads to for a rope-length. Then climb a buttress to gain the Papillons Couloir). From the brèche climb straight up (slab with a crack) for 8m and jam up a crack slanting left (IV). Belay on the ridge. Follow a system of slanting ledges slightly below the ridge on the N side (IV) which allow a gendarme to be turned. A well-defined brèche. Climb cracked slabs for 15m (III) towards a 'letter-box' with a jammed block. Belay. Get onto the jammed block to gain a first piton, traverse 3m right (the first piton helps the traverse but do not clip into it) to gain a crack which is climbed for 6–7m to an overhang. Escape on the right to avoid the overhang and go onto the S side of the step where the summit of the third step is gained up a system of flakes (V to the flakes, then III). Descend a short easy chimney for several metres, cross a small couloir and climb a crack and a short dièdre to the brèche at the foot of the fourth step. Climb for 6–7m a slab (thin crack, V), and then a ledge slanting left. Climb detached flakes to reach the summit of the fourth step. Follow the almost horizontal ridge for 20–25m to a brèche. Continue along the easy ridge (II and III) to the big ledge where

the Papillons Ridge ends. Observe on the right the descent route to the Papillons Couloir. Turn the gendarme 3009m on the left (E). This large ledge ascends diagonally from the N Ridge on the left to the brèche at 3043m on the right at the foot of the W Ridge and so skirts the foot of the final wall of the Peigne. This consists, as well as these two ridges, of the WNW Face (sometimes called the Chamonix Face, but which in fact faces Les Houches), of the NW Pillar and of the NW Face.

WNW Face: This is a concave wall above scree. Start 20m right of the Pillar up a crack system (IV) to a platform. Leave on the right and go up a series of cracks and dièdres (IV with a move of V), exiting on a large platform at the foot of a very steep wall. Above the centre of the platform climb a very open dièdre 10m high (V). The wall turns into a couloir which leads to the platform below the summit.

NW Pillar: Halfway up the slope above gendarme 3009 go up using two parallel cracks which cut across a slab, and gain the first step. Continue up a system of crack-dièdres to reach a fairly detached flake and continue straight up above to below an overhang (V) to reach the second step. Leave slightly left, then traverse right to gain a crack which looks ferocious but is in fact a fine pitch (two moves of V. Do not go left to an old sling). You are now at the foot of great monolithic slabs split by two cracks. Climb the left-hand one (A1) and leave it after 12—15m to move right (IV). Continue up a crack and then a chimney to reach the platform below the summit.

NW Face: At the end of the Papillons Ridge level with gendarme 3009 bear left towards a small platform directly below the summit. Climb a dièdre on the left (IV), then continue straight on above up short slabs (V) to an overhang. Now traverse right and, descending, climb a thin crack (A1) and pendulum into and climb a crack on the right (V). Slanting left gain 15m higher a quartz ledge (IV) level with a small niche. Straight above climb the crack with two overhangs (A1, A2), then free climb (V sup.) to a good platform. Climb the flake on the left (V sup.), then climb a second flake (IV), pass a niche and continue up a third flake (VI). Good platform. Traverse left (V), climb a flake leaning against the wall, and the dièdre (A1); then traverse left (V) to a good platform. Go up directly for 2m then slant up right (A1) and turn a corner (V) to gain a crack on the right and climb it (V). Traverse right and climb a short wall. An easy zone is now reached which leads to the platform below the summit.

Final step: From the platform climb the Lépiney Crack (V) running obliquely across the wall (J. de Lépiney climbed this with his right leg, side and arm jammed in the crack). Above, a short chimney (IV sup.) leads to a ledge on the left. Follow this ledge which descends to the left and narrows into a thin crack (A1, an easy but very exposed pitch) to the corner of a dièdre which is climbed (IV sup.) to the brèche below the summit.

N Ridge: From the brèche E of gendarme 3009 traverse left beyond the ridge and gain the huge dièdre forming the line of the route. First climb cracks (IV) for 30m. Avoid an overhang on the left (IV) to gain a chimney (IV) which is climbed for about 30m to a roof. Avoid the roof on the right (V) and go up easily to a belay. Make a delicate traverse across a slab (V) to gain on the right a typical Chamonix crack and climb the whole of it (about 35m, V then IV) to where it is closed by a roof, which can be climbed directly with an exit on the right (V), or on the left (V sup.). Climb the large chimney which follows (IV), a very steep crack (V sup.), then the dièdre (bridging). Traverse right (A1), climb a slanting crack (V sup.), then a second crack (IV, wedges) to reach the crevice between a big detached block and the wall. Exit left and for 20m go straight up a very open dièdre with a thin crack (V). Traverse slightly left, then go up cracks (IV) on the right in the direction of a niche (IV). Climb the edge of the niche (IV), then a small overhang (IV sup.) to reach the summit crest left of the summit (3–4 hrs).

Descent: Initially by the ordinary route, that is by an abseil from the summit block right of the Lépiney Crack, then down the W Ridge. Leave the ordinary route and go S to the 'dining room', continue down the ridge to reach brèche 3043, descend the diagonal ledge and then the upper part of the Papillons Ridge. When you reach the brèche above the fourth step of the lower part of the ridge, follow a ledge slanting right which leads to the bed of the Papillons Couloir. Then go back left down a dièdre which leads back to the very easy couloir which is left above its lower steps to follow a track which passes through a little brèche and leads to the Peigne névé.

The Aiguille du Peigne, West Face and Papillons Ridge (opposite page).
The North Face of the Aiguille du Peigne and the Aiguille des Pèlerins (above).

53. POINTE LACHENAL 3613m
South-South-East Face
AIGUILLE DU MIDI 3800m
Eperon des Cosmiques

From Mont Blanc du Tacul (4248m) a steep, winding ridge leads to the Col des Rognons (3415m); a little before the col is a point, only a minor snow-shoulder on the N side, but is on the S a fine ochre-coloured granite face plunging down to the glacier. This is Point 3613, also known as Pointe Lachenal to commemorate that remarkable climber and guide, killed in November 1955 at La Bédière, in a crevasse in the Vallée Blanche. In fact to set off for the Lachenal is to set off to a face apparently made for the climber, in majestic surroundings and having an elegant shape due to its purity of line, with sections rather less massive than is usual in this range.

The climbing, mostly balance-climbing, is very pleasant on solid granite with good belays, except for one belay in étriers on the artificial section. This latter, however, is not particularly awkward, since the pitons are good. The face is some 250m high and the average time needed to climb it is about 3 hrs, provided — and this is in fact the case — that all the pitons are in place. This makes it rather a short climb; I suggest therefore that rather than going back to the Aiguille du Midi by the rather boring ordinary route, you should take the Eperon des Cosmiques, which is attractive if not very difficult. Above the spur the climb joins the Arête des Cosmiques, and you will have a more extensive view. The combination of routes can easily be done in the day.

Pointe Lachenal

● **1st ascent:** P. Labrunie and R. Wohl-schlag with A. Contamine, 30 August 1959.

● **Vertical height:** About 250m (from 3350 to 3613m).

● **Grade:** TD (40 pitons in place, of which a third are big angles and wedges).

● **Time:** 45 mins from the Aiguille du Midi to the start of the difficulties. $2\frac{1}{2}$–$3\frac{1}{2}$ hrs from there to the summit.

● **Equipment:** Carabiners, étriers.

● **Starting point:** Aiguille du Midi (3800m), Cosmiques Hut (3613m), or the Torino Hut (3375m) which takes an hour longer.

● **Route** – *Outline:* The lower section of the route is a diagonal line going from the lowest point of the rock to the highest platform on the ridge on the right of the wall. The upper section follows the ridge on its S side to the summit crest.

Description: From the Aiguille du Midi, cross the Col des Rognons and go right to reach the foot of the face. Climb a narrow crack splitting a smooth slab (V), then traverse a slab left to reach and climb a wide crack (V) to a zone of blocks and terraces (V). Climb a short dièdre (V), gain a quartz ledge and climb a crack on the right to the ridge (V sup.). It is possible to leave this crack halfway up for another on the left,

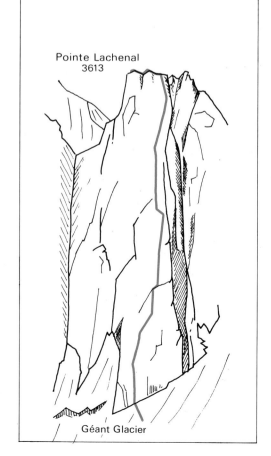

Pointe Lachenal
3613

Géant Glacier

exiting through a groove in the overhang dominating it (V).

Follow the ridge (IV and V) to a large terrace on the right side of the ridge. Cross the ridge to climb a crack running up a 50m high wall of slabs (A1). The angle eases; continue up slabs and cracks, gain the crest of the ridge on the right, climb an arête and continue easily to the summit shoulder.

If the slope is iced on the N side, it is better briefly to follow the W Ridge and traverse across onto the flat part of the glacier.

Eperon des Cosmiques
● **1st ascent:** B. Pierre with G. Rébuffat, 13 August 1956.
● **Vertical height:** About 120m (from 3600 to 3720m).
● **Grade:** D with a pitch of V, A1.
● **Time:** 1½–2½ hrs from the start of the difficulties to the top of the buttress.
● **Equipment:** Carabiners, étriers.
● **Route** – *Outline:* The route first takes a diagonal line slanting right from the couloir and crossing at its weakest point the inverted staircase barrier of roofs, and then goes vertically up by a groove system.

Description: From the couloir follow to the right a series of terraces narrowing to a thin crack which leads below the roof (IV).

Traverse 2m right and climb the overhang (V, A1). Climb the grooves in three rope-lengths (IV); bear left at the top. The route is more elegant and exposed if you gain the ridge on the left and climb it (IV sup.), but it is also possible to take the short wall preceding it and exit right. From here climb a snow slope to rejoin the route along the Arête des Cosmiques.

Climbing on the Pointe Lachenal (opposite page).
Overhang on the Eperon des Cosmiques (above).

54. AIGUILLES DU DIABLE — MONT BLANC DU TACUL 4248m
Traverse

The traverse of the Aiguilles du Diable involves climbing five outstanding summits at over 4000m in superb surroundings. When I was young and could only dream of the traverse, I thought of it as something out of a western, a sort of fantastic ride up hill and down dale, along a wild ridge with an impressive name.

Since then I have been there a number of times, even in winter, and I have found it a magnificent route with pitches often difficult and of outstanding character. The atmosphere can be felt even as low down as the Col du Diable when you come out of the shadows of the W couloir and look out over a landscape unbroken to the horizon, giving an extraordinary sense of space when you emerge into the first rays of the sun. The climb traverses one after the other; the Corne du Diable (Devil's Horn) (4064m), a short rock-climb (III); the Pointe Chaubert (4074m), in the sun but with one delicate pitch (IV sup.); the Médiane (4097m), 80m high with several moves of IV; the Carmen (4109m), whose difficulty depends on conditions, since it is climbed on the NE Face; finally, the Isolée (4114m), which you should definitely climb by the original route (V), even if it is more difficult than the

later variant (IV), which avoids the difficulty.

But of course there are descents as well as ascents, and these often involve steep and delicate abseils to get down to the brèches. The traverse is thus not only difficult but also serious, demanding high skill in rock-climbing and in mountaineering. You must not allow your mind to wander; it is essential when abseiling to follow the correct route, and to arrive at a good platform; a lot of awkward rope-management is needed. Finally there are abrupt and frequent changes from hard climbing on dry rock (as on the Chamonix Aiguilles, but here at over 4000m), to mixed climbing (as on the Tour Ronde Ridge on Mont Maudit). Here bad weather is to be particularly feared.

- **1st ascent:** Miss M. O'Brien and R. L. M. Underhill with A. Charlet and G. Cachat, 4 August 1928.
- **Vertical height:** 576m from the Torino Hut (3375m) to the Col du Diable (3951m); 297m from the col to Mont Blanc du Tacul (4248m); in all 873m (from 3375 to 4248m). Naturally the actual height involved is much greater owing to the ascents and descents.
- **Grade:** D sup., with a pitch of V. It is worth remembering that no pitons were

used on the 1st ascent. There are numerous abseils, some of which are tricky.

- **Time:** $1\frac{1}{2}$ hrs from the Torino Hut (3375m) to the bergschrund (you should allow $2\frac{1}{2}$ hrs from the Cosmiques Hut [3613m]). 2–$2\frac{1}{2}$ hrs from the bergschrund to the col. $3\frac{1}{2}$ hrs from the col to the Médiane. 3 hrs from the Médiane to the Isolée. 1 hr from the Isolée to Mont Blanc du Tacul. 11–12 hrs in all from the Torino Hut to the summit.
- **Equipment:** Crampons, carabiners, abseil rope.
- **Starting point:** The Torino Hut (3375m). It is also possible to start from the Cosmiques Hut (3613m).
- **Route** – *Outline:* This is of course shown by the line of aiguilles along the ridge, but for each of the aiguilles individually, there is no continuous line. The route uses the ground to the best advantage, sometimes on one side, sometimes on the other.

Description: From the Torino Hut ascend to the top of the Géant Glacier and the Combe Maudite to the second snow couloir after the Clocher ($1\frac{1}{2}$ hrs). It is also possible to go up the couloir beyond, which descends directly from the Col du Diable. Cross the bergschrund (about 3580m) and ascend the couloir, then slant left to gain the Col du Diable by snowy rocks and little secondary couloirs (3951m; 2–$2\frac{1}{2}$ hrs).

Follow the thin snow ridge then go up mixed ground turning the Corne du Diable on the left to the Brèche Chaubert (4047m; 30 mins). From here climb first (III, III sup.) the Corne du Diable (4064m) and abseil back to the brèche (30 mins). Continue up a smooth slab (IV sup.) and the arête which leads to the Pointe Chaubert (4074m; 30 mins). Descend the NW Face of the Chaubert with 3 abseils to the E notch of the Brèche Médiane. Turn a gendarme on its N side to gain the lowest W notch of the Brèche Médiane (4017m; 30 mins) and the foot of the Médiane itself. Slant up right by steps to reach the foot of a large 40m dièdre. This can be climbed entirely at the back (IV sup.) but generally after climbing 15m (IV) a traverse is made right (IV) to the E Ridge of the Médiane. Then climb a 15m crack (IV) to a small platform on the E Ridge. Now follow a ledge for 5–6m on the NE side on the right and climb slabs for 8–10m to regain the ridge. Descend 2m left, and cross the top of the large dièdre. The summit of the Médiane is pierced by two 'letter-boxes'; do not go up to that on the right but gain that on the left firstly to gain the summit and then to abseil directly (30m) to the Brèche de la Carmen (4078m). If an abseil were made from the right-hand window it would not lead to the brèche and at the end of the abseil you would have

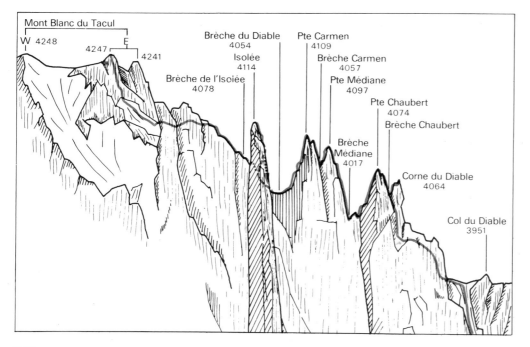

Mont Blanc du Tacul
W 4248 E
4247 4241
Brèche du Diable 4054
Isolée 4114
Brèche de l'Isoiée 4078
Pte Carmen 4109
Brèche Carmen 4057
Pte Médiane 4097
Pte Chaubert 4074
Brèche Chaubert
Brèche Médiane 4017
Corne du Diable 4064
Col du Diable 3951

to make a traverse which can be very delicate in some conditions. Climb cold cracks (IV), sometimes iced, slightly right of the E Ridge, then traverse the N side of the E horn to turn it and reach the platform between the two horns. Climb the higher, the W horn, by its E Ridge (IV) (4109m; 1 hr from the Médiane).

From the platform between the two horns abseil first down a chimney on the right, then direct to the ridge and the Brèche du Diable (4054m; 30 mins). You now reach the foot of the Isolée slightly left of the ridge; either climb this direct (III) or traverse if you have gone on up towards the Brèche de l'Isolée (4054m; 30 mins); gain cracks and climb them to below a big hanging flake (on its left you have passed an overhanging nose). Make a nice move left, protected by a piton put in fairly high up, to reach a good platform (V). This pitch

can be avoided by the Contamine variant traversing left below the overhanging nose (IV) to climb diagonally across the S Face first up a flake and then up a dièdre and a short wall (IV) to a platform.

From here the summit of the Isolée can easily be reached (4114m; 1 hr).

Abseil (25m) from the platform and continue to the Brèche de l'Isolée, follow the crest of the ridge keeping at first slightly right (easy broken rocks), then go back left by a small arête of sound rock to reach the summit of Mont Blanc du Tacul (4248m; 1 hr).

The Aiguilles du Diable: the Isolée on the left, the Carmen and the Médiane in the centre, the Chaubert and the Corne du Diable on the right; below is the Col du Diable, above is Mont Blanc du Tacul; the Combe Maudite is at the bottom, and the Grandes Jorasses are in the background.

55. AIGUILLE DU MIDI 3800m
South Face

This is a superb climb from all points of view, and not least because of its character. In 1956, when the face was unclimbed, Maurice Baquet and I felt that it was on the great slabs that we would find the most impressive and the finest route. We were right: climbing, even just being, right in the middle of these slabs is a pleasure because of their shape and their atmosphere, the texture and colour of the granite. Both the stances and the pitches are varied. The climbing is stylish: a series of fine moves, in balance, demanding suppleness and coordination. If he is to do the climb well, to feel himself at one with the rock, with the extraordinary landscape, with the sky above and the Vallée Blanche below, with Mont Blanc to the W and the Jorasses to the E, the climber should only undertake the route when he is technically highly competent and very fit. In such a case the climbing is effortless, and you will wish that the route were twice or three times as long.

Two other routes, more artificial and more traditional in line and style, have been done: on the SE Ridge, to the right, in 1957, by M. Bron, C. Bozon, A. Contamine, J. Juge and P. Labrunie; on the edge of the face, to the left, in 1963, by P. Laffont, P. Mazeaud and A. Tsinant. These too are worth climbing.
- **1st ascent**: M. Baquet and G. Rébuffat, 13 July 1956.
- **Vertical height**: About 200m (from 3600 to 3800m).
- **Grade**: TD (with 15 pitons).
- **Time**: 3–5 hrs from the start of the difficulties to the summit (as long as the pitons — of which 15 are belays — are in place).
- **Equipment**: Carabiners, étriers.
- **Starting point**: Aiguille du Midi téléphérique, Cosmiques Hut.
- **Route** – *Outline*: The route starts right of a point directly below the summit to pass between the two great roofs, and then slants left across the wall. At the summit

block it goes right onto the N Face for the original route, or takes the Cretton Dièdre which ends at the W shoulder, and follows the ridge to the summit.

Description: Just right of a point directly below the summit, climb a cracked slab then a chimney (III) to reach a platform above a small pillar separated from the face. Climb 2m left up a slightly overhanging slab (V), then using a good crack for the hands traverse right. There are now two possibilities:
– go straight up a thin crack with a wedge (A1);
– continue the traverse right, pull up onto a flake (V) and climb a slab right of the thin crack, not very steep but smooth and exposed.

You have now reached a big roof. Turn this on the left and follow an S-shaped crack (A1 and V) which splits the magnificent red slab. Descend 2m left for a stance. Climb on the right up a crack (V) and then traverse horizontally left.

Go up slightly left by a system of well-defined cracks (IV and V). Climb an overhang (A1) on the right and go slightly left again to reach a large platform. Then climb a crack system (IV) at first directly, then on the right, then left again, to reach an excellent ledge. Continue up a dièdre slanting right (IV) interrupted by a 2m slightly overhanging wall (V), then climb a crack-chimney

142

(V), which is not very steep but with poor holds. Exit on the left to a platform. Move left and climb a short step by a crack.

There are now two possibilities:

— turn on the right a magnificent obelisk of red granite and gain the shoulder E of the final arrowhead. Descend 3–4m — take care not to go too low — down the couloir NE of the brèche to climb the N side of the summit block, sometimes covered with snow and verglas (A1 and V) and then climb a 4m slab to the summit.

— traverse left (a move of V) to reach a crack (IV) which splits a large slab; when this crack becomes horizontal — for 1m — cross a corner and make a traverse which looks more difficult than it is (IV) to gain a crack (IV) interrupted by an overhang. In this way the shoulder SW of the summit block is reached. Climb the left flank of the ridge (IV) and reach the summit by a small slab (V).

The S-shaped crack on the great slabs (opposite page).

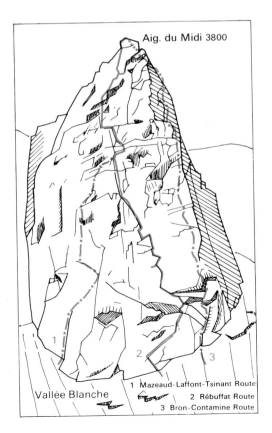

Aig. du Midi 3800

Vallée Blanche

1 Mazeaud-Laffont-Tsinant Route
2 Rébuffat Route
3 Bron-Contamine Route

56. MONT BLANC 4807m
The Brenva Spur

The Brenva Face of Mont Blanc is a high, major face of vast expanse. The climb is a technically difficult undertaking, but the combination of the names Mont Blanc and Brenva suggest an atmosphere, and this atmosphere you will feel when you leave the Torino Hut (at one time the Requin Hut was used) to go to the Col de la Fourche. The Brenva cirque, a great semi-circular wall, is there behind the crest. You spend the night at the little bivouac hut on the Col de la Fourche, or at the Ghiglione Hut just above it, and the next morning, in the middle of the night, you go downhill and into the cirque. The first light of dawn appears as you reach the Col Moore, with the morning mist dispersing in the Aosta Valley and in all the smaller valleys around.

Above the climbers is the Brenva, not too difficult at first, but awe-inspiring.

After the horizontal ridge comes the main slope, fairly easy on snow but delicate if it is iced. You come to a rock outcrop, and here there is the line of seracs. Twenty or so years ago, they were easy to cross, but now they are much more difficult with the advance of the glacier; they give an impressive atmosphere, and round off a climb with only one disadvantage: that it ends at the Col de la Brenva, leaving a further 500m to climb, these 500m being too easy to be really absorbing and coming at a point where the technical interest of the climb is much less. But your arrival on the summit is rewarding, and it is always a pleasure to go down the magnificent Bosses Ridge. If you are going down on the French side, you can go via either the Grands Mulets or the Aiguille du Goûter; if on the Italian side, you will take the so-called Aiguilles Grises Route, and then the Miage Glacier, with its gloomy barren moraines.

The first ascent of Mont Blanc by the Brenva Spur was done 15 July 1865, the day after the first ascent of the Matterhorn. The latter has quite outshone the former, because of the fame of the Matterhorn, because of the race between Carrel and Whymper and between Whymper and his own compatriots, and of course because of the catastrophe. And yet both, in their different ways, were outstanding exploits, and J. and M. Anderegg, working their way up this great snow and ice route, with no pitons and with only the equipment available at the time, are in the same category as M. Croz scaling the summit rocks of the Matterhorn, without pitons and without fixed ropes.

Leave the hut very early, do the route if possible by moonlight, make sure you are very fit; provided these conditions are fulfilled, no young climber could fail to find this route very exhilarating; he will understand what is meant by the term 'major route'. But he should also imagine what it must be like in poor weather, or during a Mont Blanc thunderstorm.

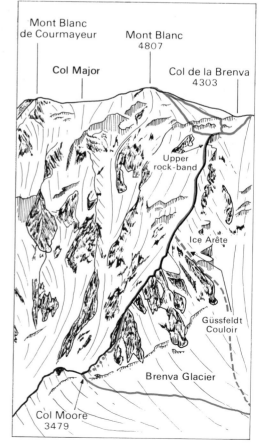

● **1st ascent:** G. S. Matthews, A. W. Moore, F. and H. Walker, with J. and M. Anderegg, 15 July 1865.

● **Vertical height:** 180m of descent from the Col de la Fourche Hut (3680m) to the Col Moore (3500m); 1307m from the Col Moore to the summit (from 3500 to 4807m).

● **Grade:** Variable according to the state of the great slope and the serac bulge, but even in good conditions, it has the feeling of a major route only to be undertaken in a period of good settled weather.

● **Time:** 1 hr from the hut to the Col Moore. 6–10 hrs from the Col Moore to the summit.

● **Equipment:** Crampons (ice-screws).

● **Starting point:** The Col de la Fourche Hut (about 3680m) or the Col du Trident de la Brenva Hut (3690m; also known as the Ghiglione Hut).

● **Route** – *Outline:* The spur gives the line itself and may be divided into four sections: the spur proper of which the mixed crest is followed to reach the horizontal snow ridge (this snow ridge may be gained directly from the Brenva Glacier by the Güssfeldt Couloir, a shorter and quicker route but more difficult; the slope of the couloir is very steep, a little exposed to falling seracs during the approach, then somewhat less so in the couloir); the great slope; the serac bulge which may be climbed directly or turned on the right; the final easy slope of Mont Blanc.

Description: From the hut (3680m) after descending the slope (pick out the best line the evening before) and gaining the glacier, cross it to reach the Col Moore (3500m). Turn the bottom of the spur on the left of the ridge and then go up it to a big step which is avoided on the left. A diagonal rake, then chimneys and short easy névés lead back to the spur which turns into a fine snow ridge, almost horizontal for a moment, overlooking on the left a bulging slope and on the right the steep and vertiginous Güssfeldt Couloir, which joins the spur to the great slope up which the route now continues, keeping on the right the rocks bounding it.

Reach the highest rocks and climb these slightly on the left, then returning right climb the serac wall barring access to the summit slopes, which are easy but cut by deep narrow bergschrunds sometimes barely visible. It is possible also to traverse right below the serac barrier on ice ledges; this traverse used to be made at the level of the rock point, but now, because of the advance of the glacier, you must take the traverse lower. To do this make an abseil (slings in place on the rock). Finally it is also possible to traverse left and find a way through the seracs to reach the summit slopes. The exact choice of route depends upon the conditions at the time, so this is a route which calls not only for technique but also for the climber's judgement and mountaineering sense.

The serac barrier above the last rock outcrop (opposite page).
The Brenva Face of Mont Blanc from the Dent du Géant (above).

57. DENT DU GÉANT 4013m
South Face

At the beginning of the ridge going towards the Jorasses and which overlooks the smiling Val Veni and the majestic Vallée Blanche, the Dent stands like a lighthouse. A familiar sight, with its pure silhouette and its simple lines, standing above the vast glacier valleys; it leans over slightly, a reminder perhaps of those tormented epochs when the Alps were born. An ever-recurring miracle in granite, always there for the delight of man. And man, naturally, has attempted climbs on all its faces, including, of course, the leaning side, the overhanging S Face. Overhang is the correct word, and I have good reason to know it; in 1964, at the top of the second rope-length, I came off and fell without touching the rock straight onto the snow 25m below — and lucky that it was snow, which falls away steeply under the face, so that I fell glancingly and not crushingly.

The first ascent of the S Face, in 1935, is a milestone in the history of rock-climbing in the range; it was here that pitons, already familiar and current in the Eastern Alps, were first used systematically, thus inaugurating the artificial techniques which were later to allow the first ascents of the E Face of the Capucin, the W Face of the Drus and other routes.

On the Géant face some of the pitons still in place date from that first ascent: the clumsiest, among them some ring-pitons. The climb lasted several days and the climbers several times needed to descend and go back to Courmayeur.

Today, the S Face of the Géant is no longer a major, or even a very difficult, climb; it is quite short, the pitons are in place, and its primary attraction is as a fine climb, varied since it is not by any means entirely artificial, very enjoyable and between 3800 and 4000m. Moreover, it is a climb which makes intelligent and imaginative use of the rock. This is why it is not direct, but contains several free-climbing traverses. Unfortunately, the rock is not always very sound.

● **1st ascent:** M. Burgasser and R. Leitz, 28 July 1935.
● **Vertical height:** About 160m (from 3850 to 4013m).
● **Grade:** TD, 25 pitons.
● **Time:** 2 hrs from the Col du Géant to the start of the difficulties. 2—3 hrs from there to the summit.
● **Equipment:** Carabiners, étriers.
● **Starting point:** Col du Géant.
● **Route** — *Outline:* Between the two summits, but slightly more below the SW summit, a relatively deep although fairly open couloir comes down. Halfway up the wall this couloir ends at a zone of terraces level with a compact bulge overlooking a pillar. The route follows the dièdre left of the pillar, then turns the bulge on the right and returns left to the terraces to continue up the whole of the couloir and exit right at the top of the brèche. A fairly uncomplicated route well chosen to fit the terrain.

Description: In the recess left of the pillar, climb the dièdre between the wall and the pillar. First you reach, after 10m or so (IV), a fine triangular platform. Continue straight up for about 15m (IV and V), traverse slightly right, climb a short wall (V) and by the arête above the pillar climb (IV sup.) to a small platform on which to belay.

Climb the slightly overhanging slab above (A1), then traverse right (A1, rather delicate; V, suspect rock) to turn the compact bulge. After a detour right, return back left

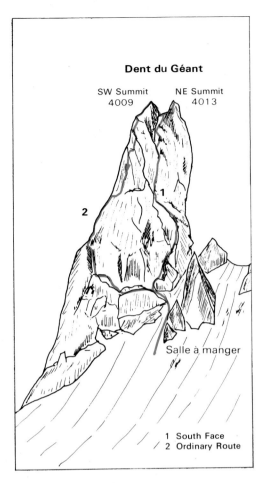

Dent du Géant

SW Summit
4009

NE Summit
4013

1

2

Salle à manger

1 South Face
2 Ordinary Route

to the foot of an open and slightly over-hanging dièdre. Climb this (A1, V) to a short wall, a ledge leading back left above the bulge and to the foot of the couloir cutting the upper section of the face. Climb straight up (IV) then, when the crack begins to overhang, climb the slab on the right (A1 and V) and return to the crack. Make an ascending traverse right to gain a dièdre from which you exit right and climb a short wall to reach a good platform at the base of the final 30m overhanging wall. Climb this mostly by artificial means (A1) bearing right, then some very fine difficult free-climbing — short walls and ledges — leads to below the brèche between the two summits.

The Dent du Géant looking at the ordinary route: the South Face is on the right, and the beginning of the Grandes Jorasses ridge in the background (right). The first pitch on the South Face (opposite page).

58. PIC ADOLPHE REY 3535m
Salluard Route

All in straight, stark lines, soaring skywards above the curving, sweeping, cold expanse of the glacier, red granite whose texture, even after sunset, seems to glow with light; such are the Pic Adolphe Rey and its E Ridge, standing sentinel at a curve in the Vallée Blanche and the Combe Maudite, at the meeting-point of two valleys. This summit, in itself so clean-cut, is only one pillar among several, all just as extraordinary, which from the Boccalatte to the NE of the Trident, from the Clocher to the Aiguilles du Diable on the other, SE, side crowd round the cathedral of Mont Blanc du Tacul. All this makes for exhilarating surroundings for the climber. And the climbing is excellent, a bit strenuous, demanding both technique and strength as one might expect in this world of stone. For all these reasons, and others too, especially the fact that it has easy access, make the Salluard Route on the Pic Adolphe Rey a very popular route.

● **1st ascent**: T. Busi with F. Salluard, 6 September 1951.
● **Vertical height**: About 300m (from 3200 to 3535m).
● **Grade**: TD, 30 pitons.
● **Time**: 4–5 hrs from the start of the difficulties to the summit.

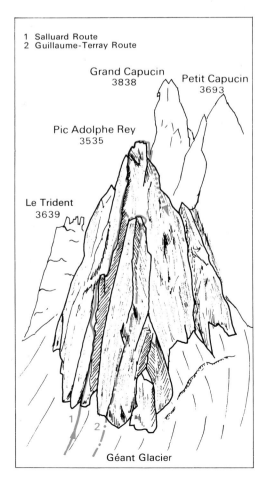

1 Salluard Route
2 Guillaume-Terray Route

Grand Capucin 3838
Petit Capucin 3693
Pic Adolphe Rey 3535
Le Trident 3639
Géant Glacier

- **Equipment:** Carabiners, étriers.
- **Starting point:** The Cosmiques Hut (3613m) or the Torino Hut (3375m). Usually the route can be done in the day by taking the first cable-car to the Aiguille du Midi or the Pointe Helbronner.
- **Route** – *Outline:* The ENE Ridge of the Pic Adolphe Rey descends in steps to the Géant Glacier. There are two routes. On the left is the Salluard Route, on the right the Guillaume-Terray Route, each taking one of two parallel ridges which join 100m below the summit (for the upper third of the ridge). The right-hand ridge descends lower to the glacier. Between this and the left-hand ridge there is a short snow slope by which the Salluard Route is approached. The line of ascent then takes roughly the S side of the ridge (except for the summit part) and so is in the sun. This makes the climbing very pleasant and exhilarating.

Description: Ascend the short snow slope right of the Salluard Route to start at the foot of the ridge which quickly steepens. Climb a wall (10m; IV sup.), an overhang (V sup.) and a crack (35m, V) to a good belay. Climb a small bulge above (5m, V) then climb a dièdre (IV) on the left which leads to a big terrace. Continue up a chimney (IV sup.), avoiding on the left the overhang closing it (V). Above either go left up a wide sloping crack leading to a short inclined wall (V) and then easy slabs which lead to terraces, or (less tiring but more difficult) traverse right (V) and climb a chimney on the N side of the ridge. Climb cracks (30m, IV sup.) up a vertical step and gain a little brèche on the ridge. Go up 40m (IV), climb a short wall (V sup.) and slant left (IV sup.) to pass through a hole. Traverse left, take a dièdre right of a chimney (IV sup.), then slant left to gain easily a brèche at the foot of the big gendarme (where the Salluard and Guillaume-Terray ridges join). Climb on the N side a wall (IV sup.), an easy ramp, although sometimes covered with verglas, and another wall (IV) to a brèche. Descend 2m on the S side, traverse left to a dièdre and climb it (V). Cross an inclined slab (20m, III) and return to the ridge (climbing several steps) which is followed easily to the summit.

Descent: From the foot of the last step below the summit, descend about 10m to a 'letter-box'. From there a 35m abseil leads to a vast terrace of blocks obvious from above. Descend easy rocks on the Petit Capucin side to gain a second terrace above a deep chimney on the SW side. Make two fairly impressive abseils: the first of about 40m (do not stop at the slings after 30m), and the second of 30m leading to the foot of the chimney from which an easy traverse (IV) can be made to the Pic Adolphe Rey-Petit Capucin Couloir which leads to the glacier.

Start of the Salluard Route (opposite page).
The geometry of granite: the Salluard in front, with the Trident and the Grand Capucin on the left (above).

149

59. MONT BLANC DU TACUL 4248m
Gervasutti Couloir

Snow routes fall into three broad categories: ridges, faces and couloirs, and of these last the Gervasutti Couloir is a prime example. It is 800m long, straight, narrow, closed in by two rock spurs and opening outwards towards the top. It is an obvious and very elegant line. In 1929, three Italian alpinists, P. Filippi, P. Ghiglione and F. Ravelli, undertook the climb, but only took the couloir to a halfway point, at which they

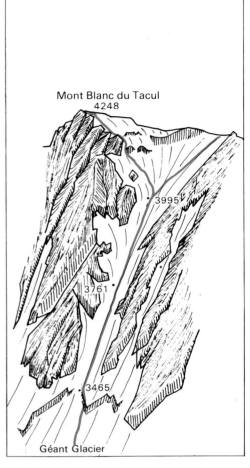

Mont Blanc du Tacul
4248

3995

3761

3465

Géant Glacier

bore right and used the rock spur on the left bank of the couloir. Five years later R. Chabod and G. Gervasutti, more confident in their judgement and in their technique, using front-point crampons, climbed the couloir direct straight to the summit. The route has since become a classic, but most climbers come out onto the summit ridge at about 4150m, right of the seracs. This makes the route less elegant but safer, since the climber spends less time below the threatening seracs, cornices and possible stonefalls; in any case whereas the exit to the right is always feasible, that to the left depends on conditions, although it is always possible to use the rocks which are often iced. The angle is steep, and the Vallot guide gives the following figures: from 3460 to 3760m, 45° (in the runnel); from 3760 to 3995m, $49\frac{1}{2}$°; from 3995m to the foot of the seracs, 55° or more.

From the technical point of view, you should be highly competent on crampons, but with the slope being so regular, I find the actual process of cramponning rather tedious, as is indeed usually the case in a couloir. My pleasure therefore comes from

elsewhere; that of climbing in an untamed world, with nothing but vertiginous and unadorned lines, and that of feeling to the depths of my being that I am following a route worthy of so much beauty. Finally, the couloir is called after Gervasutti in honour of that inspired climber, but we should not forget, if only because the two men were friends, the name of his companion the brilliant snow- and ice-climber Chabod.

● **1st ascent:** R. Chabod and G. Gervasutti, 13 August 1934.

● **Vertical height:** About 800m (from 3450 to 4248m).

● **Grade:** A very steep and continuous ice route. The direct finish can be very difficult. The whole of the route is exposed to falling seracs, cornices and stones, but the direct finish especially so.

● **Time:** 2–5 hrs from the start of the difficulties to the N Ridge of Mont Blanc du Tacul by the right-hand finish; 3–8 hrs from the start to the summit by the direct finish. In fact the time depends very much on the conditions, the climber's fitness, his technique and on the different types of snow and ice. If the slope has good snow

from start to finish, and this is rare especially on the upper part of the direct finish, then the route, despite the angle, can be climbed quickly and is almost easy. The climber will have the deep secret pleasure of having mastered the slope, its steepness, its attraction, and the snow itself. If the snow is poor, then the route will seem long, unpleasant and arduous, especially if the climber is not experienced on slopes where the snow and and ice is inconsistent and irregular.

● **Equipment:** Crampons, ice-screws.

● **Starting point:** The Cosmiques Hut (3613m) or the Torino Hut (3375m).

● **Route** – *Outline:* The couloir itself with the right-hand finish if you wish to gain the N Ridge of Mont Blanc du Tacul, and with the left-hand finish if you wish to reach the summit directly.

Description: From the Col du Midi (over the Col des Rognons) or the Col du Géant which adds about an hour to the approach, gain the slope and cross the bergschrund (3460m) by the runnel. Above climb the right bank generally but this depends on the conditions. If the direct route is chosen, go up towards the seracs, turn them on the

left and finish between the two summits. If you choose the more usual route, cross the line of the couloir at the easiest point above the narrowing halfway up, and ascend the great slope on the right to finish on the N Ridge of Mont Blanc du Tacul.

In the couloir (opposite page).
The summit ridge (above).

151

60. LE MINARET 3450m
South-East Spur and South Face Direct

The Jardin Ridge on the Aiguille d'Argentière has a large number of different towers, gendarmes and faces which provide a number of very interesting climbs, especially on the SE side of the ridge above the Améthystes Glacier. The rock is a fine red granite, and since the ridge faces the sun, climbing is truly pleasurable, especially in surroundings such as these which combine the gentle slopes of the glaciers, ideal for spring skiing, with the steep N faces of the Triolet, the Courtes or the Droites. Among these different faces, one stands out: the Minaret, on the Améthystes side of the ridge. It offers three possibilities: the ordinary S Face Route and the S Face Direct, both of these about 300m high, and the SE Spur, rather shorter and indisputably the finest route. On the other hand, considering that the approach march is minimal and that the

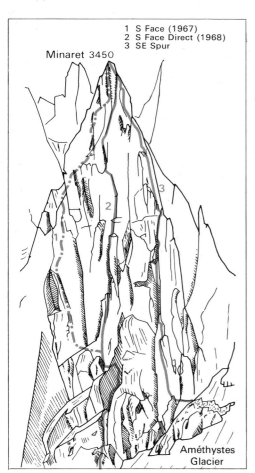

1 S Face (1967)
2 S Face Direct (1968)
3 SE Spur

Minaret 3450

Améthystes Glacier

rock itself is unusually vertical for a granite peak, it is worth coming back to do another of the S Face routes if other major routes are out of condition because of snow or bad weather.

SE Spur.
- **1st ascent:** R. Mazars with G. Rébuffat and P. de Cléry with H. Cretton, 29 July 1966.
- **Vertical height:** About 250m (from 3200 to 3450m).
- **Grade:** Sustained TD, almost entirely free-climbing (7–8m of A1-A2, numerous pitches of V and three of V sup.), 15 pitons.
- **Time:** 1 hr from the hut to the start of the difficulties. 8 hrs from there to the summit (time for the first ascent, including time to put in 15 pitons).
- **Equipment:** Pitons, carabiners, étriers.
- **Starting point:** The Argentière Hut (2771m).
- **Route** – *Outline:* The SE Spur goes up with two towers from the Améthystes Glacier, and ends at the airy summit. The first tower forms a narrow compact wall of very red granite in the form of a spire. On its right edge this spire has a small shoulder in its upper third from which an obvious groove descends forming a narrow chimney at the top and a wide couloir at the bottom. This groove forms the main line of the ascent in the lower half. Above, the route follows the ridge.

Description: From the Argentière Hut (2771m) ascend the moraine on the right bank of the Améthystes Glacier, get onto this glacier and reach the foot of the SE Spur of the Minaret at about 3150m (1 hr). Go along easy ledges to gain the groove mentioned above, here very wide, where there is a fairly obvious detached flake on its right. Here the climbing proper starts.

First tower: Go up easily for several metres, then climb a dièdre (two moves of IV sup.) to reach a poorly defined shoulder. Continue up a dièdre (a move of V) then up grooves (IV sup.). To avoid the overhang above, traverse slightly left and climb grooves (a move of V sup.), then return right to the line of the main groove (V).

There is a chimney above. Avoid the overhang start on the left (V, wedge), to bridge up this chimney (IV sup.). Continue up the chimney (IV-IV sup.) and exit right onto the shoulder of the first tower.

From there the wall facing SE above the shoulder is climbed. Initially climb steep worn slabs with excellent holds (III), continue up slabs (V) and bear left to get back onto the ridge proper of the spur. Climb the last step, made up of short walls (III), and gain the summit of the first tower. Descend to the brèche.

Second tower: Start slightly left of the ridge following a system of cracks which runs out after 5–6m below a small overhang which is climbed (A1-A2). Continue up grooves initially vertical (V, a move of A1), then bearing right (III). Climb a flake (IV sup.), pull up onto a sloping arête (V) and climb it. Climb a short dièdre (V sup.) to reach a second short wall and go up this to the top of the second tower. Descend to the brèche.

Summit tower: Climb a small slightly detached gendarme (IV). Descend 2m to climb the slab beyond (V sup.), protected by the rope passing over the gendarme. From there gain a cracked dièdre and climb it (III). Instead of going directly up from the brèche, it is also possible to descend the NE side for about 10m and then traverse right (IV sup.) to gain a large ledge well to the right. From there go back left to reach either at its start or slightly above (IV sup.) the crack running up the back of the dièdre mentioned above (III). Climb a short crack (III sup.) to gain the ridge, climb a little dièdre slightly left (V), then return to the ridge to go up a slightly overhanging dièdre with two jammed blocks (V). Climb the slab which follows using a flake (IV sup., V); the final mantleshelf is delicate as the rock is rounded (V). Go up right and climb a short wall (III).

Layback up a crack (V, shoulder to start) then climb the slab which follows to gain the ridge, which is not too steep but very rounded, by a very delicate move (V sup.). Follow this ridge to the summit of the Minaret.

S Face Direct.
- **1st ascent:** P. Beylier with G. Crétin and G. Rébuffat, 1 August 1968.
- **Vertical height:** About 300m (from 3150 to 3450m).
- **Grade:** Sustained TD, 14 pitons (several artificial aid moves).
- **Time:** 10 hrs from the start of the difficulties to the summit (time for the first ascent, putting in the pitons).
- **Equipment:** Pitons, tape slings, carabiners, étriers.
- **Route** – *Outline:* The base of the S Face of the Minaret has three small protrusions into the Améthystes Glacier. The route goes up this base on the right, then after a short traverse, as opposed to the ordinary route up the S Face which takes a big couloir-chimney on the left, the direct route takes a

line straight up for about 200m and then slants right to finish on the SE Spur 20m below the summit.

Description: Start at the base of the face at the furthest right of the three small protrusions into the glacier. Go up a system of cracks and dièdres (IV, a move of V) and, when this system runs out just below an overhanging step, traverse left to gain a poorly-defined buttress (IV, a move of V), which leads to the E end of a large terrace. This is closed on the left (W) by a big gendarme.

Do not go as far as the couloir-chimney between the big gendarme on the left and the wall on the right, but climb immediately above the terrace up a wall ribbed by many steep cracks and grooves. In spite of a slight bulge just above the start, the first pitch is easy (III and IV). The second takes a chimney (V), then a wall (A1) with an exit by a step (V). The third, after a traverse right with a big stride, follows a crack-chimney (V and A1). Above take a chimney slightly on the left (IV) and exit right to a good belay. Then gain a ledge-terrace by a system of cracks and grooves (V then IV). From here climb a deep chimney on the left which goes up to the right. After 15m make a very delicate traverse left out of this chimney (A1 and a move of V sup.).

Now go up easily (III), then again traverse left (III) to ascend a crack (V, IV then V) for two pitches to finish on the SE Ridge of the Minaret. Climb this up the two very fine last pitches (V and V sup.).

The South Face of the Minaret, with the South-East Spur on the right.

61. AIGUILLE DU PEIGNE 3192m
Vaucher Route

The S side of the Aiguille du Peigne is a high face made up of slabs — almost, one might say, of a single slab, so regular is its shape and its angle — fairly broad, seamed all the way up by thin parallel cracks, which make it appear longer and even finer. Well-defined between the two deep couloirs which bound it and heighten its effect, the Boeuf Couloir to the left·and the Peigne Couloir on the right, the wall rises straight up from the Peigne névé and narrows towards the top to the slender, soaring gendarme 3068. Above, the style of the climbing changes: you follow a ridge and then the Lépiney Crack to reach the summit once again.

The climbing is altogether very fine and very varied. Ten or so pitons, including the belay pitons, are quite enough, and the climbing is free.

● **1st ascent:** P. Labrunie, M. Vaucher with A. Contamine, 11 August 1957.
● **Vertical height:** About 600m from the start of the difficulties to the summit (from 2600 to 3192m).
● **Grade:** TD, 10 pitons.
● **Time:** 4 hrs from the start of the difficulties to gendarme 3068. 1½ hrs from the gendarme to the summit. The route is quite feasible in the day.
● **Equipment:** Carabiners.
● **Starting point:** Plan de l'Aiguille (2310m).
● **Route** — *Outline:* The route makes skilful use of the details of the wall and goes up the middle of the slabs. In the upper third, when these are barred by overhangs, it traverses right to gain gendarme 3068 up a couloir between two ridges. Above, the route follows the SW Ridge and goes up the summit block on the NW side.

Description: At the top of the Peigne névé, 10m or so right of the Boeuf Couloir, cross the bergschrund and, climb cracks and grooves (IV, IV sup.) for three rope-lengths. Then follow a horizontal ledge right for 30m and climb a wide couloir for 50m (III). Go right to climb a hidden dièdre which is marked at the start by a slight overhang (V). Continue up the dièdre following to a terrace, traverse 3m left and climb a third dièdre (V inf.), which goes up to below the overhangs at the foot of a very large and obvious block easily seen from below. Climb an overhang (V) to reach and climb the chimney forming the right side of this block (V). Climb the short dièdre which follows. Belay on the right. Bear left up rock steps and climb two chimneys one after the other (IV and IV sup.) to gain a vast terrace dominated by overhangs. From the right-hand end of this terrace traverse right to gain and climb a big open dièdre going up below a roof (V, V sup.). Exit on the right, and cross two other dièdres (IV and V) to reach a small platform.

Climb a short vertical wall (V) which gives access to a grooved couloir which leads to gendarme 3068m. For two rope-lengths climb the back and the right-hand wall of the couloir (V) to reach a terrace at the foot of a short 5m vertical step closing the middle part of the couloir. Continue up it (V) and up the slanting chimney which follows (V) and reach gendarme 3068 by easy steps and then a traverse right (IV sup.). From there follow the W Ridge and the Lépiney Crack to the summit.

The West Face of the Aiguille du Peigne and the Aiguille des Pèlerins (opposite page). On the Vaucher Route (right).

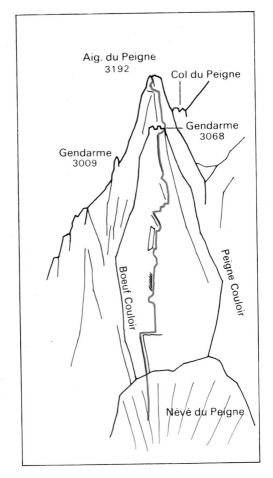

Aig. du Peigne 3192

Col du Peigne

Gendarme 3068

Gendarme 3009

Boeuf Couloir

Peigne Couloir

Névé du Peigne

62. AIGUILLE DU MIDI 3800m
Frendo Spur

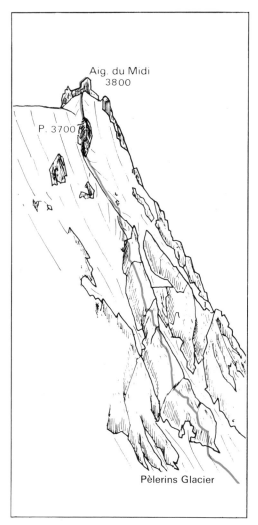

Aig. du Midi
3800

P. 3700

Pèlerins Glacier

It does not come out quite on the summit, but it is nevertheless a fine route. Firstly, its structure is pleasing: the lower section, to a point halfway up, is rock, the upper section is a snow ridge, slender, pure, almost too perfect, getting steeper the higher up you go, and finally a difficult rock rognon which finishes at the Midi-Plan traverse at about 3720m. It is also a safe route, whereas to the right and left are couloirs overhung by great seracs and often swept by avalanches.

The route becomes more difficult the higher up you go. The snow ridge can be easy, even at the top, provided it is snow, but it can be very difficult if there is ice or if the snow has not got a firm base. Above this, climbing the rock rognon is difficult.

At one time, the climb was very inaccessible; now of course things are different because of the téléphérique.

● **1st ascent**: E. Frendo and R. Rionda, 11 July 1941.
● **Vertical height**: 1218m from the start of the difficulties to the summit (from 2582m to 3800m).

● **Grade**: A mixed route, with ice sections likely to prove difficult, and a rock section of D (with a move of V).

● **Time**: 6–8 hrs from the start of the difficulties to the summit. Set out very early.

● **Equipment**: Crampons.

● **Starting point**: Plan de l'Aiguille (2310m).

● **Route** – *Outline:* In the lower half the route is on rock up the straight rock spur which runs up the left-hand section of the snow ridge. The upper section is on snow then up the upper rock rognon on the right. It is also possible to avoid the rognon on the right either by skirting the base or by leaving the snow ridge lower down to traverse right.

Description: From the Plan de l'Aiguille (2202m) follow the path and then the Pèlerins Glacier to gain the bottom of the rock at 2582m. Climb easily up mixed terrain taking a ledge ascending left to the foot of a steep step and reach the foot of a vertical snow and ice-filled system of couloir-chimneys which are followed for 100m and lead to the ridge. Go up this to a

small brèche on a horizontal shoulder. Climb cracks and steep chimneys (some passages of IV) on compact rock keeping rather to the left of the spur. You reach a shoulder at the foot of the snow slopes of the upper section of the route. Climb the crest of the snow ridge. As you get nearer the rock rognon, the ridge bulges slightly and becomes very steep. Tackle the rock rognon from the left; climb big cracked slabs which lead to an extremely steep ice chimney-couloir. Right of this couloir there are two narrow parallel cracks. Gain the one on the left and climb it until it begins to overhang. Leave it and made a delicate step (V) into the right-hand crack. Climb this for several metres and then go back to the left-hand crack and follow it to the top. You arrive below an overhanging wall. Avoid this by a horizontal traverse left which leads to the top of the ice chimney-couloir. From here the Midi-Plan Ridge is easily gained.

It is possible to avoid the rock-climbing up the rognon which is always tricky by turning it on the right. To do this go

obliquely up across the very steep snow slope, but this can only be done when the conditions are good.

Four climbers on the snow ridge of the Frendo Spur (opposite page).
The North Face of the Aiguille du Midi, with the Frendo Spur on the left of the summit (above).

63. PETIT CLOCHER DU PORTALET
East Face and South-East Ridge   2823m

The Petit Clocher du Portalet is a remarkable red granite monolith. Only the W Ridge, the ordinary and descent route, is not vertical and smooth. The other faces and ridges, although not very high, are technically extremely difficult. The SE Ridge is probably the finest route from the aesthetic point of view, being a pleasant combination of free and artificial climbing on excellent rock; the E Face, on the other hand, is full of character, so much so that because of its chimneys it is probably unique in the range. This is what makes the route so worthwhile, even if the climbing is principally strenuous; it is certainly very technical.

E Face
● **1st ascent:** I. Gamboni and M. Vaucher, 23 July 1958.
● **Vertical height:** About 200m (from 2620 to 2823m).
● **Grade:** ED with 40 pitons. Sustained and strenuous.
● **Time:** 1 hr from the Orny Hut to the foot of the wall. 4–5 hrs from the start of the difficulties to the summit. 2½ hrs from the summit to the hut.

● **Equipment:** Pitons, carabiners, étriers, 40m of rope between each person.
● **Starting point:** The Orny Hut (2687m) which can be reached from Champex by a chairlift and a good path in 1½ hrs.
● **Route** – *Outline:* In the centre of the face two cracks go up to a big deep crack cutting the face up to the summit.

Description: From the Orny Hut (2687m) cross the glacier and several moraines. Climb the steep slopes below the E Face and gain a shoulder on the left turning the step on the left. Above, two obvious cracks run up the face. 5m left of the left-hand crack climb a third very thin crack up the open slab (A1, A2). After 20m pendulum right to gain 5m lower a flake (V sup.) and get into the big crack. It is possible to make a longer pendulum and avoid the flake, but the extra section of the crack is very hard (V, strenuous). Climb the big crack (chockstones) to a good belay (V), then climb the back using the chockstones (IV sup.-V sup.). Do not go right. Leave the chimney when it narrows (V sup.). Climb a crack on the left (IV) then return to that on the right and climb the back to exit below blocks and jammed flakes at a good terrace. From here gain the summit easily.

SE Ridge
● **1st ascent:** M. Rey and C. Vouilloz, 15 June 1961.
● **Vertical height:** About 200m.
● **Grade:** TD sup. with 60 pitons. Sustained. Very good rock, coming very quickly into condition.
● **Time:** 2 hrs from the hut to the start of the difficulties. 3–5 hrs from there to the summit.
● **Starting point:** The Orny Hut (2687m).
● **Equipment:** Pitons, carabiners, étriers, 40m of rope between each person.
● **Route** – *Outline:* The ridge.

Description: Climb the steep slopes below the E Face, gain a shoulder on the left, turn the E Face by a gangway inclined outwards, then make a delicate step to reach the foot of the SE Ridge.

Start up rock steps slightly left of the crest (III) to a quartz niche. Traverse 3m right (V sup.), climb a 15m crack (A1), avoid a roof to the left (V sup.), climb a crack (A1) on the right and exit by a flake onto terraces (IV).

Climb blocks (III, IV) then a dièdre (A1, stance in étriers). Traverse below a roof (A1) and climb flakes (IV) and a more delicate aid section (A1, A2) leading to below an overhanging yellow slab. Traverse 5m left (IV, exposed); a 2m wall leads to a ledge along which it is possible to escape onto the S Face. Climb grooves for 20m (V) to gain the crest of the ridge. Climb this, then traverse left and climb further grooves

for 20m (IV sup., exposed). Traverse right (A1), climb a crack (6m, V sup.) and a step (4m, V). Move right and go up the crest of the ridge to reach a terrace with blocks (III). A slab and a chimney lead to the summit (30m, V, IV).

Descent: At first free-climbing down the crest of the W Ridge. An iron piton is reached from which an abseil is made. Keep to the ridge and make another abseil of 30m down the S side. This second abseil can be avoided by climbing down a chimney. On the S Face a system of grassy ledges lead to the brèche between the Petit and the Grand Clocher du Portalet. From the brèche ascend 30m or so N. Go along a ledge to an icy couloir with a fixed rope. Keep to ledges and gain a col leading to a small glacier tongue. Descend this. Sometimes conditions necessitate an abseil. Continue along moraines to the Orny Glacier.

The Petit Clocher du Portalet, with the North Face on the right and the East Face on the left (opposite page).
The East Face of the Petit Clocher du Portalet; the crack before the pendulum (right).
The Petit Clocher du Portalet: the East Face is on the right, the South Face on the left, and the South-East Ridge between the two (below).

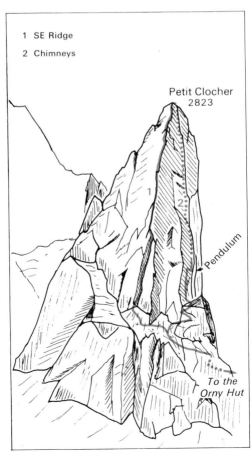

1 SE Ridge

2 Chimneys

Petit Clocher 2823

Pendulum

To the Orny Hut

64. PIC DE ROC — GREPON 3409–3482m
Traverse

In 1911, on a fine August day, Joseph Knubel emerged onto the summit of the Grépon, from the E or Mer de Glace Face. This was a fine first ascent, which culminated in the climbing of the famous crack, still today graded V sup. In 1927, Alfred Couttet stood on the summit of the Pic de Roc, a fine rock pinnacle. Finally, in 1938, Edouard Frendo combined these two fine routes and it is this combination that I suggest here.

The starting point for this climb, as for the Mer de Glace Face of the Grépon, is the Envers des Aiguilles Hut; yet in spite of its friendly guardian, it cannot quite make us forget the little Tour Rouge Hut, perched precariously on the wall, which by its atmosphere contributed so much to the climb. You had to go out and get water, and this was not always very easy. There was no light; but sometimes there was a piece of unexpected good luck, a few provisions left behind by parties which had had to retreat because of poor weather. And even to go up to the hut was to commit yourself to some extent. It seems to me not unlikely that if earlier generations loved not just climbing, but the complete experience of contact with the mountains and made of it a way of life, this, for the pioneers, was because of their inevitable bivouacs, and for the succeeding generations because of their evenings and nights in the precarious but sturdy huts where the benches and tables — when there were any; there were none in the Tour Rouge Hut, which was too small and too low — were made of real wood, with real wood-grain, which felt real, like granite, under your fingers, and not of some modern material which may be convenient, but is soulless, cold and slippery.

- **1st ascent:** J. Carrel, R. Faure, E. Frendo, R. Grière, 18 August 1938.
- **Vertical height:** About 800m from the bergschrund to the summit (from 2700 to 3482m).
- **Grade:** TD.
- **Time:** 8–9 hrs from the bergschrund to the summit.
- **Equipment:** Carabiners, 40m abseil rope.
- **Starting point:** Envers des Aiguilles Hut (2520m), but it is also possible to start from the Tour Rouge Hut (2822m).
- **Route** – *Outline:* A great Z to the top of the Pic de Roc, well-marked by the oblique ledges. Then straight up from the brèche to the summit of the Grépon.

Description: From the Envers des Aiguilles Hut go up the Trélaporte Glacier between the buttress descending from the Pic de Roc and the Tour Rouge. Cross the bergschrund and go up slabs on the left of the Tour Rouge Couloir to reach a zone of terraces level with the Grépon-Tour Rouge brèche. You can reach the same point from the Tour Rouge Hut, itself gained from the Trélaporte Glacier. To reach the hut go up the right-hand side of the glacier, cross the bergschrund or turn it on the right up the rock (IV), and traverse left across the upper snow slope above to gain the rocks above a ledge. Continue either up a chimney (IV, strenuous) or further right up a slab (IV,

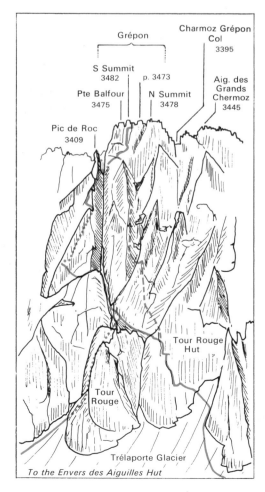

delicate) to reach a dièdre-couloir which leads to the hut. Above climb a series of chimneys (passing under jammed blocks) and, slanting left, gain the terraces beside the Tour Rouge brèche.

Cross the Charmoz-Grépon Couloir, then the Grépon-Pic de Roc Couloir to the left and go 100m up easy rock to a shoulder of the ENE Ridge coming down from the Pic de Roc. Make a traverse, initially descending, then slanting across to reach a big couloir, not visible earlier, which comes down from the ENE Ridge. Climb this first up the right bank, then up the bed or by the rocks on the right bank to the brèche on the ENE Ridge. Above, the wall is steeper and the climbing becomes more difficult. Follow a ledge left which steepens and ends at a vertical crack. Leave the ledge before this crack and climb a cracked slab (IV), then a second very steep slab to the left (IV sup.) to reach a platform (you can reach this platform from the foot of the vertical crack by descending left and then going up right again up cracked slabs, III). Follow a broken ledge right, the continuation of the platform, and climb on the left a slanting dièdre (IV)

which seems to be cut by two overhangs. Above go diagonally up right by a series of open dièdres and cracks to a little couloir. Go 5m up this, then traverse left to the SE Ridge which leads to the foot of the final pinnacle. On the right this is cut by a big slit-chimney (this makes a 'letter-box' through which you can pass onto the NW side). Climb this (IV sup., strenuous) and at the top finish to the right. Go up 2m and either free-climb (V sup.) or lasso a knob on the slab to the left below the summit and swing across to gain the summit.

Make a 30m abseil to return to the bottom of the chimney splitting the summit block. Go through the slit onto the NW side and descend to the N corner of a platform covered with a small sloping névé. From there one 40m abseil, or two abseils, the first of 30m (which leads to a narrow balcony invisible from above), and the second of 12m diagonally right from the far W end of this balcony, lead to the brèche.

On the left climb up to a platform 10m above the brèche. Climb the 10m high Frendo Dièdre (A1) exiting on the left (V) to gain a first niche and then a second 5m higher up by a deep chimney with a detached spike (V). Climb a rounded arête on the right for 10m (V) and gain a good platform by easy slabs. Other easy slabs lead from this to the end of a ledge on the Mer de Glace Route on the Grépon (found by F. Lochmatter during the second ascent and which avoids the 60m chimney climbed on the first ascent). Easy rock leads back right to a platform at the top of 60m chimney and below the 35m chimney which is climbed (IV). Climb slabs on the right, then a short strenuous crack (IV) which leads to the Brèche Balfour.

Traverse right along a flake to the foot of the Knubel Crack; at first a dièdre, this deepens into a chimney. When it is blocked by overhanging chockstones, you should move out left onto the slab which is difficult but even more alarming: you are leaving the security of a chimney to work up an exposed wall. The handhold (crescent-shaped) is small but good. There follows a sequence of delicate balance rather than strenuous moves for the feet, with the transfer of the bodyweight from one leg to the other; twice to the left, then right, the right foot on the handhold; the hands can then find very good holds for the pull-up onto the summit.

The spire of the Pic de Roc (opposite page). The Mer de Glace Face of the Grépon, with the Pic de Roc on the left (above).

65. AIGUILLE D'ARGENTIERE 3902m
North Face

The N Face of the Aiguille d'Argentière is a broad glacier wall overlooking the Saleina Glacier.

When you do the classic ski-traverse of the Three Cols in spring you see it on the right, in profile, as you come down the Col du Chardonnet, and from this angle you see the tumble of seracs coming down, but as you descend further and get nearer to the Fenêtre de Saleina, you can see the face from a distance and from in front. This shows all its beauty and the whole sweep of it. Whether it is regular and undeviating, as was the case thirty years or so ago, or chaotic, twisted, and continuously barred by lines of seracs, as it is now; its condition depends on snowfalls and the advance of the glacier. But whatever its present state and geography, it soars into the sky, admirably proportioned. Its average angle, fairly sustained, is 50°.

The actual route depends of course on the present state of the slope and especially on the presence or lack of serac barriers or bergschrunds. It can also depend on the snow, since it can sometimes be iced.

You exit onto the NW Ridge at the Shoulder and reach the summit by the ridge, or else you can go directly up to the summit. The descent by the ordinary route, the Milieu Glacier and the Argentière Glacier, is easy.

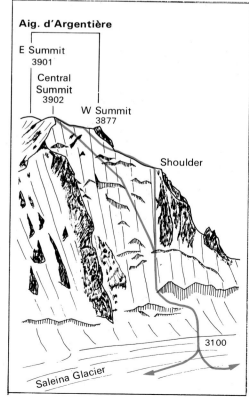

Aig. d'Argentière

E Summit
3901

Central
Summit
3902

W Summit
3877

Shoulder

3100

Saleina Glacier

- **1st ascent:** J. Lagarde and H. de Ségogne, 2 August 1926 (the N Face and the NW Ridge). B. Arsandaux and R. Gréloz, 10 August 1930 (direct finish).
- **Vertical height:** About 700m (from 3200 to 3902m).
- **Grade:** A steep slope, 50°. Danger from falling seracs.
- **Time:** 3–5 hrs from the bergschrund to the summit.
- **Equipment:** Crampons.
- **Starting point** – *From Switzerland:* The Saleina Hut (2691m), 2 hrs to reach the foot of the face. The Trient Hut (3122m), crossing the Fenêtre de Saleina (3263m), 2 hrs.

    From France: The Albert Premier Hut (2706m), crossing the Fenêtre du Tour (3336m), 2½ hrs. The Argentière Hut (2771m), crossing the Col du Chardonnet (3323m), 3 hrs.

    The last route is perhaps the most convenient, since after the climb the hut is at the bottom of the descent route, but the three other possibilities have the advantage of turning the route into a traverse — approach by one side and descent by another — as well as giving a very good view of the face and the route because you approach from a distance.
- **Route** – *Outline:* As distinct from the couloir routes such as the Gervasutti and Couturier where the line hardly varies, since the couloir itself determines the route, on face routes and particularly here on the Aiguille d'Argentière where the N Face is very broad and interrupted by serac barriers or split by bergschrunds and long crevasses, the climber has to work out his own line. It is marvellous and so uncommon in our time to have to find your own way — a true luxury. Here the route depends on the seracs, and since they are greatly enlarged and advanced the route has moved fairly far right. Higher up it is possible either to bear left to finish directly at the summit, or to finish on the NW Ridge.

    Description: Look carefully beforehand at the details and avoid as far as possible sections threatened by avalanches.

In thirty-five years the whole appearance of the Aiguille d'Argentière has completely altered; the advance of the glacier has meant that the smooth slope (above right) has become chaotic and is cut by serac barriers (opposite page).
North Face and North-East Face of the Aiguille d'Argentière with the North Face of the Chardonnet on the right and the Saleina Glacier bottom right (below right).

66. GRANDES JORASSES 4208m
Hirondelles Ridge

In 1873, when Leslie Stephen and his companions were about to make the first ascent and first traverse of the Col des Hirondelles, the great snow saddle was nameless. Below the col, on the snow, they found 'some twenty absolutely motionless black spots' and discovered, 'strangely pathetic in the midst of the snowy wilderness' the bodies of swallows killed by the storm. We wondered how it came to pass that the little company had been struck down so suddenly as their position seemed to indicate', and he concludes: 'We proposed at the time to give to our pass the name of the Col des Hirondelles.'

Naturally, the E Ridge of the Grandes Jorasses going from the col to the summit of the Jorasses is called the Hirondelles Ridge. From the Montenvers, the name seems particularly and magnificently appro-

priate. But the climber should not imagine, if he is not to be disappointed, some slender, delicate ridge with a climb to match; in reality the ridge is very different. Just behind the ridge, in fact, is the whole E Face of the Jorasses, and this prevents the ridge from being at all sharp. Moreover, the climb mostly follows the left-hand (E) side of the ridge. The climber might also be disappointed by the climbing itself. The ridge was for a long time thought to be unclimbable because of the step above the V brèche, which was said to have defeated thirty-two parties, among them Mummery with Rey, Ryan with Lochmatter, the guides of the Duke of the Abruzzi, Mayer with Dibona and Young with Knubel.

And certainly, when you arrive on the slope below the V brèche, in front of the crack, you can see that, quite apart from its

intrinsic difficulty, it is overawing, since it seems so steep as to be overhanging. Any wall or ridge seen from in front — and this is true too for ice couloirs — seems much steeper than it is. What is disappointing is to remember that Knubel, on his attempt, apparently did no more than look at the crack without attempting it, for Knubel, as a climber, had two enviable characteristics: his skill and his technique of jamming an ice-axe, just as effective in some circumstances as the use of pitons.

This is not to belittle the achievement of A. Rey, who not only climbed the pitch but did so in face of its reputation. It is a happy thought that it was a Courmayeur guide — one of those most exposed to tales of this sort — who succeeded in the enterprise.

The interest of this climb depends not so much on technical difficulty, not in any case very great or very continuous beyond the Rey Crack, as on the uncompromising atmosphere, the loneliness and the views. It is a major route, in high-mountain surroundings.

● **1st ascent**: G. Gaia, S. Matteoda, F. Ravelli, G. A. Rivetti with A. Rey and Chenoz, 10 August 1927; on 4 August 1927, Rey and Chenoz had, during a re-

connaissance, climbed the crux, the famous crack above the V brèche now known as the Rey Crack. The Courmayeur guide used three pitons for the climb.

● **Vertical height**: 623m from the Gervasutti Hut (2833m) to the col (3456m). 1025m from the Leschaux Hut (2431m) to the col. 752m from the col to the summit (from 3456 to 4208m).

● **Grade**: D, not very sustained, several pitches of IV and one of V.

● **Time**: 3–4 hrs from the Gervasutti Hut to the Col des Hirondelles depending on the state of the glacier. 5–7 hrs from the col to the summit. 3–5 hrs from the Leschaux Hut to the col.

● **Equipment**: Crampons.

● **Starting point**: The Leschaux Hut (2431m), but the Gervasutti Hut (2833m) is better.

● **Route** – *Outline:* This is given by the ridge, but the crest itself is scarcely ever followed. For most of the time the route follows the left-hand or Italian side which is less steep than the French side.

Description: From the Gervasutti Hut (2833m) gain the col by the central branch of the Frébouzie Glacier (steep slopes, large crevasses, serac barriers). This passes between the two buttresses, E and SE, of the Pointe des Hirondelles on the right and the long rock rognon on the left formed as part of the extension of the E Face of the Grandes Jorasses. Keep fairly right, that is close to the buttresses descending from the Petites Jorasses. Go past the foot of a rock ridge descending from the col and go up slopes, initially very steep, which lead to the saddle of the col (3456m).

Above and left of the col there is a slightly concave, triangular facet with its summit at the V brèche. Cross the bergschrund and initially go straight up broken rock and snow for about 100m a little right of the centre of the triangle. Then go diagonally left and climb a deep chimney to the ridge which is followed to the small pinnacle (delicate if snowed up) which precedes the V brèche (several passages of IV). From the brèche traverse left to gain the first (Rey Crack) of two parallel cracks 20m high. This is initially filled with flakes, it turns into a dièdre and finishes at a small platform (V).

Climb a dièdre to reach a second platform. Above there are at least three routes. The best is undoubtedly Gobbi's, which, instead of taking the well-marked couloir of the ordinary route to the left, goes right to a crack at the back of a dièdre which is climbed by bridging (IV) for its entire length to a platform on the ridge, whose crest is then climbed.

If the Gobbi Crack is iced up, take the couloir on the left and then return to the ridge up a long couloir. Follow the ridge which broadens and joins the Tronchey Ridge and leads easily to the summit.

The North Face of the Grandes Jorasses, with the Hirondelles Ridge on the left (above).
The Hirondelles Ridge, from the Petites Jorasses (opposite page).

67. AIGUILLE DE LA BRENVA 3278m
East Face

This is not a major summit, and it seems a little overpowered by its great neighbours, whether massive like the Blanche, or higher than it, like the Noire de Peuterey. But in spite of its modest height, it is a very individual peak, a result mainly of its structure. It is an aiguille (needle) in a quite literal sense, slender, seamed with thin cracks, made up of narrow rock flakes standing vertically. It looks as though it would tremble in the wind and, as if to underline its own fragility, it has on its N side a unique pinnacle: the Père Eternel, standing alone and isolated, precariously balanced, separated from the Aiguille by a deep cleft. The whole complex of the E Face of the Aiguille and the Père Eternel is a quite extraordinary sculpture. This is brought out particularly in the morning when the slanting rays of the sun glint on its folds of golden granite. The Aiguille de la Brenva lights up quite differently when it stands out against the mists rising between it and the Noire de Peuterey. In the autumn of 1944, several times I spent an entire week in the Torino Hut. I could scarcely take my eyes off this extraordinary sculpture.

There are several routes on the face: the Donvito Dièdre, the result of a route-finding error, short but very direct and exposed on this stark face; the two Bocca-latte Routes, dating from 1934, and, the finer, from 1935; the very hard Bertone-Zappelli Route; the route done in 1948 by J. Deudon, B. Pierre and myself. Lastly, on the right, there is one other delightful way of reaching the summit: to climb the Père Eternel first, and thus make acquaintance with the bold pole-climbing techniques beloved of the Courmayeur guides before the days of artificial climbing, then to climb the N Ridge of the Aiguille de la Brenva, with its two very difficult steps.

I have climbed the majority of these routes, but Bertone, who has climbed them all, is of the opinion that the 1948 route is certainly the most interesting of the free climbs.

● **1st ascent:** J. Deudon and B. Pierre with G. Rébuffat, 18–19 May 1948.
● **Vertical height:** About 450m (from 2800 to 3278m).
● **Grade:** TD (with five moves of V sup.). A wall unusually steep for granite. 10 pitons.
● **Time:** 4–5 hrs from the start of the difficulties to the summit.
● **Equipment:** Carabiners. Leave axes and crampons at the start.
● **Starting point:** The Torino Hut, Pointe Helbronner (the route can be done in the day by taking the téléphérique).
● **Route** – *Outline:* In the centre of the face slightly right of directly below the

summit there is a shoulder above a buttress. The route initially gains this shoulder then goes above almost straight up to finish immediately right of the summit.

Description: From the old Torino Hut, following the SW Couloir or the spur on the left bank which descends to the Toule Glacier, or from Pointe Helbronner crossing the Col des Flambeaux then the E Col de la Toule, reach the Brèche d'Entrêves (3070), descend the W side onto the Entrêves Glacier and gain the foot of the E Face of the Aiguille de la Brenva at the highest point of the glacier. Climb a vertical crack (IV) to gain a zone of terraces which lead to a chimney with an overhanging chockstone (IV), then a short dièdre (IV) and a large couloir. Go up 60m from here to the foot of a step which is climbed. The bed of the couloir is now blocked by an overhang forming a cave. Go right up a couloir-chimney (IV) with a jammed block, which turns into a dièdre. From the base of this dièdre traverse left to gain a small characteristic rock step just right of an overhanging chimney. Climb this chimney (V

sup.), then bear right to reach a shoulder, often snow-covered, at the top of the buttress below the most vertical section of the wall.

Climb up for about 15m (IV), traverse 10m right and continue bearing left up bad rock (IV). Climb up a little and traverse left to arrive below an obvious dièdre (V, a move of V sup.). Here the original route goes off to the right with a rope traverse (piton above) and continues the very difficult traverse (V sup.) to a niche filled with blocks at the bottom of a dièdre-chimney coming down from the summit ridge. Climb the dièdre (45m, IV sup., V) to a second niche, leaving this on the right by a detached flake. Climb an overhanging dièdre (V sup.), an overhang (V sup.) and a crack-chimney with jammed blocks (V, 50m pitch). Gain the summit ridge right of the summit.

From below the obvious dièdre it is easier and more direct to climb it instead of traversing right. It becomes a chimney (IV, IV sup.) at a ledge covered with blocks. Continue up to above a flake (III). Climb the slab above (V) to an overhang which is avoided to the right (V) to get into a chimney which is climbed to the summit ridge (IV and III).

Descent: Follow the S Ridge down a succession of ledges and terraces (two sections of climbing) to the Aiguille-Tour de la Brenva brèche. Cross onto the E Face. Descend the couloir going down to the Entrêves Glacier for 50m. Then make a descending traverse right (S) to the E Face of the Tour de la Brenva. Descend 70m keeping right down steep but easy slopes to the top of a smooth vertical 25m wall. Abseil down this (piton in place). Descend a very steep couloir-dièdre (abseil, piton in place). A shoulder is reached. Descend a ridge on the left for 30m. Traverse easily into the bed of the couloir which goes down to the Entrêves Glacier. If the bergschrund is bad, abseil down over it. Cross the Entrêves Glacier to the Pavillon du Mont Fréty.

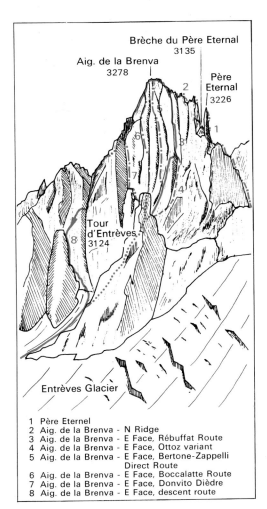

1 Père Eternel
2 Aig. de la Brenva - N Ridge
3 Aig. de la Brenva - E Face, Rébuffat Route
4 Aig. de la Brenva - E Face, Ottoz variant
5 Aig. de la Brenva - E Face, Bertone-Zappelli Direct Route
6 Aig. de la Brenva - E Face, Boccalatte Route
7 Aig. de la Brenva - E Face, Donvito Dièdre
8 Aig. de la Brenva - E Face, descent route

On the East Face of the Aiguille de la Brenva (above). The Aiguille de la Brenva and the Père Eternel, with the Aiguille Noire de Peuterey in the background (opposite page).

68. DENT DU CROCODILE 3640m
East Ridge

The Dent du Crocodile is neither an elegant nor an outstanding summit, but its E Ridge is a long and difficult climb, offering a series of pitches of high technical difficulty and typical of climbing on the Chamonix Aiguilles. Access to the ridge proper is a bit awkward and the first problem is the bergschrund (that on the Ryan-Lochmatter Ridge) which is sometimes difficult to cross, but the rest of the route is obvious. The interest of this route is derived first of all from the climbing itself; so I am suggesting a route which will appeal primarily to the rock-climber in the alpinist. The rock is excellent. The crux pitch is a large slab. P. Allain and J. and R. Leininger climbed it by a pendulum. Frendo and myself, on the third ascent, did it with a short artificial traverse — the pitons are in place.

For the descent there are three possibilities: abseiling down the ascent route; traversing to the Aiguille du Plan (30 mins) and from there down to the Requin Hut by the Envers du Plan Glacier; traversing from the Plan along the Plan-Midi Ridge to the Midi téléphérique.

● **1st ascent:** P. Allain, J. and R. Leininger, 29–30 July, 1937.
● **Vertical height:** The difficult section is about 300m high (from 3350 to 3640m).
● **Grade:** TD, a succession of strenuous pitches of IV and V, 15 pitons.
● **Time:** 8–10 hrs from the hut to the summit.

● **Equipment:** Carabiners, étriers for the slab pitch with the four inverted pitons.
● **Starting point:** Envers des Aiguilles Hut (2520m).
● **Route** — *Outline:* The Ryan-Lochmatter Ridge bergschrund, a traverse of the Plan-Crocodile Couloir to gain the E Ridge, then two separate systems of crack-chimneys and walls.

Description: After crossing the bergschrund and making an ascending traverse from left to right across the lower part of the Ryan-Lochmatter Ridge, cross the Plan-Crocodile Couloir. Climb a system of sloping ledges going up in steps (II and III) to a large platform at the base of the first, obvious, red step of the E Ridge of the Crocodile. Avoid this step on the left (III and IV) to reach a second platform at the foot of the second step where the difficult climbing starts.

Go onto the Caïman side and reach the foot of a big dièdre. Climb a deep vertical 25m crack-chimney at its back (IV and V). Continue above up a second 20m crack (IV and V) to reach a shoulder of small terraces

and steps at the foot of the crux pitch. This is a steep monolithic slab with a small buttress. At the top of this buttress traverse horizontally right (A1 and V) across the upper part of the slab to gain a dièdre (IV) which leads to a good terrace. Right of this terrace climb a vertical dièdre for 10m (V), exiting left by a delicate traverse to gain large blocks and then rock steps and chimneys which are easy (III) even if they overhang higher up. These lead slightly left. At the left end follow a slanting ledge-crack left for 25–30m and cross onto the left side of the ridge. Climb inclined slabs to gain a 30m chimney on the left (IV, exit IV sup.) which leads back to the ridge at a shoulder at the foot of the final step.

Slant easily up to gain a dièdre with a narrow 10m crack on the left and climb this by bridging (IV sup.). Climb a succession of walls and chimneys (IV) for 30m to the summit of the Crocodile.

Descent: If you descend by the same route, you will have to make 10 abseils; otherwise climb up to the Aiguille du Plan.

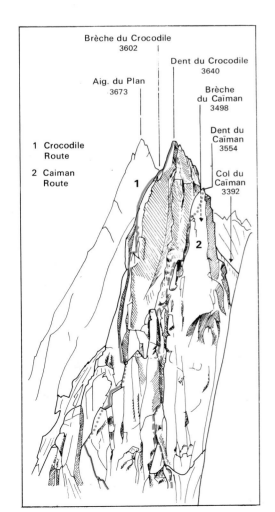

Brèche du Crocodile
3602

Dent du Crocodile
3640

Aig. du Plan
3673

Brèche
du Caïman
3498

Dent du
Caïman
3554

1 Crocodile
Route

2 Caïman
Route

Col du
Caïman
3392

1

2

*The Aiguille du Plan, the Dent du Crocodile, the
East Face of the Dent du Caïman, the Col du Fou and
the South Face of the Aiguille du Fou (opposite page).
The crux pitch of the East Face of the Crocodile, with
the Caïman in the background (above).*

69. AIGUILLE DU PLAN 3673m
North Face

The ascent of the Aiguille du Plan by its N Face is the ascent of a hanging glacier tumbling down in serac barriers and bergschrunds. The route therefore lacks the clean lines of a couloir route, but by the same token lacks its regularity or even monotony as we see; for instance, in the Gervasutti Couloir, where the angle and the style of climbing are both almost unvarying. What variety there is in the mountains, and in the pleasures and the impressions that they give us! In a couloir, with its steep and enclosed lines, the climbing is of course airy, but is principally vertiginous. Here, where the climbing follows a discontinuous line and crosses one serac leading to another, things are very different.

The N Face of the Plan is normally a difficult route which is in some years quite impossible, depending on conditions on the glacier, but it can also be relatively effortless; I have done the route myself by coming up on the first cable-car, having got home too late the previous evening to go up to the hut, although I should point out that that was with P. Habron, who is a very fast walker. But in any case you should be very fit to undertake this route, since certain pitches demand speed and confidence.

During the days before you do the route, you should examine the seracs carefully to see if the motion of the glacier is pushing any of them off balance; if so, some might over-balance and fall at any time of night or day, whether the weather is cold or sultry. Finally this is a route to be done in perfect weather, so that you can appreciate the superb view.

● **1st ascent:** P. Dillemann with A. Charlet and J. Simond, 19 July 1929.
● **Vertical height:** 400m up the rock spur, 600m up the glacier. About 1000m in all (from 2600 to 3673m).
● **Grade:** An ice-route which can be more or less difficult according to the seracs and the snow and ice conditions.
● **Time:** 5–8 hrs from the start of the difficulties to the summit. Start very early.
● **Equipment:** Crampons, ice-pitons and ice-screws.
● **Starting point:** Plan de l'Aiguille (2202m).
● **Route – Outline:** initially up the spur following the crest, turning or climbing the gendarmes, and then up the glacier, climbed by a line depending on the state of the serac barriers which have to be avoided. Sometimes you have to cross to the Col des Deux Aigles.

Description: From the Plan de l'Aiguille go up to the foot of the spur which supports the hanging glacier and rises out of the Blaitière Glacier (base at 2588m). Start on the left to gain the brèche between the first and the second gendarmes. Follow the ridge and before the second gendarme go right to regain the ridge. Turn the second gendarme on the right and return to the ridge. Just before the third gendarme, go to the right. A ledge leads to the foot of two chimneys; climb either of them (IV). Continue easily along the ridge to the foot of the hanging glacier (1½ hrs).

Gain the glacier and climb it, choosing the line most protected from falling seracs. In general keep first left then traverse right at the level of the Col des Deux Aigles, and then climb directly to the summit.

On the North Face of the Aiguille du Plan (above). View directly downwards from the North Face of the Aiguille du Plan (opposite page, left). North Face of the Aiguille du Plan (opposite page, right).

70. MONT MAUDIT 4465m
Crétier Route

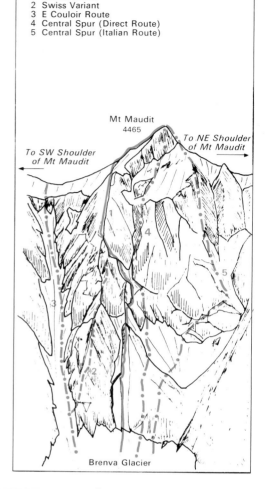

1 Crétier Route
2 Swiss Variant
3 E Couloir Route
4 Central Spur (Direct Route)
5 Central Spur (Italian Route)

Mt Maudit
4465

To SW Shoulder
of Mt Maudit

To NE Shoulder
of Mt Maudit

Brenva Glacier

The SE side of Mont Maudit, between the Tour Ronde (or Kuffner) Ridge to the E and the Brenva Spur to the S, is a complicated wall about 700m high towering above the upper cirque of the Brenva Glacier. It is a wild and isolated place. On this side there are six routes, with some variants. None of them can properly be called direct and indeed the terrain does not lend itself to direct routes. Doubtless such routes would require intensive artificial climbing; this would be the case especially on the slabs of the main part of the face, but such a route would certainly be inelegant. The first route on this side was done in 1932 and is still considered to be very hard; the Vallot guide grades it higher than the routes on the Brenva Face of Mont Blanc, including the Poire. This first route was done by the Aosta mountaineers Binel, Chabod and Crétier, a highly accomplished and quite remarkable team, excellent rock-climbers (there are pitches of IV on this route which were done by these three without pitons) and brilliant snow- and ice-climbers, with a highly developed mountaineering instinct; highly enthusiastic, safe, generous, imaginative, they preferred fine routes, with the result that their routes are first and foremost magnificent mountaineering ventures. In our day pitons, while allowing some great successes and while encouraging more and more technical improvements, laborious though some of these may be, have eliminated, not perhaps the element of risk — even in those days climbers were conscious of the dangers and made preparations accordingly— but rather the element of freedom of choice. It may be that our improved techniques no longer allow the same exhilaration as formerly.

● **1st ascent:** L. Binel, R. Chabod, A. Crétier, 4 August 1932.
● **Vertical height:** About 650m (from 3800 to 4465m).
● **Grade:** A major route in a savage, deserted setting. D sup. in the rock section but with mixed and very severe ice pitches.
● **Time:** 1 hr from the Col de la Fourche Hut (3680m) to the start of the difficulties. 6—9 hrs from there to the summit.
● **Equipment:** Crampons.
● **Starting point:** The Col de la Fourche Hut (3680m).
● **Route** — *Outline:* This can be divided into three equally difficult parts, each of great

interest. The first is mainly on rock up a red granite pillar, where the route follows an obvious chimney splitting the pillar to its top. The second is very difficult mixed climbing, slanting slightly left but with the exact line depending on conditions. The third is formed by a snow or ice ridge, finishing on the SW Ridge of Mont Maudit where climbing the cornice is not the least of the problems. Altogether the route is to the left of the great central depression of the SE side of Mont Maudit and right of the straight couloir descending between Mont Maudit and its SW shoulder. It takes a complicated massive spur which divides into two in its lower half (there is also a variant done by Geneva climbers, left of the Crétier Route in this lower half).

Description: From the Col de la Fourche Hut (3680m) descend to the Brenva Glacier and go up it towards the pillar and the long chimney splitting it.

Climb the bergschrund and the steep snow slope to gain the chimney. Climb it, then follow the dièdre on the left (IV) for 30m. Slightly on the right climb a second chimney (IV) and gain the crest of the pillar. Climb it up slabs (III and IV), and after a smooth chimney (IV) the angle eases. Turn the step above on the right. You now reach the thin snow ridge marking the top of the spur.

Above this climb the rock wall, then slant up a line of very tricky snowy, iced-up rocks to gain a snow shoulder and then the crest of a big rock step (IV). The last part of the route follows a very airy, scalloped snow ridge. The last obstacle is the final cornice on the SW Ridge of Mont Maudit, by which the summit is easily reached.

The East Face of Mont Maudit, with the Tour Ronde Ridge and Col Maudit on the right, and the Col de la Brenva on the left (opposite page). Mont Maudit between Mont Blanc on the left and Mont Blanc du Tacul on the right (above).

71. AIGUILLE DE BLAITIERE 3522m
West Face

Above the little Blaitière Glacier is a wall of compact slabs, cut by lines of overhangs; you feel in fact — and rightly, for a large part of the face has fallen away leaving a pale-coloured patch — that these are huge granite flakes several hundred metres high, sometimes split and cracked. Here you are face to face with the great war waged over the millennia between water and rock; water trickles into the rock, becomes ice and expands; the pressure then forces the granite flakes, weighing thousands of tons, apart, until they break up.

This slow erosion has made its presence felt suddenly twice in a short period of time. The route done by P. Allain and A. Fix on 10 September 1947 was wiped out by a rockfall twenty days later just after the second ascent by L. Lachenal, L. Pez, J. Simpson and L. Terray. Four years later, G. Herzog and L. Terray made a route up the rockfall area, but this too was wiped out by a rockfall in 1952 — and not perhaps before time, since the area was very dangerous and unstable. Today we use the route done by J. Brown and D. Whillans just beside the rock-fall area, but to the right of it on the granite weathered by the centuries. But who is to say whether, or when, there will be other rockfalls?

The 1954 route is very difficult and consists of a series of fine pitches, unfortunately broken up at the top just before the summit by ledges and terraces. Nevertheless, this is a very fine and very enjoyable route.

- **1st ascent:** J. Brown and D. Whillans, 25 July 1954.
- **Vertical height:** 750m from the start of the difficulties to the summit (from 2750 to 3507m).
- **Grade:** TD with 30 pitons.
- **Time:** 8–10 hrs from the start of the difficulties to the summit.
- **Equipment:** Carabiners, étriers, very large pitons or wedges for the first crack.
- **Starting point:** Plan de l'Aiguille (2202m).
- **Route** – *Outline:* This goes up the huge wall of slabs right of the pale-coloured streak, following its right-hand side, shaped like a 4; the route crosses the Fontaine Ledges and after a detour right, goes back left directly below the summit.

Description: From the Plan de l'Aiguille go up the Blaitière Glacier fairly high and just above the level of the rockfall, cross the bergschrund and slant up first to the left then to the right by a system of ledges and terraces covered with blocks. Right of directly below the rockfall, reach a corner forming a buttress. Climb this on the right, and the slab above (IV). You now arrive at the foot of the first crack, the Fissure Brown, which is vertical with smooth edges and back (VI, very strenuous free climbing; A1 using aid with wedges or very large pitons). Above continue up grooves for 7m and go left to a platform covered with loose blocks. Climb the crack above for 40m (V and VI), then a chimney and a grooved dièdre which lead to a huge platform.

On the left of the platform but still on the right of the rock fall, go up easily to a crack and climb it (V), then traverse left to a stance on a big detached block. Follow a ledge on the left and climb a short wall, then a dièdre (V sup.) capped by an overhang. Traverse left and climb a short dièdre (A2) to a piton belay on the left. Continue up the dièdre for 6–7m (A2), go right, climb a cracked wall which leads to a good belay. Climb easy slabs to a series of ledges (the false Fontaine Ledges). Traverse right to the slabs on the right bank of the large couloir which splits the face to the foot of a vertical wall, and climb these. Climb cracks left of a block to a stance on its top. Continue up a tricky crack (V sup.) and gain the Fontaine Ledges easily.

Go right and climb a steep dièdre with an overhang (VI) and then a wall right of a wet chimney (V sup.) which leads to a prominent yellow block. From the brèche behind the block make a descending traverse across some easy slabs to reach the NW Ridge and climb this (IV) to the summit. It is more elegant to gain the summit while staying on the W face and climbing a couloir-chimney (directly below the summit), then a vertical 20m wall (IV), a crack and a dièdre (IV).

Brèche 3420

Brèche 3449

Pte Centrale 3522

Pte Nord 3507

Pte Sud 3521

Reymier Couloir

Fontaine Ledge

Great Couloir

Fissure Brown

Blaitière Glacier

The Fissure Brown (opposite page).
In the dièdres above the Fissure Brown (above).
The West Face of the Blaitière, the Ciseaux and the
Aiguille du Fou (right).

72. MONT BLANC DU TACUL 4248m
Boccalatte Pillar

This is the largest and the most outstanding of those magnificent pillars which rise like organ-pipes from the Vallée Blanche to Mont Blanc du Tacul; however, it is not continuous. In actual fact it is a relatively short pillar with additions joining it at the bottom and top. Nevertheless, the quantity, the richness, the verticality of these rock spires between the two great snow couloirs, the Gervasutti on the right and the Aiguilles du Diable on the left, make up a magnificent whole. This is a succession of soaring spires of red granite, separated one from another by deep ravines which bring out their quality. This is a veritable paradise for the climber, who can enjoy not only the climb itself, but also the texture and colour enlivening the rock. He will feel himself encouraged to be creative, to be fluid in his movements. When G. Boccalatte and N. Pietrasanta came to the foot of the face in 1936, they had only too many possibilities

to choose from: all these granite columns were unclimbed and rather than proposing to climb any one particular pillar, they had the major task of making a route through this tangle of rock. This may perhaps explain their detours.

When I myself felt the appeal of this wall, I first of all followed the Boccalatte Route, without paying too much attention to the problems of route-finding, and found myself carried away by the beauty of the surroundings and in any case none too clear about Boccalatte's exact route, climbing willy nilly, spontaneously and naturally, the upper bastion of his route; this is what I mean by 'feeling yourself at one with the rock'. The weather was perfect. It was one of those days when everything seems easy and effortless, when the climber has only to follow the dictates of the rock; a day for the enthusiast, when you are happy, when everything goes right, when climbing is a

question of free give and take with the mountains.

Finally, in 1968, J. Coquegniot and F. Guillot did a particularly fine route which follows the actual edge of the pillar all the way up. This is a very daring route, graded ED, with several pitches of VI, and is more difficult and more sustained than the Gervasutti Pillar.

● **1st ascent:** Miss N. Pietrasanta and G. Boccalatte, 28 August 1936. Direct exit by the Tour Rouge: R. Michon del Campo with G. Rébuffat, 7 August 1946.

● **Vertical height:** About 800m (from 3430 to 4248m).

● **Grade:** TD with the direct finish. D if this is avoided.

● **Time:** Set out very early; as the pillar faces east, you can start climbing very early. 5–7 hrs from the start of the difficulties to the summit.

● **Equipment:** Carabiners, one axe per party.

● **Starting point:** The Cosmiques Hut (3613m). It is also possible to start from the Torino Hut (3375m), but this adds an hour to the approach.

● **Route** – *Outline:* This is given by the pillar; however, at several points where this becomes particularly steep, it can be turned. The start is left of the pillar.

Description: Go up the small glacier bay between the Pyramide du Tacul and the Boccalatte Pillar which is the pillar descending lowest onto the glacier. Climb the bergschrund at about 3430m a little right of directly below the first brèche of the pillar. Climb a slab couloir, traverse left across mixed ground and gain the brèche from which the couloir comes down.

Slant right on mixed ground to a poorly marked spur, go up first on its right (N) side then climb the crest (IV, then V and V sup.) of the Boccalatte Pillar itself on very fine red rock to the foot of a pinnacle which marks the top of this spur and turn this on the left. Continue up the ridge to reach a little snowy shoulder (from the level of the brèche it is possible to avoid this section of the climbing, if the mountain is in good condition, by climbing the easy couloir immediately left of the crest of the pillar).

Take a slightly slanting line up the very steep mixed ground on the N side of the pillar for 80m, and regain the crest of the pillar at the brèche between the second tower (above the Tour Carrée) and the foot of the Tour Rouge. Traverse right for 10m to climb ice-filled grooves (V sup.). Slant up to a small snowy shoulder, continue above and right for 20m to a crack whose bottom forms a V of red rock. Climb the crack (20m, V sup.). Go up to two inclined dièdres on the right, climb the right-hand

one (V), and gain the crest of the pillar (platform, cairn). Climb it up a slab (V) and a crack (V sup.) from which you exit right almost at the top of the Tour Rouge. Go left to gain the brèche above the Tour Rouge where the final pillar begins. Avoid the numerous small gendarmes on the right, climb the edge of the last (30m, III, IV, finish IV sup.), and reach the summit up a short snow slope.

East Face of Mont Blanc du Tacul, with the Boccalatte Pillar in the centre and the Gervasutti Pillar on the left (opposite page, right).
Climbers on the Boccalatte Pillar, seen from the Gervasutti Pillar (opposite page, left).
The Tour Rouge (right).

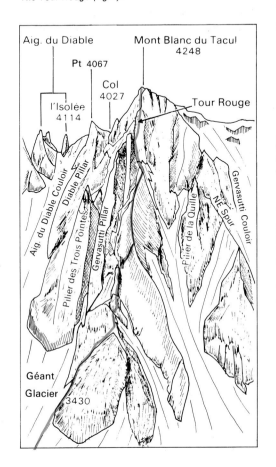

Aig. du Diable

Pt 4067

Mont Blanc du Tacul
4248

Col
4027

l'Isolée
4114

Tour Rouge

Aig. du Diable Couloir

Diable Pillar

Pilier des Trois Pointes

Gervasutti Pillar

Pilier de la Quille

NE Spur

Gervasutti Couloir

Géant
Glacier
3430

73. ROCHEFORT RIDGES 4001m — GRANDES JORASSES 4208m
Traverse

This is a magnificent traverse, always at high altitude, on mixed terrain, and taking two days. On the first day you go from the Col du Géant (3365m) to the Col des Grandes Jorasses (3825m) along the ridge passing the foot of the Dent du Géant (3900m), and going on first to the Aiguille (4001m) then to the Dôme (4015m) and finally to the Calotte (3966m) de Rochefort. This is a fairly quick and easy traverse (about 6 hrs). You spend the night at the E. Canzio bivouac hut and it is worth reconnoitring the start for the Pointe Young. On the second day, you go from the col to the summit of the Grandes Jorasses along the crest of the ridge, which varies from narrow to broad, at first rock, then mixed, then snow, and which crosses the large Pointe Young (3996m), the slender and vertiginous Pointe Marguerite (4066m), the Pointe Hélène (4045m), the Pointe Croz (4110m), which is where the mixed climbing begins, the Pointe Whymper (4184m), where the ridge broadens to the Pointe Walker (4208m); depending on your state of tiredness, on the weather and the conditions, you can continue the traverse down the Hirondelles Ridge, or go down the ordinary route, which is itself very pleasant.

No pitch is harder than IV and the difficulty is not sustained, so that en-joyment is not derived from climbing but from the atmosphere of a major route surrounding this magnificent traverse. The evening and night at the bivouac-hut in the notch of the Col des Grandes Jorasses give particular pleasure.

The place is isolated and you are very close to the mountain, aware of the closeness of wind and cloud, snow and rock. Perhaps too you will feel the satisfaction of a true mountain venture, far from hotel-like huts, téléphériques, caravans of climbers which are sometimes all too noisy; your isolation will lend to the air you breathe and the light around you (though they are in fact unaltered) a new brightness and an intensity of which you will be particularly aware in the late afternoon when, secure in the contentment of a route completed, you feel all the apprehension of the route to be done the next day.

The route should not be attempted except in good weather. It is most unpleasant to be caught by a storm on the crest of the Jorasses, especially if there is lightning, or if you are between the Pointe Marguerite and the Pointe Croz. It is here that the ridge is most slender and steepest, so that you have a superb view down slopes to the pinnacles on the N Face, and overlooking the S Face.

● **1st complete traverse:** From the Col au Geant to the top of the Jorasses: R. Schinko, H. Stange, K. Wallenfels, 21–23 July 1935. (1st ascent of the Grandes Jorasses by the W Ridge: H. O. Jones and G. W. Young, with J. Knubel, 14 August 1911.)

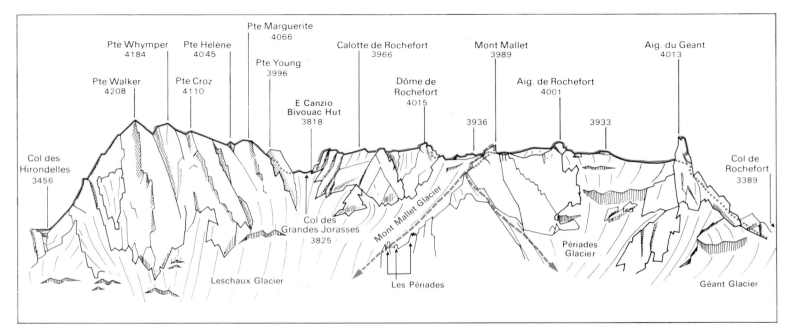

● **Vertical height:** This is relatively small (about 850m) from the lowest point, the Col du Géant (3365m), to the highest, Pointe Walker (4208m). But the total becomes much larger when all the ascents and descents are taken into account. The main characteristic of this route it is an ascending traverse.

● **Grade:** A long mixed route of which the second part is very committing. The difficult rock pitches are relatively few in number and only IV.

● **Time:** 6 hrs from the Col du Géant to the Col des Grandes Jorasses. 6–8 hrs from the Col des Grandes Jorasses to the Pointe Walker. 5–6 hrs from the Pointe Walker to the Col des Hirondelles.

● **Equipment:** Crampons, abseil rope.

● **Starting point:** The Torino Hut (3375m). It is also possible to take the first cable-car from Courmayeur.

● **Route** – *Outline:* This follows the line of the crest fairly well with Italy to the S, France to the N and some detours from time to time onto one side or the other.

Description:

1. Rochefort: From the Torino Hut (3375m) follow the ordinary route to the Aiguille de Rochefort (4001m, 3 hrs). Follow the snow ridge NE, turn the Doigt de Rochefort on the left and climb the rock step of the Dôme direct (4016m, 1 hr). Continue along the broken rocks of the ridge which becomes snow and then rock to reach the Calotte (3966m, 1 hr). Continue along the easy ridge to the top of the step above the Col des Grandes Jorasses which is descended in three abseils (1 hr).

2. Grandes Jorasses: Left of the col a couloir goes up to the ridge. Climb rocks on the right bank (IV), then fairly soon bear left up the big, not very steep but smooth overlapping slabs, broken by systems of ledges and cracks to the summit of the Pointe Young (3996m, $1\frac{1}{2}$–2 hrs).

From the summit descend first the N side, then at the brèche descend the S couloir for 30m, traverse right across the bulge of the buttress which follows (IV) and go 20m up the couloir which descends from the W Ridge of the Pointe Marguerite. Then take the rocks on the right bank of the couloir and gain the brèche between the two summits of the Pointe Marguerite (4066m, 2 hrs).

From here follow the very sharp and vertiginous ridge to the Pointe Hélène (4045m) and to the Pointe Croz (4110m). The ridge widens and becomes mixed as you continue to the Pointe Whymper (4184m) and from there to the Pointe Walker (4208m, $3\frac{1}{2}$–4hrs); 6–8 hrs from the Col des Grandes Jorasses.

Descent: If you descend the Hirondelles Ridge, look out for the abseils in the central section of the ridge.

The E. Canzio Hut on the Col des Grandes Jorasses (opposite page).
The Dent du Géant, the Rochefort Ridge, the Col des Grandes Jorasses, the Grandes Jorasses (above).

179

74. AIGUILLE VERTE 4121m
Grands Montets Ridge

From the Col des Grands Montets, the ridge goes up in a long, regular curve to the summit of the Verte. At the snow saddle of the Col it is comparatively broad and solid-looking, but as it goes further up the ridge becomes rock, and bristling with towers, at first very slender, then more massive, towards the Col du Nant Blanc. None of these towers is however sufficiently massive in itself to detract from the austerity and elegance of the route, which might indeed, were it not for this slender and indented fringing, seem monotonous and uninteresting, since the angle of the climb is very gentle. Above the col, the upper part of the ridge is in fact a glacier, the dome of the Verte, soaring and airy, its pure lines brought out by that translucent blue-green, so unique a shade but so varied, which also enhances the contrast between the straight, strong, clean lines of the serac barriers and the gentle, curving lines of the ridge itself. A truly magnificent sight! And it is yet further improved by the fact that the ridge runs between two of the steepest and wildest faces imaginable, the Nant Blanc Face to the right, concave and enclosed, overlooking far below the Mer de Glace and the Aiguilles, and the Argentière Face to the left, with its large glacier whose head and foot are both out of sight, but which, as you are nevertheless aware, runs along the foot of the great N Faces which you feel are just round the corner, on the left.

Unfortunately, on routes such as these, the climbing does not always match the surroundings. This is the case here: the intrinsic difficulty is not great and is anyway discontinuous (a few pitches of IV). Moreover, the angle being so gentle, you can console yourself with the more immediate, if more secret pleasure, of understanding the structure of a ridge and of working out the best route. This is the pleasure of unity with the mountains, of, as it were, a geological understanding when you take a certain ledge rather than the one which may look more appealing but is in fact a dead end. In such circumstances a party makes fast progress. If on the other hand such understanding is lacking, the route will be long and perhaps boring.

The exit onto the dome can be more or less difficult depending on conditions in any particular year; above it, there is usually a hard crust on the snow, which makes for good cramponning but which can also conceal wind-slab, difficult to detect.

Throughout the route you should look out for the best line and on the upper part you should always be on the alert for possible wind-slab.

● **1st ascent:** P. Dalloz, J. Lagarde and H. de Ségogne, 9–10 August 1925.
● **Vertical height:** About 900m from the Col des Grands Montets to the summit (from 3233 to 4121m), but this is along a very long ridge.
● **Grade:** This is a major mixed ridge on the Verte, where route-finding and mountaineering sense play a major part.
● **Time:** 8–12 hrs from the Col des Grands Montets to the summit.
● **Equipment:** Crampons, abseil rope.
● **Starting point:** The Col des Grands Montets (3233m).
● **Route** – *Outline:* The rock section between the Petite Verte and the Col du Nant Blanc; the first half of the ridge bristling with gendarmes is not climbed but

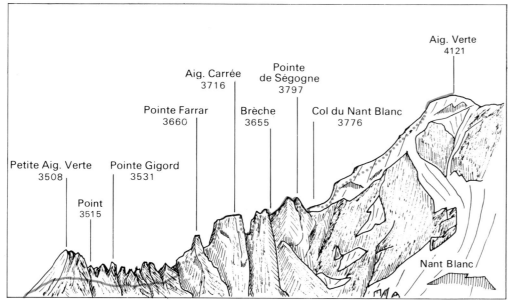

avoided by ledges on the Nant Blanc side; the second half consists of more distinct points: Pointe Farrar, Aiguille Carrée, Pointe de Ségogne, which are climbed, or turned on the Argentière side. The ice section, up the 'calotte' or dome of the Verte, is almost direct with detours depending upon the serac barriers and bergschrunds.

Description: From the Col des Grands Montets (3233m) follow the route up the Petite Verte, but 100m above the Shoulder leave this route to gain on the right by a slight descent the system of ledges on the Nant Blanc side, which traverses below the ridge (on which the most notable gendarme is the Pointe de Gigord, 3531m) and leads directly to the brèche just before the Pointe Farrar.

From the start of the ledges you should be constantly on the alert and anticipating the next pitch, because the system of ledges is not a straight line; it goes up, descends and is sometimes broken. After turning the buttresses of the Petite Verte, the ledges lead up to a couloir which is descended for 20m or so, to a point from which you go up

again to continue the traverse. When you arrive below the brèche before the Pointe Farrar, you can either climb chimneys to this brèche and on the Argentière side traverse slabs in the direction of the next brèche (3625m) between the Pointe Farrar and the Aiguille Carrée, or you can continue the traverse on the Nant Blanc side and climb the W Buttress of the Pointe Farrar to the summit and from there descend to the brèche.

Climb the Aiguille Carrée, which comes next, up a deep and sometimes icy chimney with large blocks on the Argentière side (IV). This leads to the ridge where a zone of easy-angled slabs and a short steep crack lead to the summit of the Carrée (3716m).

Descend on the Argentière side (short abseil at the end) to gain the next brèche (3655m).

The Pointe de Ségogne (3797m) which comes next is made up of a first step with three small gendarmes and a second step with two tops. From the brèche traverse on the Argentière side to climb a steep and often icy couloir on the right side (IV),

and reach the foot of the three small gendarmes which are turned on the left. Climb the second step up the ridge: a large smooth easy-angled slab (IV).

From the summit of the Pointe de Ségogne abseil down on the Argentière side towards the couloir which descends from the Col du Nant Blanc. Climb up this couloir (snow and rock) to reach the col (3776m, 4 hrs). From there the route is on ice. Climb the slopes of the calotte (dome), keeping on the Argentière side, to reach the summit. The exact route depends upon the serac barriers and the bergschrunds.

The Calotte of the Verte (opposite page).
The North Face of the Aiguille Verte with the Grands Montets Ridge on the right (above).

75. AIGUILLE NOIRE DE PEUTEREY
South Ridge
3773m

A name of legendary quality, a ridge profiled against the sky, a great reputation, magnificent climbing — all these are characteristics of the S Ridge of the Noire, and combine in a route from which dreams are made. And yet here we come up once again against the problem of the number of pitons, and here, because of the reputation of the ridge, its elegance and the elegance essential in the climber who aspires to it, the problem is a particularly grave one. At one time there were no more than eight pitons on the whole climb (and I am inclined to think that in 1950 there were only six). And yet today there are thirty. How many are we to expect in the future? It is perfectly understandable that all climbers should wish, one day, to do the S Ridge of the Noire; it is a natural magnet for eyes and ambitions. But what pleasure can you derive from the ascent if you have disobeyed the rules of the game? A sport performed in a stadium has its referees. Here, *you* are the referee, you, the climber face to face with the rock. Would it not be better to wait a while (after all, waiting is a form of progress) and then, when you are ready and fully fit to proceed, you can do the climb safely and elegantly without needing tricks which may well be a form of cheating? Putting in a piton amounts to adding an extra hold, or alternatively detracting in some way from the rock itself, its steepness, its texture, or from its height, and this, for the climber, is cheating. Any climber who really loves his sport should demand the utmost from himself, otherwise his pleasure will be mitigated or even spoilt.

The climbing here is long, not often strenuous, continuous but not sustained: there are shoulders and ledges, good belays and sound rock. The history of the S Ridge of the Noire is a microcosm of the history of climbing. It is worth remarking that while the Courmayeur guides played a big part in opening up the route, it was climbers from the Eastern Alps, used to limestone climbing, who made the first ascent.

● **1st ascent:** K. Brendel and H. Schaller, 26–27 August 1930.
● **Vertical height:** About 1100m (from 2660 to 3773m).
● **Grade:** TD with 10 pitons.
● **Time:** 7–10 hrs.
● **Equipment:** Carabiners.
● **Starting point:** The Noire Hut (2316m) is ideally situated and very pleasant.
● **Route** — *Outline:* You reach the ridge by taking a slanting line across the Pic Gamba. Above you follow the crest, fairly rounded in places, turning some steps generally on the right particularly on the lower half and a few less on the left higher up. Thanks to the towers on the ridge, the points of reference are obvious; moreover there are well-known pitches, the Welzenbach Slab, the Half Moon, the dièdre on the fifth tower.

Description: From the Noire Hut gain the foot of the Pic Gamba, the first tower (1 hr). Climb the left side of the E Spur for 50m, then a slab on the right (IV) which leads to a system of cracks and then grassy ledges. Bear right above a large rock triangle, visible from the hut, to gain the couloir from the brèche N of the Pic Gamba. Climb this for 30m, then climb the rib dividing it into two for 50m, cross the right-hand branch and then go up the rock steps of the Pointe Welzenbach to gain on the right the ridge coming down from the two gendarmes which form the second tower.

Climb this ridge direct, then on the left for 50m, to arrive at grassy terraces and reach a step. Here the difficulties begin. By a short dièdre (IV), gain a little shoulder on the crest of the ridge, climb a chimney from right to left (IV), and then a vertical slab (IV). Continue straight on, then go right to regain the ridge at the foot of an overhanging block 4m high (with a shoulder, IV). Reach on the right the brèche between the two gendarmes of the second tower. Turn the second gendarme on the right and rejoin the crest of the ridge. Avoid another gendarme again on the right, and then, from the brèche which follows, climb the ridge to the foot of a vertical step. Go again on the right, ascend ledges and then make a 60m rising traverse to arrive at the foot of the Welzenbach Slab with overlapping holds. Climb this (IV sup.) and then take other slabs and a chimney to gain the ridge and follow it to the summit of the Pointe Welzenbach (3355m), the third tower.

From here you can work out the route up the Brendel, but you may find it rather overawing, as is often the case when looking at a wall or slab from in front. Climb down easily, then make a 25m abseil to reach the brèche. Go up easily to the foot of the step on the Brendel called, because of its shape, the 'Demi-Lune' (Half Moon). Because this is alarming seen from below, many climbers have looked for its weaknesses, so that, paradoxically for one of the hardest pitches on the route, there are four ways of climbing it. The best is to reach the gap with a stride and climb up the fairly broad ridge first slightly left then almost straight up to a good platform (V sup.). The usual line is to the left of this route and starts 10m below the gap, going up a slab below an overhang and then a crack system (IV sup.) to the platform. Climb a crack (IV) left of the ridge, without going to two old iron pitons, continue up the crack (V) to a groove for the hands which leads left and allows the overhang to be avoided. Come back right and go straight up to a ledge which leads to the ridge and follow this to the summit of the Pointe Brendel (3499m), the fourth tower.

Abseil down to the brèche beyond. Turn on the left a short 10m pillar and climb the chimney on the Frêney side which separates it from the fifth tower. Make a stride to traverse to the ridge of the fifth tower and slant left (V) to reach the foot of the 35m dièdre on the fifth tower. Climb the back of

Pic Gamba 3069
Pointe Welzenbach 3355
Pointe Bich 3753
Aig. Noire de Peuterey 3773
Pointe Brendel 3499
Pt 3519
Pt 3291
Rey Couloir
2661
To the Noire Hut
Névé du Combalet

this (V) and below the overhangs closing it, traverse right across a smooth slab (V sup.) and rejoin the ridge which leads to the summit of the fifth tower (3586m).

Higher, after several teeth, there is a high step. After a line of slabs, climb two thin grooves on the right of the ridge and over two overhangs (V). Slant up right, climb a chimney, pass a large detached block on the left, climb straight up for 3m (IV) and return to the ridge which is followed, keeping left, to a shoulder. Traverse right to a couloir. Climb the couloir and by a short chimney gain the ridge and then the Pointe Biche (3753m). Reach the brèche slightly below by an abseil and over blocks. Traverse right along scree ledges and return to the ridge to reach the summit. In bad weather, particularly if there is lightning, from the brèche it is possible to traverse below the summit (climbing a short wall, III) to reach the descent route by the E Ridge.

The South Ridge of the Aiguille Noire de Peuterey on the left, with the Peuterey Ridge on Mont Blanc in the background.

76. LES COURTES 3856m
Central North-North-East Spur

This is the spur coming down lowest onto the Argentière Glacier, giving an elegant route up the centre of the face. Halfway up, it crosses to the foot of a fine red tower. From the summit of this tower a snow ridge goes up to join the final slope, which while not very steep is often icy. The first party to do the route turned this Red Tower and its slabs on the right; R. Guillard and I, on the second ascent, climbed the Tower itself; it is quite hard, but a fine climb (some moves of V), possibly more elegant than the original route and giving a rock-climbing appeal to this mixed route — although of course it may by the same token detract from its homogeneity.

There are superb views throughout the climb. From the training point of view, the Central Spur is excellent preparation, psychological and technical, for later major routes of this kind.

- **1st ascent:** J. Jonquières, A. Maillol, M. Villarem with E. Frendo and A. Tournier, 12 July 1939.
- **Vertical height:** About 1000m from the start of the difficulties to the summit (from 2850 to 3856m).
- **Grade:** A mixed route (giving a TD rock section if the Red Tower is climbed).
- **Time:** From the Argentière Hut the approach is short. Set out early, in the night, for two reasons. On the one hand the route is long, so to have good conditions for the descent as well you should reach the summit fairly early; on the other hand it is important to get used to walking and climbing at night by head-torch. This latter gives quite different dimensions to climbing: it requires new attitudes and a different sense of balance depending on crampons and on the angle of the snow, more or less steep, which cannot be seen but only guessed at when the beams of the head-torch momentarily light up a little patch of ground. The ground, grotesquely, seems almost to be moving, although the illusion is of course due to the movement of the lamp. Moreover your impressions vary according to whether you use a head-torch or a torch held in the hand. In any case it is important that the climber should feel at ease in the dark, that is to say that he should acquire at the same time a sense of balance at night and a feeling, without seeing them, for the angle of the slope while he is moving. Besides there is considerable pleasure to be gained, when you are fit, from moving and acting as if in another world. On the technical side, this training is essential for the long routes where you are obliged to set out at night. If you have not had some practice, not only will you never have the satisfaction of being 'at one' with the night, but you will also waste a lot of time

which is bad for morale at the beginning of a big route.

6—7 hrs from the bergschrund to the summit (if you take the Red Tower you should add an extra hour.

● **Equipment:** Crampons (pitons, carabiners if including the Red Tower).
● **Starting point:** The Argentière Hut (2771m).
● **Route** – *Outline:* The spur; the Red Tower is climbed or turned on the right.

Description: You can start at the first step of the spur at its lowest point (2876m) or gain the crest 100m above from the E or W. Then follow the crest of the spur up easy broken rock, with some snow patches and mixed ground, to the point beyond a small snow shoulder where the ridge comes up against the slab step of the Red Tower. Now traverse diagonally across a very steep snow slope with rocks protruding to gain the crest of a secondary snow ridge. It is also possible to traverse lower to gain earlier the couloir leading to this snow ridge, but the climber will have to choose his own route depending upon the conditions. Alternatively you can stay on the

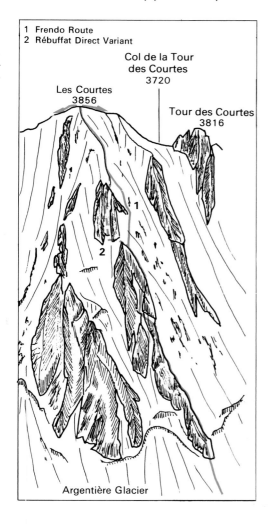

1 Frendo Route
2 Rébuffat Direct Variant

Col de la Tour
des Courtes
3720

Les Courtes
3856

Tour des Courtes
3816

Argentière Glacier

central spur, climbing the step of the Red Tower by a system of cracks with rounded edges (V) which streak the slabs on the right. Arrive at a good horizontal ridge, go left towards the crest of the ridge, and climb further cracks (V) where the wall steepens a little. Then go back left to the ridge and reach the summit of the Red Tower. Climb the snow ridge, at first horizontal, which then steepens to gain the final slopes and the summit.

View from the North Face of the Courtes towards the North Spur, with Mont Dolent and the Grand Combin in the background (opposite page).
The North-East side of the Courtes, the North Spur and the North Face (above).

77. AIGUILLE VERTE 4121m
Sans Nom Ridge

This is a magnificent route, with no serious technical difficulty (there are no very difficult rock or ice pitches), but it requires the greatest competence on mixed terrain, a good understanding of snow and ice, and considerable physical fitness in the climber himself, so that he can stick to the times given. There are two reasons for this last: considerations of safety in the couloir and on the snow section of the route, and in order for the climber to have time to admire the remarkable views from the ridge itself, for from the ridge you look down over both the Charpoua and the Nant Blanc cirques, both of them wholly remote, but very different one from the other, if only because of the effect of light on them.

To reach the ridge there are two routes: one, fairly long, up the S Face of the Aiguille Sans Nom and the other, more elegant, up to the Brèche Sans Nom and then up the little W Face of the Aiguille Sans Nom; I suggest the second, but must point out that if it is not snowed up, or if you fail to leave very early, on a cold night, it can be dangerous because of stonefall. The climber should be aware of this danger and choose the best time for the route accordingly. Naturally you should be out of the couloir before the sun reaches it, and this should present no difficulty, accidents apart; 3–5 hrs is quite enough time to reach the Brèche Sans Nom from the hut (if you wish to follow the couloir, you should leave the hut at 1 am).

You can also go up the spur descending low down on the glacier to the right of the couloir. When you reconnoitre the glacier the previous evening, you should, if you have decided on this last route, look out for the big crack which splits the middle of the lower part of the spur.

● **1st ascent:** Mlle G. de Longchamp with A. Charlet and M. Bozon, 21 September 1926.
● **Vertical height:** 884m from the Charpoua Hut (2841m) to the Brèche Sans Nom (3725m); 257m from the Brèche to the Aiguille Sans Nom (3982m); 139m from the Aiguille Sans Nom to the Aiguille Verte 1280m in all (from 2841m to 4121m).
● **Grade:** A long mixed route with a fairly hard rock section (D); very cold in the morning (climbing the Aiguille Sans Nom) and with an ice section which can be very tricky on the ridge especially if instead of climbing the two gendarmes you choose to turn them. The evening before the route reconnoitre the glacier, for it is absolutely essential to set off by head-torch and be in the couloir at daybreak.
● **Time:** 3–5 hrs from the hut to the brèche. 3–4 hrs from the brèche to the Aiguille Sans Nom. 2–3 hrs from the Sans Nom to the Verte. In all 8–12 hrs depending upon the conditions.
● **Equipment:** Crampons, 40m of rope between each climber on the ridge.
● **Starting point:** The Charpoua Hut (2841m).
● **Route** – *Outline:* The couloir to the brèche, the slightly concave small W Face of

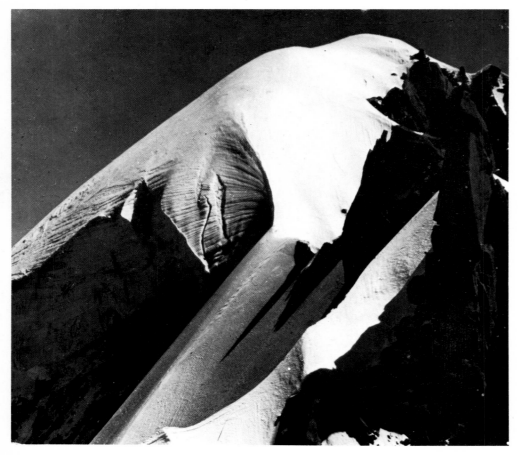

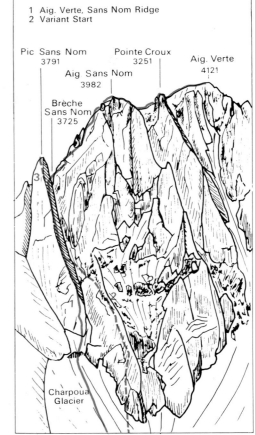

1 Aig. Verte, Sans Nom Ridge
2 Variant Start

Pic Sans Nom 3791

Pointe Croux 3251

Aig. Verte 4121

Aig Sans Nom 3982

Brèche Sans Nom 3725

Charpoua Glacier

the Aiguille Sans Nom, then the ridge proper.

Description: From the hut go up to the foot of the snow couloir descending from the Brèche Sans Nom. Climb up its bed. It is possible to avoid the lower third of the couloir and so reduce the risk of objective dangers by taking the buttress which descends fairly low onto the glacier to the right of the couloir. To do this climb the great crack dividing the base, forming two chimneys, then go easily up a zone of small overhangs and rock steps bearing left to the point where these end at a steep wall. Then traverse left to gain the couloir, about 200m below the brèche. From the brèche you can ascend the Pic Sans Nom by the E Ridge rounded into a little face above the brèche (a slab which is climbed by the crack on the left, IV). Abseil back to the brèche and continue towards the Verte.

Either start straight up the W Face of the Aiguille Sans Nom, or on the right up a short overhanging chimney (III), taken below the brèche, followed by a slab (IV) which leads to a platform. Move right to climb a chimney (III) and reach a mixed zone of short easy steps on the left not far from the ridge, which is climbed to the foot of a vertical step cut by deep chimneys. Traverse 50m right going round a little arête, and climb a system of slabs and chimneys (III and IV) cut by platforms. Go back slightly left up a slab (IV) to gain a short open chimney. You reach easy slopes. Turn on the Charpoua side a step on the crest of the ridge, then follow this to the summit block of the Aiguille Sans Nom, 6m high, which is climbed on the Nant Blanc side (3982m).

Abseil down the Aiguille Verte side, follow the ridge up mixed ground, climb a gendarme, using the rope, on the Charpoua side. Continue up the crest turning two small steps on the Charpoua side, and then a snow ridge leads up to between the two summits of the Pointe Croux (4023m). Climb the E summit descending on the Aiguille Verte side and follow the sharp crest of the snow ridge to the calotte (dome) and the summit of the Verte.

Descent: If, depending upon the time and the conditions, the Whymper Couloir is likely to be dangerous, descend by the Rocheuse Buttress, unless you have come prepared to bivouac.

Towards the calotte of the Verte (opposite page). The Sans Nom Ridge on the Aiguille Verte, with the Drus on the left, the Charpoua Glacier below, the Grandes Rocheuses, the Aiguille du Jardin and the Talèfre Glacier on the right, and the Aiguille du Moine in the foreground (above).

78. DENT DU REQUIN 3422m
North Face

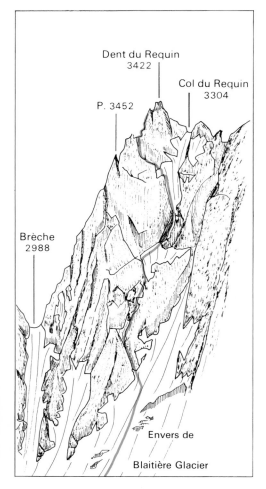

Dent du Requin
3422

P. 3452

Col du Requin
3304

Brèche
2988

Envers de

Blaitière Glacier

Above the Envers de Blaitière Glacier and the steep snow slopes overlooking the berg-schrund, the N Face of the Dent du Requin stands out, high and sheer. It is a sunless face, looking due N and moreover enclosed by the ice gullies coming down from W of the Col du Requin which descend like organ-pipes to the very depths of the dark gorges, and by the NE Ridge which goes sheer down to the Capucin du Requin and the Mer de Glace. The lines of the face are very steep, and the ice on the face itself, the upper section funnel-shaped, the lower section broader, shaped like a spring-board, add to the atmosphere of 'N Face' which is unusual in the Chamonix Aiguilles.

The rock, fine red granite darkened by facing N, is very sound and very steep for granite; it is also very compact, with huge smooth slabs to the right and especially to the left of the route. This is also very impressive, not just because of these feature-less slabs, but also because of a feeling of inescapability. But the face is not very high, no more than 700m from the bergschrund, and only 500m from the beginning of the rock-climbing; the altitude is moreover not great. From the training point of view this N

Face, as well as being enjoyable with its own particular appeal, can offer very useful experience in preparation for longer, higher routes of the same type. Finally the descent by the ordinary route is short and easy.

● **1st ascent:** J. Couttet and G. Rébuffat, 22 July 1945.

● **Vertical height:** About 700m from the bergschrund to the summit (from 2700 to 3422m).

● **Grade:** A mixed route. The rock section is TD, 15 pitons, with a very sustained 100m section between the two névés (V and A1).

● **Time:** 1 hr from the Envers des Aiguilles Hut to the start of the difficulties. 7—9 hrs from there to the summit.

● **Equipment:** Crampons, pitons, carabiners, étriers.

● **Starting point:** Envers des Aiguilles Hut (2520m).

● **Route** – *Outline:* Snow slope, rock step, central névé, narrow buttress between two snow gullies (crux), funnel-shaped upper névé of which the left edge is followed with a finish onto the top of the E Ridge.

Description: From the Envers des Aiguilles Hut go up névés, terraces and scree, then along the Envers de Blaitière Glacier to reach the base of the wall (about 2750m) and gain the foot of a well-marked spur joined to the lower step of the face left of a point directly below the summit. Climb the snow couloir bounding it to the E up the rocks of the left bank to below the brèche separating the spur from the step. Slant up a slab cut by crack-chimneys. Climb an inclined couloir-dièdre, avoid an overhang on the left and gain a terrace. Traverse right, climb vertical cracks which lead back to the left, and climb directly up to the brèche (III and IV, with a move of V sup.).

From the brèche a high wall cut by three crack systems leading to a secondary ridge can be seen above. Follow a well-marked ledge (IV) which leads to the central cracks, but before reaching them climb a wet vertical chimney (IV sup.) which gives direct access to the cracks on the left. By these cracks (III and IV, poor rock) gain the secondary ridge at the edge of an ice slope (the central névé). Above and right can be seen a narrow buttress between two ice gullies; this is the crux pitch. To reach it, climb the ice slope then skirt the wall to the right and get onto the buttress by its W side. Almost on the crest, climb a vertical 10m dièdre (A1), then cross onto the E flank and climb directly up steep slabs for 80m (V), interrupted by a slight overhang, to the bottom of the upper funnel-shaped névé.

Climb the right bank up steep loose rock (III) and reach a zone of ledges which go up left towards the NE Ridge which is followed to the summit.

North Face of the Dent du Requin (opposite page). View from the Couvercle Hut: the Dent du Requin in the centre, with the East Face on the left and the North Face on the right, with Mont Blanc on the far left and the Aiguille du Plan on the right (above).

189

79. AIGUILLE VERTE 4121m
Couturier Couloir

The main characteristic of this couloir is its elegance and this is, too, the main source of the pleasure of the climb — to be on a slope with pure sheer lines, on a route which soars straight from the glacier to the summit. There are fine views, too, in the foreground and background, especially when you have reached a certain height. For it must be admitted that, from the technical point of view, in spite of the angle of the snow (51° for the first 200m, 55° for the next 300m, and 45° thereafter), the movements made by the climber are always the same and can therefore lead to tiredness or even to boredom. It could be said that to do the Couturier Couloir, all you need is to know how to crampon; this is incorrect, of course, since you would also need good snow. As long as the snow is good, the climb is simple. The angle of the Couloir is so regular that two alpinists who fell off half-way up came hurtling down it, but emerged more or less unscathed.

The first party to make a route on this face was B. Washburn with G. Charlet, A. Couttet and A. Devouassoux, on 2 September 1929, but very early they took to the big rock rognon on the left bank of the couloir. The direct route was done three years later by M. Couturier with A. Charlet and J. Simond. Since then it has been frequently repeated and has had winter and solo ascents, being aesthetically superb, and leading directly to the Verte. The climber has the inner satisfaction of following a sheer, direct, elegant line and the joy of coming out onto a highly reputed summit. Every member of the party should be a good safe climber; not only is there a risk of muscular fatigue from the same repeated movements, but there is also an unrelieved nervous tension.

● **1st ascent**: M. Couturier with A. Charlet and J. Simond, 1 July 1932.
● **Vertical height**: About 1000m from the start of the difficulties to the summit (from 3100 to 4121m).
● **Grade**: A major snow-couloir route. Be careful to stay alert in spite of a certain monotony in the climbing.
● **Time**: 1½–2 hrs from the Argentière Hut to the start of the difficulties. 4–6 hrs from there to the summit. It is also possible to set out from the Col des Grands Montets, which adds about 45 mins.
● **Equipment**: Crampons.
● **Starting point**: Argentière Hut (2771m) or the Col des Grands Montets (3233m).
● **Route** – *Outline*: This follows the slightly curving couloir. In the upper part, depending upon the conditions, it is possible to go right up the calotte (dome).

Description: From the hut cross the Argentière Glacier in the direction of the couloir; to do this go between the base of the Grande Rocheuse Buttress and the rock rognon (2866m) and below the latter; then ascend the Rognons Glacier to the foot of the

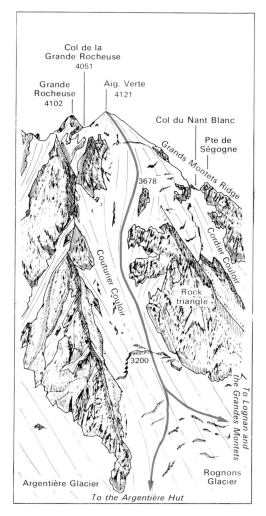

couloir. If you come from the Col des Grands Montets, after descending the Rognons Glacier, traverse right below the Grands Montets Ridge and the NW Face of the Verte (beware of falling seracs).

Climb the bergschrund up the runnel and go up either right or left of the centre of the couloir where there is a risk of snow slides and occasionally avalanches. Halfway up follow the curve of the Couloir to the right and from there either go straight up or climb up right to gain the summit by the calotte (beware of wind slab).

Towards the calotte of the Aiguille Verte (opposite page, left).
Towards the middle of the Couloir (opposite page, right).
The calotte of the Verte (right).

80. PETIT DRU 3733m
North Face

This is a fine big face, in superb surroundings; it gives magnificent climbing and remarkable views, everything that the climber could wish for. It was attempted as early as 1904 by that well-known team Ryan and Lochmatter; it was first descended in 1932 and ascended in 1935; it has now become a classic.

In some poor seasons, because the ice never melts out of the cracks, it is impossible or at least extremely hard. In good conditions, however, it can be done quickly. On 14 August 1946, I did it in an afternoon, not to set up some sort of record, but simply because it was perfect weather, because it was the last day of the holidays for my companion René Mallieux, and because the next day, 15 August, was the Fête des Guides in Chamonix, and I wanted to be there. We went up on the first train to Montenvers — at that time it only left Chamonix at 8.30 and went slowly — crossed the bergschrund at 13.10 and were on the summit at 19.30. René was delighted and so was I.

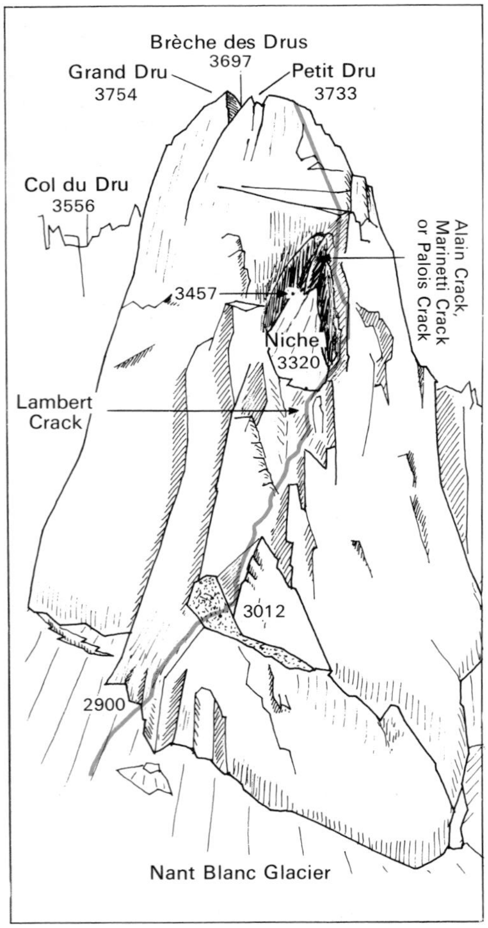

But the best way to do the climb is to set off from a bivouac on the terraces, or under the rocks, of the Drus rognon. The face is steeper than are most granite faces and the rock is very sound, except in the first couloir. The belays are good. The climb is mostly up cracks and therefore strenuous; it can be very awkward for climbers unused to Chamonix cracks.

- **1st ascent:** P. Allain and R. Leininger, 31 July – 1 August 1935.
- **Vertical height:** About 800m from the start of the difficulties to the summit (from 2900 to 3733m).
- **Grade:** TD with 10 pitons (4 pitches of V). Danger of falling stones below the niche. Quite a lot of verglas on the upper part of the climb.
- **Time:** 6–10 hrs from the start of the difficulties to the summit.
- **Equipment:** Carabiners; carry an axe and a light pair of crampons per party.
- **Starting point:** Bivouac on the rognon at the foot of the face.
- **Route** – *Outline:* Above the couloir giving access to the zone of terraces, go up diagonally left to right to reach the pillar beside the Niche.

Description: From the bivouac climb the upper slopes of the little Dru Glacier or the crest of the rock rognon at the top of the moraine, and make for the snow ridge separating the Dru Glacier from the Nant Blanc Glacier. Cross this at the best place and go up the Nant Blanc Glacier to skirt the foot of the Drus, and start the climb up the first couloir. It is easy, deep, with poor rock, and gives access 100m above to a zone of terraces covered with stones and snow. Make a rising traverse right to gain the left side of a large triangular pillar. Climb cracks and chimneys for about 100m (III with a move of IV) to reach the point where the pillar joins the wall proper of the face. Going diagonally up to the right a chimney formed by cracks (IV) can be seen of which the most obvious is a 15m jamming crack (IV, strenuous). Traverse right along a small ledge to reach a vertical wall cut by a

10m crack (the Lambert Crack, V). Climb this, turn an overhang on the left then go up a couloir-chimney full of ice which leads to the bottom of the Niche. Make a rising traverse to the right (usually ice, rock steps and slabs in dry years) to a large platform on the edge of the W Face. Continue up a couloir with large blocks to a second platform also on the edge of the W Face and stop to look at the nearby West Face Route. From here go up a sort of depression left of the monolithic buttress which overlooks the platform. By a traverse left gain a vertical 20m chimney. Climb this and exit left by a dièdre to a platform, then climb a short 3m crack to reach a stance. Do not take the wide crack going up above but descend 1m to the left to climb a dièdre with

[Diagram labels]

Brèche des Drus
Grand Dru 3754
3697
Petit Dru 3733
Col du Dru 3556
Alain Crack, Marinetti Crack or Palois Crack
3457
Niche 3320
Lambert Crack
3012
2900
Nant Blanc Glacier

a crack (IV) which leads to a platform on the edge of a vertical wall (impressive view of the Niche). Climb a vertical 20m crack (III and IV) to a slight hollow overlooked by a vertical wall. Climb this directly (V, exposed) or avoid it on the left (sloping ledge, V) and reach the foot of the Allain Crack. Do not climb this. Traverse right through a 'letter-box' and make a stride right to the Martinetti Crack which slants up a zone of slabs. Climb this crack (IV for 15m, then V when it steepens and narrows). Finish left up a slab. Good belay. Climb a crack on the left with a flake (V), then a 4m cracked wall (V, strenuous) and then gain on the right the third large platform on the edge of the W Face.

On the left climb cracked rocks for 40m (IV) which lead to a snow ledge. From here the climbing can become mixed. Climb a wall, go up a system of chimneys (IV) to the first quartz ledge 150m below the summit (to the right there is a finish traversing onto the Bonatti Pillar). Go left into a couloir (large blocks at the start) and climb it for 60m to reach the second, sloping quartz ledge (which, if you wish, leads to a hole through the Bonatti Pillar 50m below the summit, and allows an escape onto the S Face and then in two pitches to the ordinary route at the foot of its difficult pitch).

Above climb the back of the last, often icy, chimney to reach the summit.

North Face and West Face of the Drus.

81. MONT BLANC 4807m
Innominata Ridge

This is a great Mont Blanc route and one of the finest. In spite of its name, it is in fact only half a ridge. It is in the middle of that great wall of deep couloirs and extraordinary red granite pillars, those of Frêney to the E and those of Brouillard to the W; the wall which is the central feature of the S Face of Mont Blanc, created and forced upwards to the sky forty million years ago. This is an imposing and stark environment.

For the Innominata as for the Peuterey Ridge, there is a long approach; nevertheless, in poor weather at 4000m, a retreat and descent by the Brouillard Glacier is less dangerous than by the Rochers Gruber. It can therefore be said that, up to a certain altitude, the route is less committing. But the ascent of Mont Blanc by the Innominata Ridge is in any case a major route, a mixed route where you are affected less by the

1 Innominata Ridge
1a, 1b, 1c—Variants
2 S Pillar of Frêney
3 Pilier Dérobé
4 Central Pillar of Frêney
5 N Pillar of Frêney

Mont Blanc de Courmayeur 4748

S Pillar

N Pillar

Central Pillar
Pilier Dérobé

Tour Rouge

Pte Eccles 4041

Col Eccles 4000

technical difficulty (pitches of III and IV) than by the height and the loneliness, though this latter is mitigated by the Eccles bivouac hut at 3850m.

The rock, good red granite, is sound. The route makes the most skilful use of the terrain. There is one dangerous section: the traverse of the great couloir, where there is danger of stonefall. There is a very steep section on the final ridge, but the main things to be feared on the Innominata Ridge, as on all major routes, especially those on the Italian side of Mont Blanc, are wind and bad weather. Because of its height and its exposure, there is no protection on this side of the mountain from the W wind which whips straight over the Col de la Seigne. This is a route not to be undertaken except in good conditions, in settled weather and when you are really fit. I did the route once on 17 October. The days may be short in October, but the colours are magnificent. It was a day of perfect peace, of total solitude; a day of joy and comradeship for the three men who were that day climbing Mont Blanc.

● **1st ascent**: S. L. Courtauld and E. G. Oliver with A. Aufdenblatten and A. and H. Rey, 19–20 August 1919.
● **Vertical height**: 1260m from the Monzino Hut to the Eccles bivouac hut; 957m from the hut to the summit (from 3850 to 4807m); 2217m from the Monzino Hut to the summit.
● **Grade**: A mixed route, very serious, at high altitude. Pitches of IV.
● **Time**: 5–7 hrs from the Monzino Hut to the Eccles bivouac hut. 7–12 hrs from the hut to the summit.
● **Equipment**: Crampons.
● **Starting point**: At one time it was usual to start from the old Gamba Hut at 2663m. Then in 1939 the C.A.I. built a first bivouac hut near the top of the Pointe Eccles. The platform on which that was built was so exiguous that even though the hut was small, it tilted over to the right. It was destroyed in 1952, so that this magnificent face regained its true stature and loneliness. Then a new bivouac hut was built in 1958, a little lower down, about 200m below the Pointe Eccles, and protected by a large overhanging block.
● **Route** – Outline: The large well-defined ridge over the Pointe de l'Innominata and

the Aiguille Croux is part of the summit wall of Mont Blanc. This means that above the Col Eccles, the Innominata Ridge looks more like a wall. The general line of the original route ressembles a figure 4: a direct ascent, a traverse left and a return diagonally right to the summit ridge of Mont Blanc.

Description: From the Monzino Hut to the Eccles bivouac-hut: Go up to the little Châtelet Glacier and ascend it towards the right. Cross a short area of polished slabs, then take an ascending line slanting left towards the base of the S Ridge of the Innominata which is crossed at the foot of the first gendarme to reach, with a slight descent, the Brouillard Glacier (look at the photograph of the Aiguille Croux-Innominata Route). Cross the glacier which there forms a small plateau towards the left of the foot of the rock buttress which descends from the summit ridge of the Innominata. Climb the bergschrund on the left of the buttress and slant across the slope – do not go straight up it – to reach the Col du Frêney (3600m). Climb a steep, often icy, slope towards the Pointe Eccles and reach the bivouac hut by slanting up left, first up a névé and then up mixed terrain of rock and snow.

From the Eccles bivouac hut to Mont Blanc: From the bivouac hut gain the ridge descending to the Col du Frêney, go up this and climb the short wall to reach the Pointe Eccles (4041m) keeping right, and from

there the Col Eccles (about 4000m). Follow the snow ridge which leads to the foot of the great rock step; do not go left, climb the ridge on good granite (III) somewhat on the Brouillard side, to the foot of two red towers. Climb a chimney and gain a ledge, climb by a crack (IV) the 5m wall which follows on the right of the first tower. Turn this on the right (E) and gain the brèche to the N of the tower. Leave the second tower on the left and follow a horizontal snow ridge to the foot of the second step. Avoid this on the left towards the great snow couloir. Cross this rapidly at about 4250m, above the place where it steepens. Gain and climb a rock rib to a narrow ice couloir at the foot of an over-hanging red tower which goes up obliquely left; climb this couloir to the great rock buttress closing the great couloir. Climb this buttress keeping almost to the crest on the W side (rock steps, snow slopes and ridges); it ends in a snow ridge about 150m high. Continue up this ridge or up the slope to the left to reach the Brouillard Ridge at about 4650m. Follow this and turn off left to gain directly the summit of Mont Blanc.

The snow ridge at the foot of the second step (opposite page).
The South Face of Mont Blanc; on the right the Chandelle and the Frêney Pillar, lower right the Innominata, the Innominata Ridge directly below the summit, on the left the Brouillard Pillars and the Brouillard Ridge (above).

82. LES DROITES 4000m
North Spur

Opposite the Argentière Hut is the huge majestic N Face of the Droites; of that great wall of couloirs and pillars running without a line of weakness from the Verte to the Triolet and beyond to Mont Dolent, this is the most impressive section, being nearest to the hut and the highest. It curves slightly outwards; that is to say that its N Spur protrudes a little from the NW Face to the left, a massively simple wall of snow slopes where we find the Davaille-Cornuau Route, and the NE Face on the left where the Lagarde Couloir soars upwards between the pillars, one of the finest routes made by that outstanding alpinist. The N Spur is therefore on the apex between two faces and the route moves from one to the other. This is a mixed route, never very difficult but long and

1 NE Couloir (Lagarde Couloir)
2 N Spur
2a Variant Start
3 W Summit, N Spur

Les Droites E Summit 4000
Brèche des Droites 3944
W Summit 3984
Col des Droites 3733
Col de Aig. Verte 3798
3775
3500
3384
Argentière Glacier

sustained. Except on the final section it is not particularly beautiful, but it is impressive and thought-provoking. The Vallot Guide gives an angle of 56·5° from 2926m to 3400m on the lower section which takes the NE side, and then of 61° from 3384m to 3626m for the central section. This sort of angle would be very considerable on an ice route, but is less alarming on a mixed route as here, with a fair number of rock sections. Higher up the angle eases. It is always better to belay, but it can sometimes be possible for an evenly-matched party to move together. The route is done fairly frequently each year and on good days several ropes may be on the route together. At such times particular care should be taken to avoid stonefalls. In any case you should set out very early, using head-torches, even if the distance from the hut to the bergschrund is short.

● **1st ascent:** C. Authenac with F. Tournier, 20—21 July 1937.
● **Vertical height:** The spur is 1210m from its base at 2790m to the summit. The usual route starts at 2926m which gives a height difference of almost 1100m (from 2926 to 4000m).
● **Grade:** A major route in high mountain surroundings, TD.
● **Time:** 9—15 hrs from the hut to the summit.
● **Equipment:** Crampons, ice-screws and ice-pitons.
● **Starting point:** Argentière Hut (2771m).
● **Route** — *Outline:* The couloir on the NE side left of the lower buttress, then from the brèche 3407m the spur on its NW flank to the shoulder, followed by the summit ridge.

Description: From the Argentière Hut, cross the Argentière Glacier and enter the little glacier bay, without going too high, to start up the first couloir left and above the lower buttress of the spur. Above the bergschrund, climb the bed of the couloir up steep and sound rock to the foot of the gendarme on the left of the couloir. Where the couloir widens, gain the saddle between the gendarme and the wall. Go straight up then bear right, cross over the ridge of a snow-capped pillar to gain and climb a long deep couloir, at first up the rocks on the left bank and then up the bed, to the deep brèche of the N Spur (3407m).

Climb the snow crest to the foot of the wall which follows it, then climb an icy 40m couloir-chimney at first on the left bank and then on the right to a shoulder at the foot of a vertical step of the ridge. Slant right up an ice slope to a horizontal ledge. Several metres above the ledge climb a couloir on the left (blocks covered with verglas), which leads back to the ridge, where several short steps lead to the foot of a great barrier of smooth slabs.

Bear right up a system of chimneys and ledges, pass behind a detached flake at the foot of the great smooth slabs. Get into and climb another ice couloir using large blocks on the left bank, then a couloir-chimney with a recessed overhang on the right bank to gain the ridge (3500m). Slightly right climb a deep couloir with large overhanging blocks to finish at a snowy platform. Climb blocks for 20m or so and traverse horizontally right over steps and detached flakes to reach the edge of very steep ice slopes. Traverse these horizontally for 20m level with two rock outcrops. From the second outcrop slant up right to reach a chimney very steep at the start. Continue up a chimney-couloir interrupted by overhangs; climb the bed for 20m, then go up broken rocks to reach a shoulder with a snow cornice. Climb a vertical 10m crack, pull up onto a little shoulder. Traverse snow and ice diagonally left (30m) to reach a long couloir with easy snowy blocks which leads to the brèche at the top of the couloir.

Then continue up the very fine terminal ridge: there are gendarmes and pinnacles linked by snow ridges. Follow the crest turning obstacles by ledges on the E side, then avoid a first group of towers by a rising traverse on the N Face and a second group on the E flank. Climb the snow ridge to the summit.

The North Face of the Droites with the North Spur between the sunny and the shadowy sides.

83. AIGUILLE NOIRE DE PEUTEREY
West Face
3773m

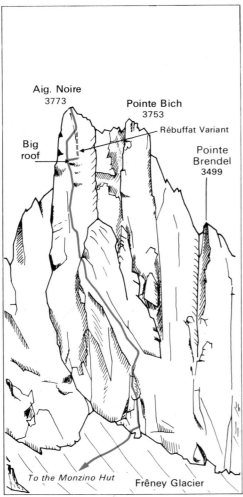

Aig. Noire
3773

Pointe Bich
3753

Rébuffat Variant

Big
roof

Pointe
Brendel
3499

To the Monzino Hut   Frêney Glacier

This is a superb rock-climbing route, not so continuous or sustained in standard as the Punta Gugliermina, but with a very strenuous, indeed very difficult pitch, despite the pitons in place on a very overhanging dièdre (about 15m high) on the upper third of the Face, the most difficult section of the climb. The face is beautiful, very isolated, cold, even unfriendly. The grey rock is sound on the difficult sections, but can be poor on the easier central section. V. Ratti and G. Vitali took nearly three days on the first ascent, B. Pierre and I took two on the second; now that the pitons are in place, especially in the dièdre, it is a day's climb.

● **1st ascent:** V. Ratti and G. Vitali, 18–20 August 1939.
● **Vertical height:** About 650m from the start of the difficulties to the summit (from 3320m to 3773m).
● **Grade:** TD with 50 pitons, not very sustained but with one very hard pitch even if – and this is the case – the pitons are in place.
● **Time:** 3–4 hrs from the Monzino Hut to the start of the difficulties, depending on the state of the glacier. 9–10 hrs from there to the summit.
● **Equipment:** Carabiners, étriers.
● **Starting point:** Monzino Hut (2590m).
● **Route** – *Outline:* The Face can be divided into three sections: the base, which after a short traverse is fairly steep where you go straight up, the easy middle section where you go up diagonally, the very steep summit wall which is climbed directly almost in the centre.

Description: From the Monzino Hut (2590m) either go up directly passing below the Aiguille Croux, or over the Col de l'Innominata to the foot of the face going beyond the point directly below the couloir from the S Brèche of the Dames Anglaises. 50–60m right of the fairly large bergschrund of this couloir get onto the rock. Gain a ledge and in two pitches (III) reach the foot of a narrow chimney with two jammed blocks (V, then IV) and climb it. Exit right onto the small platform of a buttress going up to an overhang. Make a stride left and go through a 'letter-box'. Go back right above the overhang; climb a line of crack-chimneys (a move of IV sup., then 30m of IV) to the horizontal brèche on an arête giving access to a huge scree couloir which continues as a

crack to the brèche left of the Pointe Bich. Here the Boccalatte Route goes off left towards the Pointe Bich and the Ratti Route goes left to the summit.

Go up the couloir but leave it left as soon as possible (do not go up more than 60m because the slabs cannot be climbed) for a spur, climbing a system of cracks (III and IV) immediately right of the crest of the spur (which lower down becomes a vertical wall bounding the 'letter-box'). Gain the top of the spur, climb the snow arête which covers it to the brèche which separates it from the wall. Continue up bad rock on the left (III), reach a couloir-chimney and climb it. Higher climb an arête for three rope-lengths obliquely right; this is cut by short walls with chimneys which can sometimes be icy (two pitches of IV sup.). Climb an inclined slab on the right.

You have reached the end of the middle zone and arrived at the foot of the first dièdre, the start of the main difficulties. Climb this at first up the back, then on the left, then again up the back and pull up onto a jammed block (30m, V, a move of V sup.). Reach the foot of the second dièdre, vertical then slightly overhanging (V, A1, athletic and strenuous) finishing right onto a slab below an overhang. Climb straight up a crack for 5–6m (IV sup.), then, instead of continuing up the line of cracks (the Ratti-Vitali Route on the first ascent) traverse the open slab on the right for 15m (V, exposed) – this is the route followed by B. Pierre and G. Rébuffat on the second ascent. Climb up overlapping flakes (IV) and return left towards a zone of terraces forming the edge of a great cirque of gently sloping slabs. Climb a couloir which becomes a dièdre (IV), finishing on the left. By a dièdre on the right, gain the little brèche on the summit ridge just right of the summit.

The West Face of the Aiguille Noire de Peuterey: on the right in the far background the ordinary route, in front of this the South Ridge, on the left the Dames Anglaises (opposite page).
On the West Face: the dièdre pitch (above left).

84. AIGUILLES DE CHAMONIX
Aiguille du Midi-Grépon Traverse

This is a superb ridge route, very varied and very enjoyable. A fast party can do it in the day, at least as far as the Col des Nantillons, but there is much to be said for bivouacing on the route, a way of staying longer and more enjoyably in the midst of that extraordinary chain of Aiguilles. It is a good idea to do the route as two ropes of two for several reasons: firstly it will mean that you have two 60m ropes, which will mean you need only one abseil down the lower step of the Dent du Caïman, and secondly, it is always delightful to see one's companions strung out along the ridge; it gives the scale of the mountains, and makes for a happy feeling of unity between man and rock. This route, up hill and down dale, is the most varied imaginable: rock sections, ice sections, ascents, descents and abseils, some of them very fine, and taking place now on one side of the ridge and now on the other.

● **Vertical height:** For the whole traverse you are between 3800m (Aiguille du Midi) and 3482m (Grépon) at an average height of 3500m.

● **Time:** By setting out very early from the Aiguille du Midi or the Cosmiques Hut it is possible to do the route in the day, in 16–18 hrs. But the usual times for the sections are as follows: Aiguille du Midi-Aiguille du Plan 3 hrs; Aiguille du Plan-Dent du Caïman 3–4 hrs; Dent du Caïman-Col du Fou 4–7 hrs; Col du Fou-Col des Nantillons 4–6 hrs; Grépon-Plan de l'Aiguille 3–5 hrs; making 17–25 hrs in all.

● **Equipment:** Crampons, carabiners, pitons, 1 axe per party, a 60m abseil rope (120m of rope).

● **Starting point:** Cosmiques Hut (3613m) or the Aiguille du Midi (with a bivouac there). It is possible to set out very early, at night: the route to the Aiguille du Plan is simple to follow, easy and you will already have done it. It is also possible for a fast party to take the first cable-car.

● **Route** – *Outline:* For two days you follow the summit ridge of the Aiguilles, climbing most of the summits, avoiding some of them if you wish (Pointe Chevalier, Pointe Lépiney).

Description: From the Aiguille du Midi (3800m) go along to the Aiguille du Plan (3673m). After climbing the summit, descend the final rocks by the ascent route and turn the summit on the left. Gain the ridge halfway between the Aiguille du Plan and the Dent du Crocodile and follow it to the latter summit (3640m).

From the Crocodile descend either on the right (E) or on the left (W) climbing down the upper rocks, and reach a narrow balcony. Make a 35m abseil on the Caïman side to gain level steps on the ridge. Descend these to make a second abseil on the Chamonix side diagonally for 40m (it may be worth putting on crampons, depending upon the conditions) and make a descending traverse to regain the crest and reach the Brèche du Caïman (3498m). Move left to climb the Dent du Caïman on the Chamonix side; its first feature is a small, fairly steep face. Go up left, then straight up, climbing a short steep wall, and then continue diagonally left to reach a comfortable balcony on which to belay. Climb the 12m high step above almost straight up for the first 4m using a C-shaped flake, then on the right and finally straight up (IV). Climb easy rock to reach the summit (3554m).

From the summit of the Caïman make a short abseil of 10m on the Envers side which leads to a sloping terrace on the right (you can also climb down). From this terrace a slightly diagonal abseil of 35m on the Envers side gives access to a ledge which is followed right. Make a delicate step (V) at a break to get onto the top of the second step of the NE Ridge of the Caïman. Go onto the Chamonix side, descend easily for several metres. Make a long abseil (40m) slightly obliquely to reach a snowy ledge; descend this to the summit of the first step

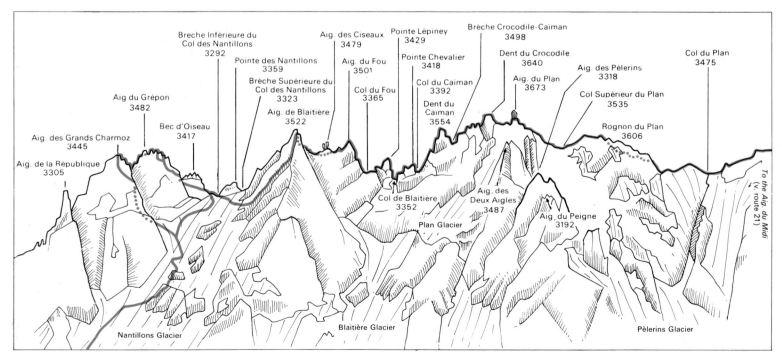

of the ridge which is split at the start for several metres by a couloir-chimney in the bed of which there is a large block. From there make a single 60m abseil to the Col du Caïman (3392m) or two 30m abseils. Go along the level ledges of the col taking a slanting line across a snow terrace on the Chamonix side below the summit of the Chevalier to a chimney which leads to the summit (3418m). Return to the snow and regain the ridge after the gendarme to the N of the Aiguille Chevalier. Descend the Chamonix side to the top of a step which is descended by a chimney on the Envers side (an abseil may be convenient) to reach the Col de Blaitière (3352m).

The aiguille beyond is the Pointe Lépiney. Climb steps to reach the shoulder W of the top. From there traverse right on the Envers side by ledges (easy at first and then delicate) to gain and climb a 15m chimney slightly overhanging at the start. At the top the angle steepens; climb a crack and go up a slit to reach the summit (3429m). Make a 15m abseil to reach a terrace on the Chamonix side and from there the W shoulder, keeping to the Chamonix side by

an easy ledge. Climb along the N Ridge to a step which falls away sharply to the level area below. Make a 30m abseil (delicate start, first on the Envers side, then going onto the Chamonix side) to reach the level area which leads to the Col du Fou (3365m).

From the col you climb the SW Ridge of the Aiguille du Fou. Go up to the foot of the first wall. Climb either a 10m crack overhanging at the start (V, strenuous, with a shoulder) or the slab on its left (A1). Steps lead left to the foot of a dièdre with a thin 10m crack at the back which you climb (V). Return right up two steps. Climb a crack-dièdre slanting left (III) to reach a good platform. Go left up rising ledges covered with blocks or climb on the right a series of steep cracks for 20m (III), and reach a large terrace. Bear right to where the ridge is hollowed out into a big couloir. You can climb straight up a wall and then a flake which bears right to a ledge leading back left, but altogether this is very difficult (V sup.). It is better to reach and climb a jamming crack (IV) left in the corner of the hollow with an overlapping base. Above continue up a narrow 10m chimney (IV)

and then up a crack-dièdre which you leave near the top to climb the cracked slab on the left side (IV). You reach a huge terrace. Then on the Envers side climb a slab then a deep chimney (III) to reach a little shoulder and gain on the right the terrace below the summit block. From here on the right gain the summit (V, 3501m).

From the Fou traverse below the Ciseaux and gain the Brèche de Blaitière. On the way climb one of the three summits. Descend by the Bregeault Ridge and gain the Col des Nantillons to climb the Grépon. To do this go up rising ledges leading to the CP Terrace. From here descend to the brèche and climb the spine of the jammed block. Traverse left, reach the dièdre of the abseil and climb it (III). Reach terraces and go up ledges to the top of the couloir which on the left, on the Nantillons side, comes down from the diagonal route which slants up from the Charmoz-Grépon couloir.

The Aiguille du Plan in the centre, the Aiguilles de Blaitière on the left, and on the right the ridge going to the Aiguille du Midi and Mont Blanc du Tacul.

You can of course go straight up to the Brèche Balfour and climb the summit block by the Knubel Crack, the Dunod Crack or the Lochmatter Crack, but it is pleasanter to follow the Charlet Route which follows the couloir on the left for a short while, then climbs the summit part of the W Face of the Grépon and comes out at the brèche S of gendarme 3473. The description is as follows: directly below the summit, start up a chimney to a jammed block and pull up (IV), and there leave this chimney to climb a slab on the left (IV) below a very clean-cut overhang. Traverse obliquely left up a crack (III) and reach a fine terrace. Climb a steep chimney for 20m and pass a jammed block. Through a 'letter-box' gain, on the left, a less steep couloir-chimney and go up it (III). Then climb a chimney ending below an overhang. Climb the overhang (IV sup.) and go up a slab to the brèche S of gendarme 3473.

From there it is pleasant, instead of going straight to the summit, go across to the great gendarme nearby, for the ascent of this is in itself a very fine pitch. From the brèche go straight up an open chimney and, when you reach the overhangs closing it, traverse left to climb a flake on the Nantillons side and then return right up the summit block of the great gendarme which you climb on friction holds, laying away from the ridge. Then return to the brèche and climb the summit of the Grépon from there and then descend to the Col des Nantillons to reach the glacier and the valley.

Climbing the great gendarme on the Grépon (left).
In the centre the Pointe Lépiney and the Aiguille du Fou, the Aiguille de Blaitière on the left, and the Grépon on the right (opposite page, above).
From the Aiguille du Midi to the Grands Charmoz, the whole route seen from the valley (opposite page, below).

85. PETITES JORASSES 3649m
West Face

Seen from the French side, the Petites Jorasses look like nothing more than a shoulder on the ridge running from the Aiguille de Leschaux to the Col des Hirondelles, and they are rather overpowered by the Grandes Jorasses, being lower and less well-proportioned. But to make up for this, the French side has an outstanding wall, curving slightly outwards and crossed at several points by rows of dark overhangs. The left-hand side going straight up from the glacier faces more to the W; it is on the latter that we find a superb route, very difficult and very sustained but never laborious and always technical, without violent contrasts. It needed a very developed mountaineering sense to think of, then work out a route up this W Face, an immense bastion 700m high. It is all the more overpowering because of the overhangs, or, to be more exact, roofs, which

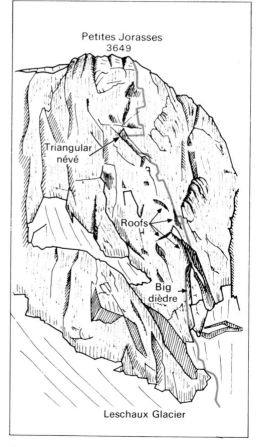

Petites Jorasses
3649

Triangular névé

Roofs

Big dièdre

Leschaux Glacier

204

are all that offer a focus on the smooth, slightly rounded slabs, always sheer and almost monotonous with their unbrokenness and their perfection; rather than a succession of slabs, this is a single slab 700m high. It is just as well that there are overhangs to add variation and scale.

From the aesthetic point of view, the face is not particularly beautiful, but for the climber engaged on it, its sheer lines dropping away on all sides give a very strong and individual impression, and the climbing is not only very difficult but a real joy for anyone having the necessary technical ability.

I was lucky enough to do this climb with Philippe Deudon and it was a delightful experience from every point of view; I was on a great face with a very strong partner whose climbing is a joy to watch — his every move positive, leisurely, rhythmical, supple. He is the son of another climber in the first rank both because of his climbs and because of his personality, and with whom, winter and summer, in the Mont Blanc range and in the Dolomites, I have done a number of routes.

Finally, apart from the beauty of the climbing on this face, this is an example of the most outstanding route-finding, which means that except for a few metres, the climbing is free with some fine, sheer 30m pitches. The rock is excellent, but fairly compact and without much friction. Though the face is steep, all the climbing can be done in balance, without arm-strength. These days all the pitons needed, about thirty or so, are in place.

● **1st ascent:** M. Bron, A. Contamine, P. Labrunie, 20–21 August 1955.
● **Vertical height:** 700m (from about 2950 to 3650m).
● **Grade:** Very sustained TD with pitches of V sup. particularly in the central section. At the bottom the rock is often wet.
● **Time:** 12–15 hrs.
● **Equipment:** 15 carabiners, étriers.
● **Starting point:** Leschaux Hut (2431m).
● **Route** – *Outline:* Left of directly below the summit, above a little glacier bay, climb an obvious 200m dièdre which ends below the roofs. After a traverse right between the roofs, the route gains another dièdre then reaches the central zone formed by the wall of slabs and goes up to the triangular névé almost directly below the summit. There is a traverse right to turn the slight arête on the upper part of the face. The route goes up the W side of this arête and then up slabs to the summit.

Description: From the Leschaux Hut go up the glacier and climb a steep snow slope to reach and climb the great dièdre at the start (V, a move of V sup.) to below the

big roofs. Traverse right (V, a move of V sup.), continue up two dièdres and gain the arête on the right (V sup.). Slant up to the right and climb the narrow section (V) of a wet couloir. Go back left along ledges above the great dièdre, climb up a couloir, then gain the slabs up a crack (V sup.) and a dièdre (V sup.). Climb an overhang (A1) and the dièdre which follows (V sup.) and

continue more easily to slant left along a ramp towards the triangular névé. Climb this. Reach a good ledge, make a slightly descending traverse for about forty metres (IV sup., a move of V) to get round the arête and climb the chimney behind it. The angle eases off. Climb directly on the N Face up open dièdres and slabs, then traverse obliquely right and go back left up slabs (IV sup., a move of V) to reach the summit.

Opposite page: the great dièdre at the start (above left); the end of the traverse after the névé (right below); a belay (above).
This page: the A1 overhang (above left); the big traverse, with the North Face of the Grandes Jorasses and the Leschaux Glacier in the background (above right); the traverse below the névé (left).

86. MONT BLANC DU TACUL 4248m
Gervasutti Pillar

This very clean-cut pillar, straight as a die, gives a superb climb, on excellent rock, in awe-inspiring surroundings. It is parallel to the central pillar (Boccalatte Pillar) on Mont Blanc du Tacul, but it is shorter, steeper and more sustained, all of which gives it a rare restraint and elegance. It was to attract the attention of Giusto Gervasutti, an outstanding climber, for whom this face of Mont Blanc du Tacul had a great appeal. In 1934, with R. Chabod, he did the first ascent of the NE Couloir (Gervasutti Couloir), a superb ice route; on 8 August 1946, with P. Bollini della Predosa, he climbed the central pillar (Boccalatte Pillar), a mixed route. A month later, on 16 September of the same year, with G. Gagliardone (with whom he had done the first ascent of the E Face of the Grandes Jorasses) he made an attempt on this rock route, and was killed while abseiling down to try and unjam the rope, in the middle of the storm which had forced them to turn back. Throughout the Mont Blanc range, and beyond, this tragedy provoked enormous grief, as had done, a

few years earlier, the death of another outstanding climber Emilio Comici, who had also been killed while preparing an abseil.

The ascent of the Gervasutti Pillar is now classic, all the finer for being entirely free-climbing.

- **1st ascent**: P. Fornelli and G. Mauro, 29–30 July 1951.
- **Vertical height**: About 800m (from 3400 to 4248m).
- **Grade**: TD with 20 pitons, pitches of V sup. and VI. The main difficulties are found in the first 300m.
- **Time**: 7–10 hrs from the foot to the summit.
- **Starting point**: Cosmiques Hut (3613m) or the Torino Hut (3375m).
- **Route** – *Outline*: This is simple, the route being marked by the pillar which is fairly sharp.

Description: From the Col du Midi or the Col du Géant gain the foot, crossing the bergschrund left of the central pillar (Boccalatte) directly below the couloir between it

and the Gervasutti Pillar on the left. After a steep snow slope start the first step right of the lowest point of the pillar, up a crack which leads to the crest (V then IV sup.). Do not take a more difficult crack, with jammed blocks, further right. On the crest climb a dièdre and exit left onto a small ledge (V, IV). Continue straight up, traverse left (V) then right up easy rock to the foot of the central step. Climb a grey dièdre (25m, IV sup.) and reach a platform on the left on the crest of the pillar. Continue up a crack (IV, strenuous). Go through a 'letter-box', then over a little roof on the left (IV sup. or A1) and go up the left edge of the pillar. Gain directly (V sup., VI) a platform at the foot of a large tower split on the left by a crack (the pitch of VI can be avoided by taking cracks leading up to the left end of the platform). Climb the crack for 10m (IV), traverse right, reach the edge of the pillar, climb it (V, V sup.) and gain a platform. From here either climb an easy dièdre right of the ledge and right of a large red roof, and an overhanging crack (10m, A2) leading to a platform above the roof; or free-climb on the left — make a 3m horizontal traverse (V) to gain the back of a small red dièdre and climb it (20m, IV and V) to the large red roof, traverse 2m left and climb it up overhanging flakes (V and V sup.).

A short ledge (IV) and chimney (IV sup.) and several blocks lead to a brèche. Left of

the pillar climb a long chimney ending as a crack (70m, grooves, III, IV, V), a slab, blocks on the right, then a 10m dièdre with a detached flake (V) which lead to an ice ledge. Follow this; after 6–7m you can climb a crack overhanging at the start (A1), or you can continue to a large triangular block, climb it (IV sup., strenuous) and make a rising traverse left (V sup., VI) to gain the top of the crack mentioned earlier.

A crack (IV sup.) leads to a long rising ledge (100m) of ice and rotten rock at the foot of the final step. A crack (V) leads to a brèche. Traverse several metres left, descend 10m to the base of two long chimneys. Climb the left-hand one (IV sup., ice) to reach the top of the Gervasutti Pillar at the foot of the Red Tower. Climb the left flank of the Red Tower by a short couloir and the easy broken rocks of a secondary rock rib to reach the brèche beyond the Red Tower. Climb the final pillar to reach the top of Mont Blanc du Tacul.

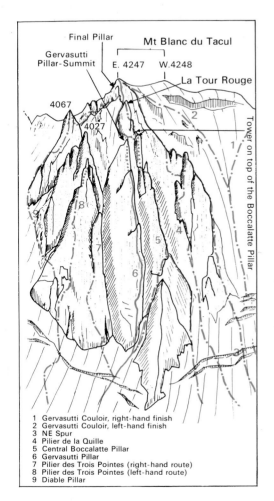

1 Gervasutti Couloir, right-hand finish
2 Gervasutti Couloir, left-hand finish
3 NE Spur
4 Pilier de la Quille
5 Central Boccalatte Pillar
6 Gervasutti Pillar
7 Pilier des Trois Pointes (right-hand route)
8 Pilier des Trois Pointes (left-hand route)
9 Diable Pillar

On the right Mont Blanc du Tacul and its pillars:
the Boccalatte Pillar from the side, the Gervasutti Pillar
in front and the Aiguilles du Diable in the centre
(opposite page).
On the Gervasutti Pillar (above).

87. POINTE GUGLIERMINA 3893m
South-West Face

This is a magnificent pure rock climb; undoubtedly the most difficult route done in the Mont Blanc range before the war, a period when free-climbing sometimes attained the very highest level. The SW Face of the Gugliermina is quite different in structure from the other great faces of the range. Here the rock has many of the features of limestone, and the climbing, primarily balance-climbing, very exposed, reminds one of the great Dolomite faces. The climb is yet further enhanced by the approach, short but very beautiful, up the Frêney Glacier, and by the descent, towards the Aiguille Blanche – both make for something quite superb. From the summit of the Gugliermina you can also continue towards Mont Blanc over the Aiguille Blanche and the Peuterey Ridge.

Finally, the thought of Boccalatte and Gervasutti, climbers outstanding in vision and in technique, should also add to the pleasure of the route.

● **1st ascent:** G. Boccalatte and G. Gervasutti, 17–18 August 1938.
● **Vertical height:** About 600m (from 3300 to 3893m).
● **Grade:** TD with 25 pitons, sustained for 400m, exposed due to the exceptional steepness of the pillar and to the quality of the rock which is poor at several places. There is no pitch as hard as the overhanging dièdre on the W Face of the Noire just across the way, but the route as a whole is more difficult. In fact these two routes have very different characteristics, with difficult artificial climbing on the Noire and free-climbing on this route. But free-climbing, by its very nature, is always finer than aid-climbing.
● **Time:** 3–4 hrs from the Monzino Hut to the start of the difficulties. 7–9 hrs from there to the summit. In all 10–12 hrs.
● **Equipment:** Etriers, carabiners, ideally 40m of rope between each climber.
● **Starting point:** Monzino Hut (2590m).
● **Route – *Outline:*** The rock rognon at the top of the glacier directly below the summit, the Schneider Ledge (which you leave half-way between the glacier and the Schneider Couloir), the easy central section the buttress itself which is the most obvious feature of the face, and then the traverse left at its top to gain the SW Ridge which leads to the summit.

Description: From the Monzino Hut gain the lower plateau of the Frêney Glacier either directly when the glacier is in good condition (at the beginning of the season) passing below the E Face of the Aiguille Croux, or going over the Col de l'Innominata (when the glacier is too crevassed). To do this go up the little Châtelet Glacier towards the col, climb a barrier of glaciated rock on the right, a snow slope on the left and continue up a couloir-chimney to reach the col. Descend the steep and rotten couloir on the Frêney side by an abseil to reach the snow, and go up the very crevassed glacier.

Go up to the top of the rock outcrop (3292m) directly below the Pointe Gugliermina. Above the glacier the base of the Gugliermina is cut by two parallel ledges

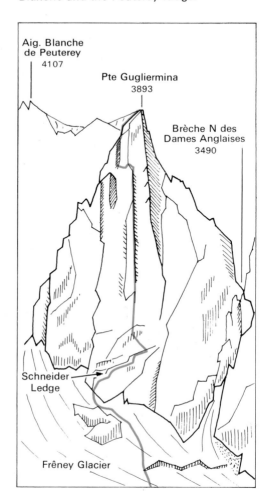

ascending to the right, one above the other. Take the upper ledge (the Schneider Ledge) which passes below an overhanging shelter-stone (good bivouac site) and leave it to go up for 100m in the direction of the great pillar of the Gugliermina right of the great depression. Climb the slabs of the pillar which is poorly defined at the bottom, then follow the crest for 200m (IV, a move of V, sustained) to a 5–6m high flake detached from the wall. Climb the chimney formed by this, exit on the right, climb an open dièdre on the right (V then IV). The edge of the pillar overhangs. Leave it to climb a rib obliquely left towards a chimney-couloir at the top of the great depression (V, exposed). Climb this chimney-couloir and reach a large ledge of blocks which is followed left to the end. Climb a smooth dièdre (A1, finish V) to reach a big spike (with sling) 10m higher and on the left (a bad stance right of the spike). From here make a descending rope traverse diagonally left, then climb two dièdres and arêtes to reach a sloping ledge with a difficult pull-up (V sup.). Climb terraces and cracks (one of IV, one overhanging A1) to reach a ledge on the SW Ridge which bounds the face on the left 30m higher than the big shoulder of this ridge. On the other side of the ridge, climb slabs on the left (V, a move of V sup.), then continue more easily to the summit.

Descent: From the summit abseil down to the Gugliermina-Epée Brèche (a pinnacle to the NW). From here go left (N) to go round a buttress and so gain the ordinary route up the Aiguille Blanche de Peuterey, from which you descend by the Schneider Couloir and ledges. This choice of route for the descent is advisable because it is quicker and safer, particularly in bad weather, than descending by the Dames Anglaises Brèche and its couloir, which is always in a precarious condition, particularly at the end of the season.

On the Gugliermina Spur (opposite page).
The Pointe Gugliermina, from in front (right).

88. AIGUILLE DU TRIOLET 3870m
North Face

Above the Argentière cirque, bounding at its remotest and most hidden point the great wall of N Faces of the Verte, Droites and Courtes, some thousand metres high, very difficult, very awe-inspiring, is the N Face of the Triolet, which unites a tumbling glacier and a rock wall. The route I propose here is one of the finest and most difficult ice routes in the range. It was done for the first time in 1931 by R. Gréloz and A. Rochs, technically very gifted climbers from Geneva, with that excellent mountaineering and snow sense which so many Genevans have. At that time the main problem of the face was a problem of conditions; this is a problem which has lessened over the twenty years since the first ascent. Of course, on any snow and ice route, success always depends on the quality of the snow; nevertheless, these days, with the technical advances made possible by front-point crampons and by ice-pitons and screws which allow good belays and abseils (both of which were impossible earlier on), it is possible to

undertake this climb even if optimum conditions do not prevail everywhere on the face. It is this, as well as the Face's intrinsic beauty, which explains why there are a number of ascents every year.

As is the case for any glacier face, the N Face of the Triolet changes year by year. The snow, annually accumulating above and slowly compressed to form ice, moves downwards, adds weight to and extends the rows of seracs. The slope is very steep, 53° at the bottom and even steeper in the middle. The angle towards the top depends on the route taken; you can go straight up as did A. Contamine and L. Lachenal, but normally you traverse right above the big serac barrier and then either come back left to get to the summit or exit directly onto the ridge of the Petites Aiguilles du Triolet. From the summit there are superb views.

● **1st ascent**: R. Gréloz and A. Rochs, 20 September 1931.

● **Vertical height**: About 800m from the bergschrund to the summit (from 3100 to 3870m).

● **Grade**: A major ice route on a very steep slope calling for excellent technique and a sound balance, physical and mental.

● **Time**: 1½ hrs from the hut to the berg-

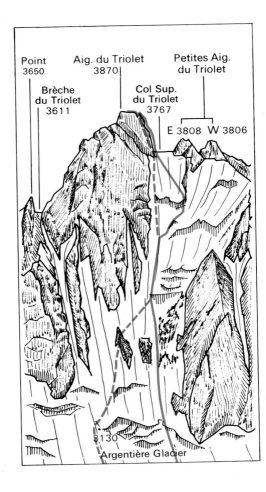

Point 3650
Brèche du Triolet 3611
Aig. du Triolet 3870
Col Sup. du Triolet 3767
Petites Aig. du Triolet
E 3808 W 3806
3130
Argentière Glacier

schrund. 4–8 hrs from the bergschrund to the summit.

● **Equipment:** Crampons, ice-pitons and ice-screws. It is worth having plenty of rope, so that the pitches can be made long.

● **Starting point:** The Argentière Hut (2771m).

● **Route** – *Outline:* First the right bank of the slope with the ice seracs (that is below the right section of the rock base of the Triolet), then a traverse right below the upper serac barrier and a return left.

Description: From the Argentière Hut (2771m) go up to the head of the Argentière cirque. Climb the bergschrund if possible at the point where you can go straight up above in a straight line without traversing the runnels; usually this will be on the right or left of the rock rognon to the right. Sometimes it is a temptation to try to go further left to climb past pointed rocks which stick out of the ice; this is rarely a good solution, since ice forms faster near rocks and the rocks will also impede the establishment of a good rhythm, if only by tempting you to unnecessary belays.

Skirt the first serac barrier on the left and, before the rocks, traverse right across the slope between the two barriers. Avoid the second on the right and continue either directly towards the summit ridge of the Petites Aiguilles du Triolet, or go back left at the top of the second barrier to continue directly towards the summit.

The North Face of the Triolet seen from the Courtes (opposite page).
On the North Face (above and opposite page).

89. GRAND CAPUCIN 3838m
East Face

The Grand Capucin is an extraordinary red granite tower with an E Face rising steeply out of the Géant Glacier. Particularly noticeable are the rows of overhangs which at one time suggested it was unclimbable,• but Bonatti found a winding route which goes over some of the overhangs, but in general works its way up between the great roofs; the climbing is quite literally, geometrically vertical, something quite exceptional on granite.

I was lucky enough in 1953 to do the fifth ascent of this superb route; at that time there were very few pitons in place. I have been back several times since and W. Bonatti's route has become a 'via ferrata'; you can scarcely find 10 metres of climbing free of pitons. A pity — the whole atmosphere of the face is changed. But however much I regret this proliferation of ironmongery, I am still convinced that the E Face of the

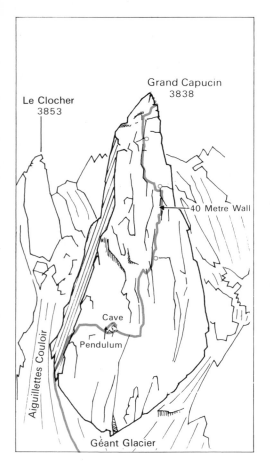

Capucin is a marvellous route, intricate, making clever use of the rock. It is exposed, on vertical slabs in between rows of overhangs and roofs, and somewhat strenuous — though this last is not in fact unpleasant, even if you are used to limestone climbing and rather prefer delicate balance-climbing.

● **1st ascent:** W. Bonatti and L. Ghigo, 20–23 July 1951.
● **Vertical height:** About 490m from the bergschrund to the summit (from 3400 to 3893m). The height of the climb itself is about 350m.
● **Grade:** ED with 40 pitons in place; however the number of pitons now in place on the wall is much greater, more like 200–250. This, quite apart from the aesthetic aspect, is technically quite unnecessary and indeed incomprehensible. If a climber, after all, wanted to clip into every piton, this would take him a considerable time and make the whole climb extra tiring; moreover the pitons are so close together that the étriers would more or less overlap. Unfortunately it is the case that using too many pitons brings the grade of the climb down, and turns the Capucin into an artificial, and regrettably laborious, climb.
● **Time:** 10–20 hrs from the bergschrund to the summit.
● **Equipment:** 30 carabiners (used on the 40m wall), several pitons, étriers.
● **Starting point:** The Torino Hut.
● **Route** – *Outline:* In spite of a superficial simplicity, the structure of the Capucin is fairly complex; in fact the immense slabs cut by cracks and dièdres continually run into barriers of overhangs. Demonstrating on this great first ascent in 1951 an exceptional sense of rock and route-finding ability, Bonatti succeeded in passing these, and in reaching the summit where more than once the route seemed to have come to a dead end. This means that you do not follow a direct route, but an intricate route, which makes detours based on an understanding of the rock. This means a certain number of traversing pitches which have the disadvantage of taking time without gaining height. But conversely, these are magnificent pitches and that after all is what counts; if we are there, it is because of a love of climbing. Moreover, the Capucin apart, traverses are often among the finest of

pitches on routes, giving not only fine climbing but a sense of discovery.

Here the general line of the route is given by a line of cracks and dièdres, which rarely lead into one another, being often closed by overhanging steps. These are turned on the left for three pitches, on the right for the pitches to the top of the 40m wall, again on the left, then on the right to gain the ledge-terrace below the great summit overhang.

Description: From the Torino Hut go across to the Couloir des Aiguillettes left of the Grand Capucin. Climb this for 100m or so and reach on the right a zone of terraces which are sometimes snowed up. Cross these easily, descend slightly and

Le Clocher 3853

Grand Capucin 3838

40 Metre Wall

Cave

Pendulum

Aiguillettes Couloir

Géant Glacier

reach a break. Either traverse across a sloping slab with tiny holds (V, V sup.) or go up a crack on the right (IV) below a roof from which you descend on the rope into a short slanting dièdre to gain an earthy ledge with a cave. Follow this ledge right to the third dièdre. Climb this for 15m (IV) and exit left (V) towards a stance and blocks. Climb a second dièdre (IV), traverse left (V) and pull-up onto a small ledge. Continue up a short chimney formed by a flake (V, III). Climb a dièdre leading to a narrow ledge. Continue up the dièdre and, without going too high as the pitons would suggest, traverse right (V) along the base of a sloping slab below the huge overhang to a slanting dièdre. Climb this to the roof and traverse right below it to pull up onto a small terrace (the first Bonatti bivouac).

Climb the grooves above for 20m, gain a small ledge 3m to the right. Climb a deep dièdre (IV), go over a roof on the right. Leave the dièdre and traverse right along a thin horizontal crack; make a stride into a chimney on the right between the wall and a flake (with snow in the bottom) which leads to a large platform at the foot of the 40m wall. Climb the 40m wall (V sup.). It is possible to take a stance in étriers halfway. I personally enjoy long pitches and I always climb this as one pitch. You come out on some big steps (second Bonatti bivouac), right on the edge of the N Face, by which it is possible to escape by abseiling.

Climb a short wall (IV) on the left and follow a ledge left to reach a crack slanting slightly left. Climb this (V), turn a roof on the right (V sup.). Then go up cracks below a small roof. A traverse right leads to a small ledge and a crack (V) above leads to a poor niche (third Bonatti bivouac) below a roof. Traverse left below the roof (V) to get into and climb an overhanging dièdre with an exit left (stance in étriers). Continue up a wide crack in an inclined slab (V), then up a vertical crack and slabs on the right to a vague hollow. Take the crack on the left which goes up to below a huge overhang (IV). Traverse slabs (V) right and pull up onto a ledge in the corner to the right of the roof. A dièdre (IV) leads to the Shoulder. Turn to it on the right, descending slightly, cross onto the N Face (IV, often snowed up) and ascend a dièdre (IV sup.) to snow ledges near the summit.

Descent: This is made on the N side of the very steep W Face which overlooks the Brèche du Grand Capucin, the side used by E. Augusto with E. and H. Rey and L. Lanier in 1924 on the first ascent, made using a pole and large pitons.

Pitons for the abseils are in place (test them and the slings). From the brèche, descend the E Couloir over poor rock, very

dangerous particularly in dry years (abseils). Gain the snow couloir between the Petit and the Grand Capucin and then the glacier.

The East Face of the Capucin. The climber, visible halfway up, gives the scale (above).
On the 40m wall pitch (opposite page).

213

90. MONT BLANC 4807m
Route Major

This is the finest route on the Brenva Face of Mont Blanc. It lies between the Sentinelle Rouge on the right, a more elegant but less interesting route going directly to the summit, and the Poire (Pear) Route on the left, which is much harder and very dangerous. The Route Major is a mixed route, primarily ice but including some rock sections, one of which at least is very difficult. These are extraordinary surroundings, remote and unspoiled, especially very early in the morning when the sun, glancing over the horizon, strikes the rock outcrop cutting through the seracs on the summit dome of Mont Blanc; it heightens the contrast, the harmony between two materials and two colours: rough-textured red granite and blue-green, geometrically shaped ice.

The climb is hard primarily because the rock is very compact and because of the altitude at which it is done. It is essential to leave very early, to be wholly on the alert and to move very fast when crossing the main couloir, and to keep to time. The climb should be undertaken only in settled weather.

● **1st ascent:** T. Graham Brown and F. S. Smythe, 6–7 August 1928.
● **Vertical height:** 1328m from the Col Moore to the summit (from 3479 to 4807m).
● **Grade:** A route of great seriousness presenting ice and rock difficulties. D at altitude.
● **Time:** 8–12 hrs from the Col de la Fourche to the summit. Set out very early; it is essential you should be on the ridge at night, or at least by daybreak.

first on the left for 15m (III sup.), then up the back with a detour left in the middle. This is the most usual line.

— it is also possible to turn the short buttress descending to the snow on the right and then climb the same chimney or another chimney 5m further right.

— a third possibility is to climb the rock step up its left side. Above a semi-circular ledge climb a dièdre chimney (III then IV) topped with an overhang (V).

Climb to the top of the step which leads to the serac barrier. The height of this varies from year to year. Climb this and continue up easy slopes to gain the summit ridge and then the summit of Mont Blanc.

The rock step on the Major, seen from the Brenva Spur, and the seracs on the Col de la Fourche (opposite page, right and left).
Traverse of the Great Couloir (left).

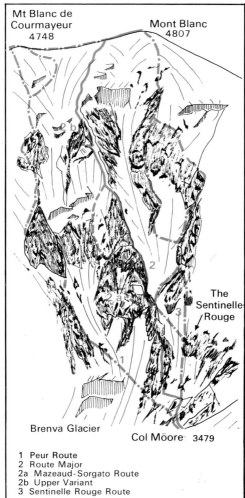

1 Peur Route
2 Route Major
2a Mazeaud-Sorgato Route
2b Upper Variant
3 Sentinelle Rouge Route

● **Equipment**: Crampons, pitons, carabiners.

● **Starting point**: Col de la Fourche Bivouac Hut (3680m) or the Trident Bivouac Hut (3690m).

● **Route** — *Outline*: From the bottom of the great couloir which descends from the dome of Mont Blanc, go diagonally across towards the spur with rock steps which constitutes the line of ascent.

Description: From the Col Moore go round the Brenva Spur and traverse to the Great Couloir coming down from the dome of Mont Blanc. Cross this as quickly as possible above the final gully to gain the bottom of the great buttress which forms its right bank. Climb this buttress to a step which is turned on the right on the Great Couloir side. Beside the step there is a slender gendarme with a bivouac site. Return to the buttress above the step. It is possible to reach the same point by traversing from the left bank of the Great

Couloir at this level. This depends upon the conditions.

The ridge will be snow and rock alternately. After a very short snow ridge (4035m), climb slabs on the right. Traverse left and climb chimneys to reach a second snow ridge, longer and thinner. Climb a small rock wall and a third very long ridge leading to the upper rock step (about 4115m). Climb the first barrier of the step by a 5m chimney couloir and go up the snow ridge to reach the foot of a characteristic vertical wall which is the most difficult rock obstacle of the route. There are several ways of climbing it:

— at the top of the snow slope traverse right below the rocks to a dièdre between the step itself and a short buttress facing the snow slope. Climb a short difficult crack (IV) in the back of the dièdre, then continue up the edge of the short buttress and go right into the snow couloir which leads to the foot of a long chimney, which is climbed

91. AIGUILLE VERTE 4121m
Nant Blanc Face

This is the outstanding mixed route on the Verte, and one of the finest of its kind in the range. The angle is very great, but the route above is all sheer and unbroken. This is because of the lines of the face funnelling down from the top of the wall directly below the summit; lower down the face broadens, but it has no defined shape, so that you have the impression of an immense waste of ice. There are no particular features. The face gets very little sun except at the end of the afternoon. The wall is therefore monotone, and feels cold and inhospitable. This might suggest that the route is unpleasant, but not at all, quite the contrary. Our pleasure here is an almost militant one; a feeling of warmth combating the surrounding cold, which is of course an essential factor in making the climb safe; sunshine and sunlight can wait for the summit.

With J.-P. Charlet, I was lucky enough to do the second ascent. His uncle Armand had done the first seven years before. This meant that, for me, not only was the face steep, remote and very difficult, but that it had an aura around it. I am scarcely exaggerating when I say that at that time doing the face as a second ascent of one of Armand's routes was possibly more difficult than doing it unclimbed. The aura was enhanced by the moment we chose to do the Face, since it is a face which can never be in perfect condition: if the rock is dry, the slope is ice, and if the slope is snow, there is verglas on the rocks. At the bivouac my feelings were compounded of enthusiasm and apprehension, but the latter vanished at the bergschrund. We were pleasurably fit, relaxed, at one with that world of ice. Everything went well and that same evening, by the Couvercle and the Charpoua, we got back to Trélachamp on foot; this was in 1945.

The Nant Blanc Face of the Verte is today a classic route, still technically very difficult and demanding a certain mental strain; you must go quickly so as to be finished before the day warms up and of course before the sun gets onto the Face.

● **1st ascent:** D. Platonov with A. Charlet, 22 August 1935.

● **Vertical height:** About 900m from the bergschrund to the summit (from 3200 to 4121m).

● **Grade:** A major steep mixed route rarely in good condition, in impressive surroundings.

● **Time:** 6–8 hrs from the bergschrund to the summit.

● **Equipment:** Crampons.

● **Starting point:** Bivouac on the rognon at the top of the Dru moraine below the Pointe Farrar, or at the Col des Grands Montets.

● **Route** – *Outline:* Between the Grands Montets Ridge and the Sans Nom Ridge, the Verte presents a huge wall. The Direct Route described here confines itself to the central section. High up the line is determined by a huge funnel facing largely W below the dome of the Verte and takes the left side. Lower down the line follows a great snow slope (facing largely N), first narrowing into a couloir which is taken almost direct.

Description: From the Drus bivouac cross the glacier to pass between the base of the rock buttress supporting the hanging glacier between the Sans Nom Ridge and the rock outcrop just below it. Go diagonally up the glacier and reach the bergschrund at the bottom of the great Nant Blanc snow face (about 3200m). Cross the bergschrund, climb the snow slope for about 200m. Above it hollows into a couloir (it is also possible, depending upon the conditions, to use the rocks on the right bank) which leads to the foot of the rock band supporting the buttress on the left edge of the funnel. Climb rock covered with verglas up this band

which gives access to the hollow. Climb this until it is lost in the snow slope which leads to the dome. Pass between the serac barriers, usually on the left, and reach the summit.

The exit from the Nant Blanc Face (opposite page). The Nant Blanc Face of the Aiguille Verte, with the Drus on the right (above).

217

92. PETIT DRU 3733m
Bonatti Pillar

It may be true to say that the soaring rocks of the Drus are symbolic of will; Walter Bonatti is also a symbol of that quality, a man of unshakeable but imperturbable will, thorough-going and safe. To achieve this quite outstanding first ascent, Bonatti spent six days on the face. Even today this is a quite astonishing feat, especially if you remember the obstacles, dangers and difficulties that he had to overcome. He had first of all to visualise, then work out, a route up the spur, then to absorb the structure of the rock sufficiently well to avoid dead ends and follow a continuous route. Then he had to be strong enough mentally and physically to do the route, and to have the force of character to spend six days alone on it. On the other hand, the expedition up the pillar was an exhilarating enterprise worthy of Bonatti's steel, and

we can only be grateful for his amazing success.

So fine a route is naturally a temptation for many climbers; quite a few of them unfortunately have not been good enough to do the route fairly, and more and more pitons appear every year, so that more and more climbers set off on it, and put in more and more pitons. The result is that this outstanding route has become, as the Fontainebleau climbers say, the 'autoroute du Sud'. Will a similar fate soon overtake the American Direct?

There are two ways to reach the foot of the pillar: you can either go up the couloir, which is logical and elegant, but also dangerous because of the possibility of stonefall, or you can go down the Flammes de Pierre Ridge, as Bonatti did on the first ascent; this avoids the danger for you, but adds to the danger for others in the couloir, for the rock on the Flammes de Pierre is so poor that you may well send down some rocks.

The climb thereafter is superb and exhilarating; the rock is sound and finely coloured.

● **1st ascent:** W. Bonatti, 17–22 August 1955.
● **Vertical height:** About 400m from the bergschrund to the bottom of the buttress; about 600m from the bottom of the buttress to the summit (from 3100 to 3733m).
● **Grade:** ED, with 200 pitons, very sustained. Rope up 40m apart.
● **Time:** 1½–2 hrs from the bergschrund to the foot of the buttress. 15–20 hrs from the foot of the buttress to the summit.
● **Equipment:** 30 carabiners, pitons including wood wedges and/or American angles, étriers.
● **Starting point:** Bivouac on the top of the moraine (reached from the Montenvers or the Col des Grands Montets), or even on the Flammes de Pierre.
● **Route** – *Outline:* The couloir, which you follow up the left bank as far as possible, then the pillar with a pitch left to reach the great terrace, and an ascent of the right-hand side.
Description: Avoid the bergschrund of the couloir by taking to the rocks on the right (V inf.) which are followed as far as possible instead of the couloir itself. Higher climb a step (V), then go up snow to reach

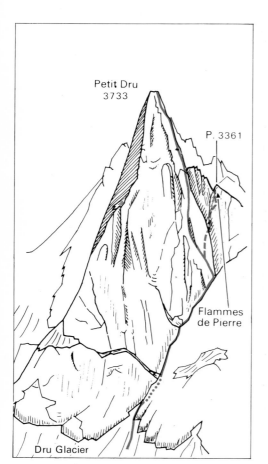

Petit Dru
3733

P. 3361

Flammes
de Pierre

Dru Glacier

the foot of the Flammes de Pierre. Traverse left towards the small ledges at the foot of the pillar. Climb flakes or a dièdre on the left to a good terrace (IV sup.). Climb a short wall and on the left get into and climb a 30m dièdre (V, wedges) which leads to a good ledge. Traverse right, laying away from a big flake, and climb a dièdre (called the Green Lizard) for 40m. When it begins to overhang, exit onto a platform (V). It is also possible to reach this platform by climbing directly above the ledge to below a great roof and then bearing right (A1, V) up a dièdre to avoid the roof.

Gain two terraces and reach the foot of a big dièdre on the left. Climb this direct for 25m (V), then go left along a little ledge and go up its left edge (V), which is the crest of the arête itself. Go round this and climb a dièdre which narrows into a crack (VI, A1, V) and leads to a platform. Continue up a very wide crack (A1) and go left along a sloping ledge. Climb a crack, laying away (IV), and reach a narrow stance at the foot of a vertical wall. From the belay, traverse right for 3–4m (V) and climb the wall (A2, wedges). Climb a crack (V, A1) for 5m to reach and climb the bottom of a flared, vertical chimney, sometimes covered with verglas (V), which leads to the big platform on the edge of the Pillar itself, level with the Flammes de Pierre.

Climb up for 30m (IV) and reach the foot of two cracks along a ledge. To the right of the belay climb the left-hand crack for 10m. Step round the pillar to gain the other crack on the right. Reach a small niche (V). Climb the overhang above the niche (wedges, A1) and go straight up for 15m to rock steps at the foot of the red slabs. Climb these for two rope-lengths at first up a slightly slanting dièdre (V, A1), then up a crack (V, A1). You reach terraces right of the crest of the Pillar (bivouac site). From here there are three possibilities: to climb the black roof as on the second ascent of the Pillar; to avoid the black roof on the right by traverses and pendulums, following the route of the first ascent; the best solution is the third, to go left. To do this, climb a dièdre and exit left (V) onto rock steps, climb a slab (IV), a dièdre slanting right and a 50m vertical crack (A1) up the open slab. At the top traverse right (V) to reach a small niche (by making a long traverse right from the niche it is possible to get onto the ordinary route up the Drus). Go diagonally up left by a sort of ramp (IV) to a small ledge on the edge of the pillar. Continue left up a slanting crack (V) to a niche. Above climb straight up a crack system and a short vertical dièdre (V). Two pitches (IV) lead to a ledge of shattered rock. Follow this to the right to a break and reach the shoulder at the foot of the final step in two easy pitches.

Climb overhanging chimneys (a move of V, A2) and reach in four pitches the second quartz ledge which is linked left, through a hole, with the N Face, and along which it is possible to go right onto the ordinary route. But in any case you are near the summit which is easily reached.

Walter Bonatti (opposite page).
On the Great Slabs (right).

93. AIGUILLE DU FOU 3501m
South Face

Although it has been famous now for several years because of its great and very sustained difficulty, at first sight the S Face of the Fou does not look a very attractive route. Situated as it is above a couloir, in between two great rock shoulders, much diminished by the effects of perspective, the American Route might appear little more than a training route. But once you have climbed that steep couloir, crossed a bergschrund which can sometimes be awkward and gone up gullies very exposed to stonefall, and once you arrive at the foot of that great monolithic wall, under the overhangs, you will soon forget those first impressions.

The summit is only 3501m high. The wall itself is no more than 300m high, but it is of extreme difficulty, a difficulty due to several factors, not least its unusual appearance and conformation.

All the other walls in this range are seamed with couloirs, lined with arêtes and spurs. The Fou is unique in having a flat, smooth, vertical surface, a simple diamond shape in red granite; it is bounded by four straight, pure lines, and right up the centre is the route.

The most outstanding achievement of those who first climbed it, remarkable American climbers very well trained on granite and in the Mont Blanc range, is to have discovered a route which, in its beauty and purity, is worthy of that wall. It gives a quite extraordinary impression.

Because the S Face is entirely vertical, with no features other than some thin cracks, the climber may be said to be clinging to the face, rather than on it; technically it is the only S face of its kind. It is very hard and very sustained, and will remain so until it is 'invaded' by pitons. The climbing is almost entirely free, a series of delightful moves.

● **1st ascent:** T. Frost, J. Harlin, G. Hemming and S. Fulton, July 1963.
● **Vertical height:** About 700m from the hut to the start of the difficulties; about 300m from here to the summit (from 3200 to 3501m).
● **Grade:** ED with 80 pitons.
● **Time:** 15–25 hrs.

- **Equipment**: Carabiners, étriers, a selection of pitons and wedges.
- **Starting point**: Envers des Aiguilles Hut (2523m).
- **Route** – *Outline:* After the ascent of the couloir and the start up the centre of the face, the route follows a line of cracks to the right; these lead to the great diagonal crack which is climbed direct to the summit.

Description: From the Envers des Aiguilles Hut go up the Envers de Blaitière Glacier to the Aiguille du Fou. Go up toward the foot of the S Face up the left side of the great couloir to the bergschrund at about half height. Cross the bergschrund on the left and return to the centre of the couloir to climb up the runnels (danger of stonefall) and reach the foot of the S Face, bounded by two couloirs.

Climb two pitches up a slab of rotten rock in the left-hand couloir to reach, after a short traverse right, a good ledge. You have now reached the foot of an overhanging section (a 7-shaped overhang). Climb a very steep cracked slab (V, V sup., VI, with a rope move) leading to the foot of a 40° overhanging slab which is climbed by a crack going up on the right (A1, A2). This leads to a good platform.

Climb a slanting crack on the right (V, A1) to reach the foot of an obvious 15m dièdre. Do not take this but traverse 3—4m right to gain a vertical 45m crack leading to the bottom of the diagonal crack (V, V sup., VI, very athletic). A first pitch (V) up a sloping ramp leads to a little platform. After a very delicate move (VI) and a short traverse left (V sup.), you reach the foot of an overhanging crack and climb it (V sup., VI) to take a stance in étriers below a big obvious roof.

Traverse this roof to the left (4m, VI) to go up a ramp, cracked at the start (VI, A1), which becomes a compact slab (VI, A2). You reach a flake.

At this level leave the great diagonal crack by a vertical slab (A1, A2, VI) which leads, after a short overhanging traverse right, to a fine platform (the only good bivouac site on the face).

Climb a dièdre for 40m (V, V sup.) which ends at a sloping ledge. Follow this 15m right and so reach a big area of slabs. Climb this for about 60m up a line of cracks slightly slanting left (V sup., VI very sustained, no resting-place). After three pitches go up a section of less steep cracks to reach the summit of the Fou (IV sup., V) after an almost entirely free climb.

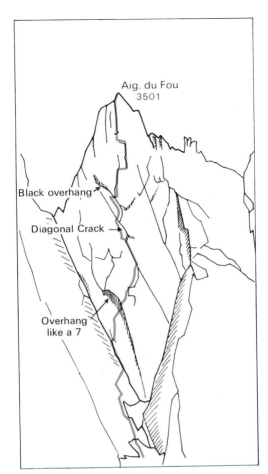

Opposite page: View looking down the 50m wall (left). The Pointe Lépiney and the Aiguille du Fou (above). This page: On the 50m wall (top). On the diagonal crack (bottom).

94. LES COURTES 3856m
North Face

This is one of the greatest ice routes of the range, and this for two reasons: first the series of very steep ice pitches at the top of the first third of the face, and second the sustained angle of the face, an angle which never lessens. The N Face of the Courtes is framed between the Central Spur to the left and the NNW Spur on the right; it is not an unbroken ice slope, and indeed has a number of buttresses and little rock spurs, which lead to some narrow couloirs and ice bulges. The face is broad enough to accommodate two parallel routes with a number of variants and connections between them. The finest is the Swiss Route, the most direct; it follows the right-hand side of the face, where the snow slopes are unbroken; it is also the most difficult. Between this and the Central Spur, there is the left-hand route, which, although not quite in the same class as the right-hand route in difficulty or in technique, is nevertheless a very great route. When you remember that the right-hand route was done in 1938, you will realise that at that time ice climbing techniques had already reached an extremely high level.

- **1st ascent**: C. Cornaz and R. Mathey, 31 July 1938.
- **Vertical height**: About 800m from the bergschrund to the summit.
- **Grade**: An extremely steep ice slope.
- **Time**: 6–10 hrs from the bergschrund to the summit.
- **Equipment**: Ice-pitons and ice-screws. Remember that the first ascenders climbed the route without all this equipment.
- **Starting point**: The Argentière Hut (2771m).
- **Route** – *Outline:* From the Argentière Hut cross the glacier towards the bottom of the couloir. Cross the bergschrund and go straight up towards the narrow section of the couloir at the top of the first third which is the steepest section (you might possibly climb the rocks in the ice on the left bank of the couloir). Then the couloir widens but although it remains steep, the angle eases slightly. In the upper third it is possible to go directly to the summit or to bear right to gain the snow ridge at the top of the NNW Buttress.

The North Faces of the Courtes and the Droites (opposite page, above).
On the North Face (left, and opposite page, below).

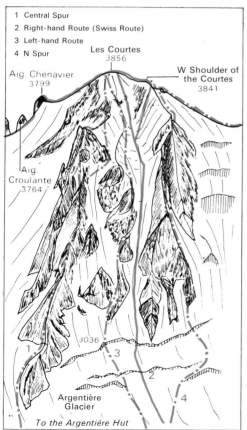

1 Central Spur
2 Right-hand Route (Swiss Route)
3 Left-hand Route
4 N Spur

Les Courtes
3856

Aig. Chenavier
3799

W Shoulder of
the Courtes
3841

Aig.
Croulante
3764

3036

3

2

1

4

Argentière
Glacier

To the Argentière Hut

95. MONT BLANC 4807m
Peuterey Ridge

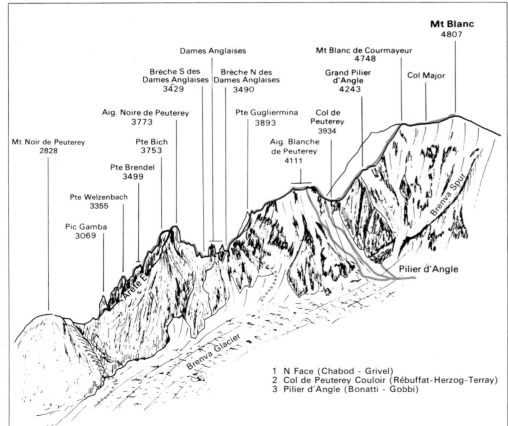

Dames Anglaises

Brèche S des
Dames Anglaises
3429

Brèche N des
Dames Anglaises
3490

Mt Blanc de Courmayeur
4748

Mt Blanc
4807

Aig. Noire de Peuterey
3773

Pte Gugliermina
3893

Grand Pilier
d'Angle
4243

Col Major

Mt Noir de Peuterey
2828

Pte Bich
3753

Col de
Peuterey
3934

Pte Brendel
3499

Aig. Blanche
de Peuterey
4111

Pte Welzenbach
3355

Pic Gamba
3069

Arête L

Brenva Spur

Brenva Glacier

Pilier d'Angle

1 N Face (Chabod - Grivel)
2 Col de Peuterey Couloir (Rébuffat-Herzog-Terray)
3 Pilier d'Angle (Bonatti - Gobbi)

This is a route of great magnitude, undoubtedly the finest route up Mont Blanc. It has none of the rock-climbing difficulty of the Innominata, but there can be very serious ice-climbing difficulties, and it is primarily a route on which the climber is very much committed; the Col de Peuterey in poor weather is a much more serious proposition than the Col Eccles; you can escape only by the Rochers Gruber, and I speak from experience when I say that this is, by no means easy, and that crossing the Frêney Glacier towards the Col de l'Innominata is highly dangerous because you are passing underneath the great serac barrier at its head.

You need to be very fit so that you can keep up a good pace in spite of the altitude; this is a route where safety depends on speed. In good weather, this is a superb route, the finest parts being the ridge between the Pilier d'Angle, and the exit onto the Brouillard summit ridge.

There are several ways of doing this climb. The simplest, that described here, is to gain the Col de Peuterey, either, and this is the finest and most logical route, by the Aiguille Blanche, or alternatively by the E side of the Brenva Glacier. But there are also several other very hard routes:

— doing the ridge as a whole, that is climbing the S Ridge of the Noire, descending the N Ridge and following the crest to the Dames Anglaises, the N Brèche of the Dames Anglaises, and so to the classic route on the Blanche. This is a very long route, demanding at least one bivouac. It is elegant but heterogeneous; it follows the whole length of the ridge, but the ridge itself is very uneven in standard.

— gaining the summit of the Aiguille Blanche de Peuterey either up the SW Face of the Pointe Gugliermina or up the Chabod-Grivel Route on the Brenva Face of the Blanche; this last is a superb ice route.

— gaining the Peuterey Ridge by the Bonatti-Gobbi Route up the Pilier d'Angle; this is a superb, first-class route, long, very difficult, very beautiful, which follows the diagonal line dictated by the structure of the face, rising directly from the base of the Pilier d'Angle to the Shoulder of the Ridge.

These different routes add new dimensions to the classic traverse of the Peuterey Ridge in terms of difficulty either on rock (Noire de Peuterey-Gugliermina) or on ice (Blanche-N Face) or on mixed terrain (Bonatti-Gobbi Route) — a new dimension of considerable scale. Several reasons make it worth having done the Ridge at least once before undertaking these more demanding alternatives: knowledge of the route, experience of high altitude, and knowledge of

one's own behaviour and resistance in case of poor weather.

● **1st ascent**: By the Aiguille Blanche de Peuterey: L. Obersteiner and K. Schreiner, 30–31 July 1927. By the E side of the Col de Peuterey: G. Herzog, M. Herzog, G. Rébuffat and L. Terray, 15 August 1944.

● **Vertical height**: 1344m from the Monzino Hut to the Col de Peuterey, to which must be added 177m for the ascent of the Aiguille Blanche; about 600m from the Brenva plateau (the Col de la Fourche Hut) to the Col de Peuterey; 927m from the Col de Peuterey to the summit (from 3934 to 4807m).

● **Grade**: A very serious route at high altitude from which it is difficult to retreat.

● **Time**: 6–12 hrs from the Monzino Hut to the Col de Peuterey. 4–7 hrs from the Col de la Fourche to the Col de Peuterey. 5–10 hrs from the Col de Peuterey to the summit.

● **Equipment**: Crampons (bivouac gear).

● **Starting point**: Monzino Hut (2590m);

Craveri Bivouac Hut (3490m); Col de la Fourche and Trident Bivouac Huts (3680/3700m).

The Aiguille Noire de Peuterey from the side: the South Ridge, the North Ridge, the Dames Anglaises and the Pointe Gugliermina (opposite page).
The North Face of the Aiguille Blanche de Peuterey (above).

The Peuterey Ridge: from left to right, the
Aiguille Noire, the Dames Anglaises, the Aiguille Blanche,
the Col de Peuterey, Mont Blanc de Courmayeur and
Mont Blanc (above).
The Aiguille Blanche de Peuterey, the Col de Peuterey,
the Pilier d'Angle from the Frêney side, with the
Innominata Ridge in the foreground (left).
View looking down the main slope of the Peuterey
(opposite page, above).
Mont Blanc de Courmayeur (opposite page, below).

● **Route** – *Outline:* Formerly the start used to be up the couloir to the N brèche of the Dames Anglaises; now the Schneider Ledge and Couloir are taken, which lead diagonally from the foot of the Pointe Gugliermina to the Arête de la Blanche. Then follow the summit ridge over the Aiguille Blanche, the Col de Peuterey, the Pilier d'Angle (Eckpfeiler) and Mont Blanc. Coming from the Col de la Fourche cross the Col Moore to reach the foot of the Col de Peuterey Couloir badly exposed to falling stones coming from the Pilier d'Angle and the final rock step. Set out very early and climb it by night.

Description: From the Monzino Hut go up the Frêney Glacier, either directly if it is not too crevassed early in the season, or over the Col de l'Innominata, towards the Pointe Gugliermina. Go up between the base of this point and the rock rognon. Continue along the Schneider Ledges diagonally up to the right leading to a slanting couloir. Climb this; it leads to a brèche overlooked by a slender gendarme on a secondary SW Ridge between the wall of the Pointe Gugliermina and the SE Ridge of the Blanche.

On the right go up a couloir and then easy rocks to gain the SE Ridge of the Blanche. Follow the ridge, then on the Brenva side slant across to avoid by some distance, and fairly low down, the Pointe Gugliermina. Return to the ridge above the Pointe Gugliermina and follow it to a brèche (about 3900m). From this brèche descend on the Brenva side, then return to the ridge and keep on the Frêney side to where the ridge turns from rock to snow and leads to the SE summit (4107m). Descend a chimney on bad rock to reach the snow ridge leading to the central summit (4112m). Avoid this summit on the Brenva side. Return to the crest, then traverse the flank of the snowy rocks of the NW top (4104m). Then make three abseils to descend to the Col de Peuterey. From here there are two possibilities:

— continue along the ridge and reach the shoulder of the Pilier d'Angle after turning a large obvious gendarme on the Brenva side; this is the most elegant solution, and the least exposed to stonefall.

— traverse 150m left to below the large gendarme and go straight up to the shoulder of the Pilier d'Angle (this is quicker).

Then follow the ridge above the large gendarme turning a step on the right. Continue along the ridge and the large slope which leads to the corniced summit ridge. Go along this to Mont Blanc de Courmayeur and then to Mont Blanc itself.

96. GRANDES JORASSES 4208m
Pointe Croz — Central Spur

The N Face of the Grandes Jorasses literally fascinated the climbers of the thirties and forties, and still continues to fascinate today's; even now, the face is as admired and as coveted as ever. It is high, awe-inspiring, beautiful, in superb surroundings. It soars upwards between the Col des Grandes Jorasses to the W and the Col des Hirondelles to the E, and its summit ridge parallels the lines of the base down below on the glacier.

Not only its structure, but its appearance is imposing: grey and red granite, bold, undeviating, unchanging, contrasting with the flowing, curving glacier, eternally present and eternally on the move. Without the sweep of the glacier below, immobile yet ever shifting, the Grandes Jorasses would lose much of their attraction.

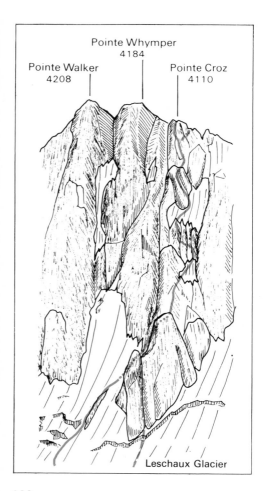

For many years, the N Face was thought to be unclimbable. In all probability the first to make an attempt on it, in 1907, were those inspired climbers G. Winthrop Young and his guide J. Knubel.

The first serious assaults came however only after 1928, and in the first instance on the Walker Spur; Gasparotto, Rand, Herron and Zanetti, with A. Charlet and E. Croux reached the foot of the first slab section.

In 1931, two Germans, Heckmair and Kroner, made an attempt on the Central Couloir. A few days later, in the same couloir, two other Germans, Brehm and Rittler, were killed either by an avalanche or by stonefall. From that time onwards a constant stream of the best climbers of the time passed through the Leschaux Hut, all heading for the Walker Spur.

In 1933, however, Gervasutti and Zanetti, refusing to follow the crowd blindly, made an attempt on the central spur which comes out at the Pointe Michel Croz; they reached 3500m.

In the following year, on 5 July, A. Charlet and R. Gréloz were the first to make an attempt; but Charlet headed left towards the crest of the spur and its overhangs, when he would have done better to go right below the névés.

On 30 July, no fewer than four ropes were to be seen simultaneously strung out along the spur: German (Peters and Haringer), Austrian, French (A. Charlet and F. Belin); the latter retreated at 3600m unfortunately for Charlet was superb on ice and Belin unequalled on rock; and Italian (G. Gervasutti and R. Chabod).

In deteriorating weather, all the parties turned back except the Germans. These, however, having overcome the crux, were also obliged to turn back, and on the descent Haringer slipped and was killed. Peters came back alone and returned a year later with another companion: Meier. After a first attempt which was halted by stonefall, the two Germans made the first ascent on 28–29 June 1935.

A few days later, the climb was repeated by G. Gervasutti and R. Chabod, Loulou Boulaz and R. Lambert, and then by T. Messner and L. Steinauer.

Much later, on 4 July 1947, when the guides' training course for which I was responsible had done a considerable number of major routes, I felt we could attempt the Central Spur. On that 4 July, seven of us set out in three ropes: G. Michel and myself, Vergez and Muller, Lachenal, Brechu and Revel; we did the route in the day. But immediately afterwards, at 10.00 that evening, as we were bivouacking on the Italian side, G. Michel was carried away by stonefall.

This very imposing route is shorter and less difficult than the Walker Spur; since it is mixed, it has been much less downgraded by too many pitons than the Walker Spur.

● **1st ascent:** M. Meier and R. Peters, 28–29 June 1935.
● **Vertical height:** 1000m (from 3100 to 4110m).
● **Grade:** Several pitches of V, but more than the difficulty of some individual pitches, what counts is the length and setting of the route. There are objective dangers at several points: in the couloirs which go up the first and second towers, and then below the two névés.
● **Time:** 12–15 hrs from the start of the difficulties to the summit.
● **Equipment:** Crampons, pitons, carabiners.
● **Starting point:** Leschaux Hut (2431m).
● **Route** – *Outline:* The line is determined by the spur itself. For 100m above the second tower and up to the brèche of the final ridge of the Pointe Croz, the W side, on the right of the Spur, is followed. Higher it is possible to finish direct or by a traverse right.

Description: From the Leschaux Hut (2431m) go up the Leschaux Glacier towards the right bank of the great central couloir. Then after crossing the bergschrund go up the fairly steep slope and then climb the couloir which ends at the brèche above the first tower.

Climb the ridge on the left bank of the couloir, then the couloir itself or the right bank to the brèche of the second tower (danger of stonefall in the two couloirs). Go up the crest, at first easily for 60m, then, also for 60m, up two pitches of IV. Then make an ascending traverse towards the right across the very steep (50°) slope of the central névé to reach the base of a couloir-dièdre at the top of the névé. Start up the back of the dièdre, then go sharply right to climb slabs and cracks on the left bank (IV). Then return left and climb at first straight up the back of the dièdre, then climb the steep slabs (V) on the left which lead to the upper névé (all this step between the two névés is exposed to stonefall).

Climb the very steep upper névé to the foot of rocks which are followed on the right to the point where a couloir-chimney goes

up left to a well-defined brèche, about 150m below the summit of the Pointe Croz. Climb on the right of the buttress for 60m and then there are two possibilities:
— either finish directly at the Pointe Croz. Climb the dièdre-couloir between the crest of the spur on the left and a secondary ridge on the right for 30m. This leads left to the foot of the final wall and the final pitch is very difficult (V; this is the original and most elegant route).
— or traverse right to go round the base of the secondary ridge mentioned above and climb the very open couloir right of this ridge to a little brèche. Traverse 6—7m right of the brèche (IV sup.) and climb slabs with flakes above. At the top of the flakes make a 15m abseil right into a little couloir and climb this to the summit ridge W of the Pointe Croz.

North Face of the Grandes Jorasses. left to right: Col des Hirondelles, Hirondelles Ridge, Pointe Walker (4208m) with the Walker Spur coming up to it, Pointe Whymper, Pointe Croz where the Central Spur finishes, Pointe Hélène, Pointe Marguerite, Pointe Young, and the Col des Grandes Jorasses.

97. GRANDES JORASSES 4208m
Walker Spur

On this huge and mysterious face, nature has marked out a clear line. The N Spur, going directly from the lowest point of the face right up to the summit, is a true rock-climber's route. It is 1200m high; it looks solid and yet slender. On its left is the Hirondelles Ridge, all harmony and exposure; on its right is a vista of couloirs and spurs going to the Col des Grandes Jorasses. The first ascent was led on 4, 5, and 6 August 1938, at sight, by a quite exceptional climber whose talents were equal to the face: Riccardo Cassin, with L. Esposito and U. Tizzoni, all of them trained to a high pitch on the Grigna limestone. Nowadays the N Spur has none of the mystery of that period, and the standard of the climb has been very much lowered by the growing number of pitons put in and left in it. Cassin used only fifty pitons and left four; now there are some two hundred in place, including some expansion bolts. This explains why quite a few climbers today think, not unreasonably, that the mixed Central Spur is more difficult than the Walker.

From experience I know that the N Face of the Grandes Jorasses by the N Spur of the Pointe Walker is a route to dream of, perhaps the finest in existence. But, once again, if the climber wants the route to live up to his dreams, he must himself climb to the highest standard. Success is not a matter of scrambling up anyhow.

Because it faces N, the route is sometimes out of condition for a whole season because of snow and verglas. This means that in seasons when it is in condition, there are usually, on any fine day, three or four parties strung out along the ridge. Finally, you must remember that the W wind can sometimes prevail over the the N wind, and that this brings storms: some parties have found this out to their cost, and certain climbers, among them some of the best, have escaped only by the skin of their teeth.

- **1st ascent:** R. Cassin, L. Esposito and U. Tizzoni, 4–6 August 1938.
- **Vertical height:** 1200m (from 3000 to 4208m).
- **Grade:** ED with 50 pitons, TD with more than 50 pitons. Many pitches of IV and V, a move of V sup., and 1 move of VI, well distributed along the whole route. The rock is generally very good except high up

in the 80m chimney (the Red Chimney). There are several bivouac sites, particularly between 3900 and 4000m on the ridge. But now it is usual, given the number of pitons in place, to finish at the summit in the day. Watch out for stonefall in dry years.

- **Time:** 12–15 hrs from the start of the difficulties to the summit. Contrary to what you might imagine, the Walker Spur is not a true N face. If you can keep to a fast time (to do the route in the day), then you can spend a fair time climbing in sunshine. In fact, at the start the route takes the left side of the pillar, that is the E side; then it goes up most often on the right, except at the top, and so is exposed to the setting sun.
- **Equipment:** Crampons, pitons, étriers.
- **Starting point:** The Leschaux Hut (2431m).
- **Route** – *Outline:* The Spur is fairly massive at the bottom above a rock rib and a snow slope. Cassin climbed the first step direct. On the second ascent I made a route to the left – the 30m dièdre – which avoids the big step. Above the bands of snow the route takes the 75m dièdre and then traverses right – diagonal abseil – to climb the Grey Tower. The Spur becomes less steep and you reach the triangular névé. Then comes the long Red Chimney splitting the final step and leading to the last easy slopes.

Description: From the Leschaux Hut reach the foot of the Spur across the Leschaux Glacier and cross the bergschrund at the base of a snow cone.

100m up this snow couloir follow the hanging snow bands on the left which go across the pillar for about 100m. Regain the rock and follow an ascending and slightly sloping ramp for two pitches, at first on the right then on the left, to reach the foot of two cracks (30m dièdre, first step).

Start this pitch up the left-hand crack for 15m (V, V sup., athletic) and gain the crack on the right by a delicate traverse (VI). This leads to a good platform at the foot of an overhanging zone (V). From the belay traverse right for 3 to 4 pitches (usually traversing along an ice band) to gain the crest of the spur. Go up very broken rock for several easy pitches to reach the foot of a very steep buttress.

Now take the right flank of the pillar to climb a great dièdre which is often wet (the

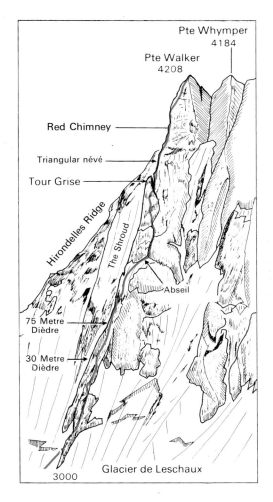

Pte Whymper
4184

Pte Walker
4208

Red Chimney

Triangular névé

Tour Grise

Hirondelles Ridge

The Shroud

Abseil

75 Metre
Dièdre

30 Metre
Dièdre

Glacier de Leschaux

3000

75m dièdre, IV, IV sup., V). At the finish of the dièdre follow slabs, then a short chimney, which leads to a good ledge below an overhanging zone. Traverse for about 15m (V) and make a diagonal abseil of 8–10m to reach an overhanging crack-chimney and climb it.

Climb an easy ramp for a pitch, leading to a large block. You are now at the foot of an area of vertical slabs (the Black Slabs). Start up a short crack ending below over-hangs which you avoid by a short traverse left which leads to a crack. Climb this for 8–10m (V, V sup.) to arrive at a sloping ledge. Continue up the slabs following a small ascending crack going right (V). You reach a zone of depressions closed by a gently overhanging couloir (V sup.) which you climb to reach a good ledge leading towards the couloir which bounds the pillar on the right. Do not go into this couloir, but climb directly up an area of compact and unattractive slabs (grey slabs). Now gain, on the right side of the pillar, the crest of the arête (V, V sup.). Climb this arête, usually on its right side. You arrive at a mixed zone leading to a hanging névé (the triangular névé).

Climb this névé to the foot of the final step. Make a 25–30m traverse right (delicate moves) to reach an area of vertical chimney-cracks (red chimneys). Climb these for three pitches (vertical and often shattered rock, IV sup., V) to reach the foot of an over-hanging buttress. Avoid this by a traverse right (delicate at the start, V). Go into the easy couloir ascending to the left which leads in several pitches to the final shoulder below the summit. From this shoulder, two pitches (there is often a snow cornice) lead to the summit.

Opposite page: the Black Slabs (above) and the 30m dièdre (below).
This page: On the final pitches (above);

98. PETIT DRU 3733m
West Face – American Direct

In 1952, after a number of attempts, L. Berardini, A. Dagory, M. Laine and G. Magnoni reached the summit of the Drus by the W Face. They had done this magnificent ascent in two stages: 1–5 July they had climbed up from the bottom of the face by the couloir and ledges as far as the 90m dièdre, and then 17–19 July, having traversed to the same point from the nearby second main platform of the N Face, they had found a route up the upper part of the face. A superb achievement.

Ten years later, two American climbers, G. Hemming and R. Robbins, went straight up from the base to the 'jammed block' at the foot of the 90m dièdre, where they joined the 1952 route; this direct route, elegant and very hard, is known as the American Direct. It is indeed one of the finest extreme climbs of the range, if not the finest. It is exceptional also in that the climbing as far as the 'jammed block' can be done entirely free and needs, for this, no more than thirty pitons (without counting belay pitons). Airy and exposed, this is a route with several very strenuous pitches; it is to be hoped, though the hope is probably vain, that it will not be invaded by pitons. Once past the 'jammed block', the classic route has plenty of pitons, but the pitches wind their way through a superb series of roofs and great slabs. The exit onto the N Face, which is sometimes, covered with verglas, gives a new and subtle flavour to this great rock route.

● **1st ascent:** G. Hemming and R. Robbins, 24–26 July 1962.
● **Vertical height:** About 1000m from the start of the difficulties to the summit (from 2700 to 3733m).
● **Grade:** ED with 30 pitons. Above the 'jammed block' the climbing is artificial, with the pitons in place. An advantage of the Direct Route is that it is not exposed to stonefall, which is unfortunately the case with the 1952 route, particularly on the ascent of the couloir.
● **Time:** 12 hrs from the start to the 'jammed block'. 7 hrs from the 'jammed block' to the summit. 19 hrs in all.
● **Equipment:** Pitons, carabiners, étriers.
● **Starting point:** Bivouac at the top of the Dru moraine.
● **Route** – *Outline:* After ascending the base the route takes a system of crack-chimneys aiming for the great dièdre which comes down from the Niche des Drus. Then it goes right to reach the 'jammed block'. Above, after the 90m dièdre, there is a diagonal abseil into a system of crack-dièdres which gives a line through the great roofs. It leads to the third terrace on the N Face, and the finish is up that route.

Description: Start up the base a little above and left of the lowest point of the rock on the Dru Glacier, at the level of an area of slanting ledges on the right. Follow these almost to their right-hand end. Climb a short steep slab (V), then a small overhang (V sup.) and follow a vague dièdre (V) to a belay with a rock spike. Climb a crack on the right which widens into a chimney (V sup. then V), leading to a less steep zone below a half-moon-shaped slab. Go up slightly right, then turn the slab to the left and reach a large ledge above the base. Bear right along the ledge. Climb a short wall (IV sup.) to reach a ledge which is followed left (II and III) to where you can make a slightly rising traverse right (V sup.) to gain the line of crack-dièdres. Climb these for five pitches. The first pitch (40m) starts with a flake which is climbed by a strenuous layback (VI, then VI sup. or A1, V at the end). The following pitch goes over an overhanging block (V sup.) following a cracked slab (VI). Then you climb cracks and dièdres with a section of bad rock (V sup., VI). The fourth pitch goes over an overhang and then takes a dièdre (V sup.). Belay below a block. Climb the overhanging crack above to the left, and then slabs to a good belay (V sup., VI). You are at the foot of an obvious dièdre.

Climb over a block, move left, then climb close to the crest of the arête separating this dièdre from another further left (IV sup.). Reach the bottom of the great dièdre descending from the Niche des Drus (Mailly Dièdre) and climb this for a pitch (V), then

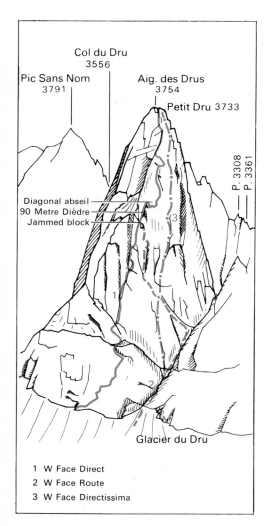

Col du Dru
3556

Pic Sans Nom
3791

Aig. des Drus
3754

Petit Dru 3733

P. 3308
P. 3361

Diagonal abseil
90 Metre Dièdre
Jammed block

Glacier du Dru

1 W Face Direct
2 W Face Route
3 W Face Directissima

traverse right along a ledge to the foot of a system of cracks. Climb these (V then V sup.) and reach a small belay at the foot of the chimney beside the 'jammed block' on the left. Climb this (IV sup., IV). Climb the great dièdre above (the 90m dièdre): this gives one pitch of IV sup., two pitches of A1, A2. Traverse right along a flake (IV), then make a diagonal abseil right to the Germans' Terrace (fixed rope). Climb a vertical wall on the right (V, A1). Traverse right and climb a double crack (V). On the right take a steep crack (V and V sup.) to a belay below the roofs. Climb 'The Bolt' between the roofs (IV sup.) and continue up a large dièdre (IV sup.). Turn an overhang on the left (V), then climb the back of the dièdre on the right (V, A1) to a belay at the foot of vertical flakes. Climb these (IV-V) and reach a niche at the back of the dièdre. Above a crack-dièdre (V) leads to a large terrace on the edge of the N Face. Climb the crest of the arête (IV sup.), then bear left to reach a first ledge covered with verglas. Climb the couloir-chimney above (blocks, IV sup.) to a second, quartz ledge about 50m below the summit (by which you can reach 'The Hole' on the right and go onto the S Face) and then go up to the summit.

The Direct on the Drus (left).
The 90m dièdre (opposite page).
The Grade VI layback (below).

99. LES DROITES 4000m
North Face

This is a mixed ice route, which can for several reasons be called a major one. In the first place there is the structure and general appearance of the face, framed by two spurs (the NE Spur to the left and the NW to the right), so that it appears both vast and enclosed: the upper section is mixed, hollowed out, concave, funnel-shaped, and the lower part is snow, convex, rather rounded, with a huge ice bulge like a shield. Then there is the slope itself with its particular characteristics due to its angle and structure: lower down it is shrouded in a layer of ice of variable thickness, sometimes covered with enough snow to hide the underlying slabs and sometimes thin and translucent so that they are visible; the upper section is made up of smooth, rounded granite slabs, often covered with verglas and seamed by ice couloirs. In fact the whole climb, from top to bottom, is vertiginous and sheer, with no protruding, reassuring rocks to act as relief. Moreover the face is at an awkward angle; a little steeper, and even the fact that it is north-facing would not allow the ice to adhere.

This then is a very severe face, indeed unusually unwelcoming; there are no platforms, no resting places and no recognisable landmarks, for nothing stands out on this mixed terrain. For all these reasons, and principally because it scarcely lends itself to pitons, unlike the Bonatti Pillar, the Walker, or even the Frêney Pillar, it seems improbable that the N Face of the Droites will ever be downgraded, or become popular and lose its character. It will always remain remote and untamed.

- **1st ascent:** P. Cornuau and M. Davaille, 5–10 September 1955.
- **Vertical height:** 1000m (from 3000 to 4000m).
- **Grade:** The NW Face of the Droites remains at ED level, as distinct from rock routes which are downgraded quickly and easily (because of the number of pitons which can quintuple in a few years), because given its ice and mixed nature it lends itself less to pitons, and because the configuration of the ice itself changes each year.

This route calls for very safe and confident ice technique and a definite physical and mental balance. In bad weather retreat is difficult. The difficulties are sustained and almost continuous. The face lacks ledges, platforms and terraces, even of modest dimensions.

- **Time:** 25–30 hrs from the start to the summit. A rope on very good form and above all very experienced on ice will be able to do the route under good conditions in one day.
- **Equipment:** Crampons, pitons, ice-pitons, ice-screws. Long ropes.
- **Starting point:** The Argentière Hut (2771m).
- **Route** – *Outline:* Roughly speaking the wall falls into two sections: the lower section, of greater height than the upper section, consists of the great snow/ice slope (which is usually climbed on the right-

hand side almost directly below the rock promontory which descends from the upper step), while the upper section consists of a complex step in the form of a large funnel made of granite slabs (sometimes covered with ice, often with verglas by the water melting from the snow higher up) and ice couloirs. The first third of this step is very steep and very smooth both in the rock and in the ice sections. There are two ways of climbing this step, and this is an advantage, for the climb depends upon the conditions. The two lines are almost parallel. That taken by the first ascenders, rather to the right, follows a depression which led them to the

The diagram on the left shows:

1 NE Spur
2 NE Variant
3 N Face
4 N Spur

Les Droites

E Summit 4000
Brèche 3944
W Summit 3984
Tour des Droites 3948
Signal Vallot 3843

Lagarde Couloir

Argentière Glacier

summit ridge right of the E summit. The line taken by the second ascenders goes up more directly to the E summit by a succession of walls and couloirs.

Description: Climb the bergschrund on the right-hand side of the face and go up the initially extremely steep slope, which then eases a little in angle to the bottom of the rock spur which comes down from the final ridge (a comfortable bivouac site on the lower rocks).

Above there are two possibilities:
— skirt the spur on the left to the base of the great step and go up to the right up a very steep ice couloir-dièdre descending from the great couloir below the Brèche des Droites (3944m). Go up this dièdre for 25m, reach a little cone of snow at the foot of a great slab bounded on the right by a crack-chimney. Climb this, then go up cracked slabs (A1) and a jamming crack on the left to reach a small platform above the couloir. Continue straight on above (V), then return right towards the arête up a secondary ice couloir. Arrive at the edge of the great couloir. Cross this slanting left and reach the upper part of the step. Climb this, bearing left across very steep mixed ground and gain the summit ridge a little right of the E summit.
— go left (the line taken on the second ascent) to go up towards the E summit. Above the ice slope get onto the first rock wall and climb this up rock covered with verglas and couloirs. Above climb very difficult couloirs and chimneys (some sections of artificial on ice and rock). Take a diagonal line towards the right behind a flake, then to the left up a very steep couloir and a vertical wall (V, A1) to gain a fairly obvious buttress. Then continue to the snowy top of the summit part of the NE Spur.

On the North Face of the Droites (opposite page, and right).

100. MONT BLANC 4807m
Central Pillar of Frêney

Although the difficulties of this route are not extreme (except perhaps for 60m of climbing on the Chandelle at over 4500m), the Central Pillar of Frêney is and will remain an outstanding Alpine route. Not only is the foot of the face difficult of access (to get there is in itself a not inconsiderable snow route), but there is a serious risk of poor weather which would involve a very difficult retreat; this means that the climber undertaking the route is seriously committing himself, and should have excellent mountaineering sense. The route is similar to all the routes on this side of Mont Blanc in that it is only a part of a very long expedition.

● **1st ascent:** C. Bonington, I. Clough, J. Duglosz and D. Whillans, 27–29 August 1961; R. Desmaison, P. Julien, I. Piussi, Y. Pollet-Villard, 28–29 August 1961.

● **Grade:** A route of great character which you should only undertake when very fit. The route up the Chandelle (60m high) is VI, A1-A2, and is now completely pitoned which reduces the difficulty.

The base supporting the Chandelle, without being of extreme difficulty, is still very difficult given the altitude. But the technical aspects apart, the most obvious feature of this route is the physical and moral commitment that it requires. Other routes present greater and more sustained difficulties, but none demands such powers of decision and such exact mountaineering judgement, this because of the remoteness and the difficulty of retreat in case of bad weather. The Frêney Pillar is the most striking example of how the difficulty of a route is made up of several factors besides the difficulty of the climbing itself.

● **Time:** 4–8 hrs from the Col de la Fourche Hut to the Col de Peuterey, 6–8 hrs from the Col de Peuterey to the foot of the Chandelle, 4 hrs for the ascent of the Chandelle, 3 hrs from the top of the Chandelle to the summit of Mont Blanc. This makes 17–23 hrs in all from the hut to the summit.

● **Equipment:** Crampons, pitons, carabiners, étriers, bivouac gear.

● **Starting point:** Col de la Fourche Bivouac Hut (3680m) or the Trident Hut (3690m). It is also possible to set out from the Monzino Hut (2590m) or bivouac at the Col de Peuterey (3934m).

● **Route – Outline:** Above and left of the upper Frêney Plateau rises the great wall running from the Peuterey Ridge on the right to the Innominata Ridge on the left. On this wall the Central Pillar stands between the N Pillar (Gervasutti) and the S Pillar (the Hidden Pillar, so-called because less obvious than the others). It is formed by four great steps separated by easier zones. The first is climbed up the centre, the second on the right of the pillar, the third more on the left, and the fourth, the Chandelle, by a fairly complex line of cracks avoiding the overhanging areas.

Description: From the Col de Peuterey make a long traverse up the curve of the snow towards the foot of the Central Pillar (the bergschrund is sometimes tricky). Several pitches up mixed ground lead to the foot of the first step, which is climbed in the centre by an obvious line of cracks (two or three pitches, IV sup., V). Easy broken rock then leads to the foot of a very steep step. Go up on the right of the step. The first pitch goes up flakes and grooves to a small platform at the bottom of a dièdre. Climb the face right of this dièdre, go over an overhang and get into the crack in the back of the dièdre. You are now almost on the right-hand edge of the spur.

Two pitches up hanging snow bands and a ramp ascending to the left lead to the foot of a very obvious crack-chimney. Climb this (V, V sup., very sustained) to gain mixed ground above, which leads along an arête to the foot of the Chandelle.

A first pitch up a dièdre, slightly overhanging at the finish, leads to a good platform (possible bivouac site). Climb a cracked slab to reach the foot of an overhanging zone and avoid this by a traverse right (V, V sup., VI very sustained, no ledge). You are

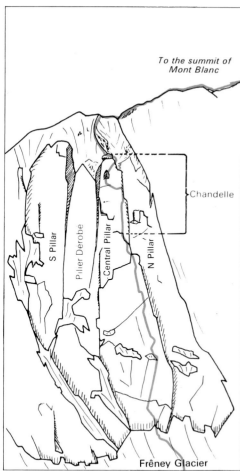

now at the foot of a great chimney-dièdre, largely overhanging, which leads to a good ledge (V, V sup., A2). From the belay go up a short 7–8m wall (IV) and traverse left to the edge of the pillar. Continue for three poorly defined pitches up slabs (IV, IV sup., V) to gain the summit of the Chandelle. A short abseil leads to a brèche. Go up fairly steep mixed ground (45°) to reach the Brouillard Ridge, and continue along this to the summit of Mont Blanc.

Bivouac on the Pillar (opposite page).
The Frêney Pillar from the Col de Peuterey (bottom right).
Reaching the summit of Mont Blanc (above right).

THE WOULD-BE MOUNTAINEER

And now summer is at an end, and you are rich with the experience of the mountains.

For the winter you will be left with good and bad memories (the two often go together) of the routes you have done; you will remember above all the ridges and the faces you glimpsed and studied and longed for as you climbed. These on gloomy days will be the subjects of your dreams.

But reality too will be yours: you will go to outcrops to perfect your technique (true joy will come for you from climbing free and well). You will have your memories, too, of what you did the previous summer, with certain indelible moments: a moment of tiredness at high altitude, a route where you made a mistake, a ridge where you took a wrong turning, a bergschrund or a crevasse which was difficult or impossible to cross, unexpected bad weather. You are rich in memories, but also rich in ambitions: so many routes to do, and beyond the Alps so many peaks.

Training grounds are often small limestone outcrops; you will become used to verticality, to narrow stances, to tiny, hidden holds. You will develop a technique based not on brute strength but on balance and litheness; in the mountains, later, this will bring you more pleasure and less exhaustion. To know deep in yourself that you are climbing well is a source of joy.

Skiing too will help you. You will gain a knowledge of snow, become accustomed to living in snow. Do not imagine that as a mountaineer you must despise piste skiing. By doing a maximum of downhill runs, using téléphériques, you will acquire skill as a skier and then, in spring, you can set off on skis for the Three Cols, Mont Mallet, the Haute Route, Mont Blanc.

And then a new summer will open before you . . .

*
**

In writing about these climbs, I have rediscovered those who accompanied me on the great adventure.

Together we toiled over moraines and shivered through bivouacs, together we were warmed then burnt by the sun, caressed by the breeze, then whipped by the wind. Together we scraped ourselves on granite, or twisted our knees on the way down scree.

There have been abseils on wet rope which were difficult — abseils where the abseil rope was difficult to retrieve, or even jammed. We were shaken by lightning, by its unexpectedness, its roar, its smell.

Together we knew and shared apprehensions, doubts, fears; and yet it was there, far above, that we learnt of the life, the ardour, the strength, that burned deep within us. All that made for solid, unalloyed, inner happiness was there, in our souls, and we did not know it.

And then there was friendship.

On the Clochers-Clochetons, on the Pic de Roc, on the Sans Nom and the Peuterey, I have rediscovered you, my faithful companions. Here Jean gave me a shoulder; there, Lionel shared a lemon with me; on the ridge, Edouard freed the abseil rope; elsewhere, Henri taught me to cut steps.

Henri, you above all; to the world you may appear insignificant; to me you were a true 'big brother' in the mountains.

I wish all alpinists a big brother, a man to inspire love and respect, to keep an eye on your roping up, to take an almost tender care of you while introducing you to that tough and arduous life.

A man to let you share his moments of exaltedness, at 4000m, to introduce *you* to the summits around, much as a gardener might introduce you to his flowers.

A man to be envied, whose home is the mountain hut and whose world is the mountains. And the friendship of a man of such riches is beyond price.

L'Apprenti montagnard, les cinquante plus belles courses du massif du Mont Blanc
(Editions Grand Vent, 1946).

PHOTOGRAPHS

The letter following the page number indicates the position of the photo on that page, according to the following code: A = above, B = below, L = left, R = right, C = centre.

Front cover: R. Bonnardel — G. Rébuffat. Back cover: G. Rébuffat Collection.
E. Bayle: pp. 87, 203 (A). D. Belden: p. 37. D. Bertholet: pp. 51 (B), 78, 79. G. Bertone: pp. 11, 14 (B), 67 (A), 148, 150, 167, 175, 198, 207, 208, 209, 210 (A), 211. A. Blanchard: pp. 34 (AL), 36, 218. R. Bonnardel: pp. 31, 98. A. Braconnay: p. 14 (A). H. Candle: pp. 143, 231 (B). C. Cassin: p. 236. A. de Chatellus: pp. 49, 62, 108, 141, 176 (R), 180, 183. J. Coqueniot: pp. 6, 15, 17, 35 (BR), 94 (R), 95 (B), 151, 190, 203 (B), 204 (AB and D), 205 (AR and AL), 214 (R), 216, 221, 231 (A), 237 (A). M. Darbellay: pp. 23, 83, 158, 159 (B). B. Denjoy: pp. 53, 62, 63, 68, 97, 119, 124, 132, 133 (A), 137, 188, 194. J.-C. Droyer: pp. 176, 184, 215, 220 (L), 222, 223 (B), 230 (B), 232, 233, 234, 235. D. Fourrès: pp. 224, 227 (B). J. Franco: pp. 61, 111, 116, 191, 226 (B). I.G.N.: pp. 120, 171 (L). Y. Komori: pp. 171 (R), 175. H. Kondo: pp. 40, 54, 55 (B), 89, 96, 115 (A), 139, 173. F. Lespinasse: pp. 58, 104, 110, 114, 156, 157, 162, 164, 204 (AL), 212, 220. U. Manera: pp. 106, 107, 115 (B), 206. H. Miyazaki: p. 142. J.-P. Motti: pp. 138, 149. P. Nava: pp. 10, 77 (L and C, black and white prints from colour negatives), 95 (A), 102. G. Ollive: pp. 13, 16, 30, 76, 92 (R), 136, 223. A. Re: p. 100. G. Rébuffat Collection: pp. 18, 19, 28, 32, 33, 34 (B), 35 (A and BL), 38, 39, 42, 43, 45, 48, 51 (A), 52, 54, 55 (A), 59, 60, 64, 65, 66, 67 (B), 74, 75, 77 (R), 80, 81, 82, 84, 86, 88, 90, 92 (L), 94 (L), 99, 101, 103, 105, 112, 113, 117, 118, 126, 127, 128 (L and B), 129, 130, 131, 133 (B), 135, 144, 145, 146, 153, 154, 155, 159 (A), 160, 163 (A), 166, 169, 174, 178, 179, 189, 190, 195, 202, 205 (B), 210 (B), 213, 227 (A), 230 (A), 237 (A). V Renard: p. 170. P. Rouaix: pp. 41, 70. S. Shirahata: pp. 123, 199, 226 (A). M. Vaucher: p. 122 (R). B. Washburn: pp. 47, 55, 56, 57, 65, 69, 71, 73, 85, 91, 93, 109, 122 (L), 125, 128 (A), 147, 161, 163 (B), 165, 168, 172, 177, 181, 193, 195, 197, 201, 217, 225, 229, 233. B. Wittich: p. 121. C. Zappelli: pp. 46, 214 (L).

Impr. Jean Mussot - Paris.